George Washington Centennial Memeorial
Excerises, Mount Vernon, December 14, 1899;

G Washington.

GEORGE WASHINGTON

Centennial Memorial
Exer

MOUNT VERNON D

GEORGE WASHINGTON

Centennial Memorial Exercises

MOUNT VERNON, DECEMBER 14, 1899

———

Record by the M W Grand Lodge of Colorado
A F & A M

———

DENVER COLORADO
THE W F. ROBINSON PRINTING CO, PRINTERS
1903

E 312
6
F85

To the Memory

OF

WORSHIPFUL BROTHER GEORGE WASHINGTON,

INSCRIBED ON THE

CENTENNIAL OF HIS DEATH

BY THE

M. W. GRAND LODGE, A. F. & A. M.

OF THE

STATE OF COLORADO;

WHICH WAS ADMITTED TO THE

UNION OF STATES

ON THE

CENTENNIAL OF THE DECLARATION

OF INDEPENDENCE

WHICH WAS MADE EFFECTIVE

BY WASHINGTON

THROUGH HIS PRACTICE

OF THE

VARIOUS MASONIC VIRTUES.

The M. W. Grand Lodge of Colorado

A. F. & A. M

GRAND MASTER'S OFFICE.

GLENWOOD SPRINGS, COLO , March 28, 1903.

ROGER W WOODBURY, Denver, Colo .

Dear Brother Woodbury—I have just received a letter from Past Grand Master A A Burnand, in which he advises that suitable likenesses of the Colorado representatives to the Washington Centennial Memorial exercises at Washington's tomb be published in our memorial volume. I fully concur with him and will as Grand Master instruct you to please see that suitable cuts or halftones are procured of the Colorado representatives, that is, the five who were at Mount Vernon The expense at best cannot be great, and I regard this volume as one that will reflect great credit on this Grand Jurisdiction

With best wishes for your health, I am,

Fraternally yours,

MARSHALL H DEAN,

Grand Master

ROGER WILLIAMS WOODBURY,
Past Grand Master of Colorado.
Chairman Colorado Washington Centennial Memorial Committee.
Died July 11th, 1903.

Introduction.

—

The Masonic Memorial Exercises which took place at Mount Vernon on the centennial anniversary of the death of Worshipful Brother George Washington, were formally inaugurated by the Most Worshipful Grand Lodge of Colorado in 1893, in response to a recommendation in the address of Grand Master William D Wright, made on the suggestion and request of Past Grand Master R W Woodbury

The official recommendation was referred to the Committee on Jurisprudence, consisting of Past Grand Masters R W Woodbury, James H Peabody and William D Todd This committee reported at the same Grand Communication in favor of the proposition, and presented a method of procedure Execution of the same was entrusted to a committee to serve until the close of the proposed memorial exercises, and Past Grand Masters R W Woodbury, William D Wright and William D Todd were appointed as such committee, who reported progress to the Grand Lodge from year to year

The first circular of the committee was sent to all Grand Masters and Grand Secretaries in the United States They were requested to recommend the formal approval of their Grand Lodges, and to appoint committees to report to, and co-operate with, the Colorado committee

The irregular dates at which the various Grand Lodges assemble made progress slow, and a year elapsed before all had convened Quite a number of Grand Masters at once gave hearty and patriotic endorsement Some neglected it until another year From the Grand Masters it went to Grand

Lodge committees for consideration. Some approved and committees were promptly appointed. Others advised delay One or two, and perhaps more, disapproved

Then the idea run the gauntlet of praise or ridicule of the various Committees on Foreign Correspondence.

After many discouragements, several circulars and scores of letters, the co-operation of Grand Lodges was slowly obtained, until, when the committee had been engaged three years at their work, enough Grand Lodges had acquiesced to ensure a national character to the memorial exercises on the lines originally proposed.

All the preliminary work having been accomplished, and it having been determined that the exercises could only take place at Mount Vernon, the Grand Lodge of Virginia was then formally invited to arrange all details, with Colorado guaranteed as a faithful supporter to the end The invitation was accepted, with special acknowledgements to the Grand Lodge of Colorado for its inception of the Memorial, and for the services it had performed

The Colorado committee continued in frequent correspondence with the Virginia committee, not only in the raising of money for the Virginia committee, but in an advisory capacity generally

The Memorial Exercises were perfected and carried out by the Grand Lodge of Virginia substantially as outlined by the Colorado committee early in their work

Because of the national character of the exercises, and the conceded fact that they memorialized "the largest figure in all merely human history," and the almost certainty that they will be repeated by untold generations as long as Freemasonry continues to exist, have impelled the Grand Lodge of Colorado to round up its work by putting in imperishable form the principal records pertaining to its inception, progress and culmination, and also the exercises which took place in Colorado simultaneously with the national exercises at Mount Vernon   It is to be regretted that a majority of the Colorado Lodges failed to report their memorial proceedings to the Grand Secretary , and it is also to be regretted that the requests of this committee for copies of the addresses delivered before local Lodges were not all responded to   This volume contains all the addresses that were received by the committee or the Grand Secretary

The correspondence carried on by the committee is mostly omitted While of local interest, as showing the volume and scope of the work of the committee, it does not possess such a general and permanent interest as to justify its being perpetuated in this volume

ROGER W WOODBURY,
Chairman

Preliminary Preparations
and
General Arrangements

Washington as a Mason.

A detailed account of the Masonic incidents of Washington's life is of intense interest to Freemasons, but a few facts only can be presented in this book

He was initiated in Fredericksburg Lodge, Virginia, on the 4th of November, 1752, a few months before he reached the age of twenty-one He was passed on the 3rd of March following, and raised on the 4th of August   The records of the Lodge showing the above facts are still preserved, as is also the Bible upon which he was obligated

After the War for Independence the Lodge at Alexandria, then working under the Grand Lodge of Pennsylvania, elected to become subordinate to the new Grand Lodge of Virginia, and petitioned the latter for a charter, with George Washington as Worshipful Master.   On the 28th of April, 1788, the charter was duly issued to "Alexandria No 22," and contained the following phrase   *   *   *   "do hereby constitute and appoint our illustrious and well-beloved brother George Washington, Esq , late General and Commander in Chief of the forces of the United States of America," etc

On the 20th of December in the same year Washington was re-elected Master for the year commencing with St John's Day, December 27, 1788

After his death it was the desire of the members that the Lodge name should be changed so as to embrace that of their illustrious first Master, whereupon the name was officially changed to "Alexandria Washington Lodge No 22 "

The most conspicuous event of Washington's Masonic record was the laying of the corner-stone of the National Capitol at Washington, on the 18th of September, 1793. He was then President of the United States, and acted as Master upon the invitation of Dr Dick, then Master of Alexandria Lodge

There is no doubt but that in the minds of his Masonic compeers after the war he was regarded as the Great Patron of the fraternity of America, and many were led to believe that he had held official rank as General Grand Master The Grand Lodge of Pennsylvania and others sought to create a general grand mastership and elevate Washington to that office, and a medal was struck two years before his death, bearing his bust and name upon its face, with Masonic emblems and the letters "G W. G G. M." upon the obverse

   *   *   *   The story of Washington as a Mason must now be left, though with reluctance, and the formal record of the inception, progress and culmination of the Centennial Memorial Exercises at his tomb, begun

FROM THE ADDRESS OF M W WILLIAM D. WRIGHT, GRAND MASTER OF COLORADO 1893

The story of "the days that tried men's souls" is a record of which Masonry may well be proud The first overt act of resistance to taxation was when in the twilight of a December day in 1773, a band of patriots, disguised as Indians, threw overboard the tea in Boston harbor Masonic records of colonial times are said to establish the fact that the act was committed by a body of Masons, who left a Masonic Lodge room for that purpose

WILLIAM D. WRIGHT,
Past Grand Master of Colorado.
Member Colorado Washington Centennial Memorial Committee.

The famous midnight ride of Paul Revere was in April, 1775   His cry of alarm aroused the farmers to prepare for the battle of Lexington, the first conflict of the War of Independence   Longfellow writes

> "And yet, through the gloom and the light,
> The fate of a nation was riding that night,
> And the spark struck out by that steed in his flight,
> Kindled the land into flame with its heat"

He did his work and served the great cause with freedom, fervency and zeal, for Paul Revere was a Mason, and afterwards became Grand Master of Masons in the State of Massachusetts

July 4, 1776, after a long and solemn debate over the consequences of the act, the members of the first Continental Congress, pledging to each other their lives, their fortunes and their sacred honors, attached their signatures to a simple scroll   That scroll was the Declaration of American Independence   It was drafted by Thomas Jefferson, a Mason   *   *   *

Benjamin Franklin, then Master of a Masonic Lodge in Philadelphia, in many respects the wisest and greatest man of this day, was a member of the committee afterwards appointed to draft the Constitution of the United States

The first President of the Republic, the immortal Washington, was a Mason   He took the oath of office with his hand resting upon a Bible, which had just been taken from a Masonic altar. As Grand Master of Masons just a hundred years ago yesterday, he laid the cornerstone of the capitol at Washington   His pictured form, clothed masonically, looks down upon us from its honored station just above the Grand Master's chair as I now address you   It decorates the walls of nearly every Masonic Lodge in the land   By universal consent of civilized men, he is the largest figure in all merely human history, and his name stands first upon the roll of Masonry's illustrious dead. Acting now upon a suggestion originally made to me by Past Grand Master R W. Woodbury, Chairman of our Committee on Jurisprudence, I respectfully recommend the appointment of a committee to report at this session, with a view to the holding of national Masonic memorial services at the tomb of Washington, at Mount Vernon, on the centennial anniversary of his death, December 14, 1899 The report of such committee, together with the action of this Grand Lodge thereon, would then be presented to all other Grand Lodges in the United States, for such action as they may think best Should this suggestion happen to meet with their approval, as such Grand Lodges meet annually, it would not give too much time in which to properly consult and make suitable arrangements

REPORT OF COMMITTEE ON JURISPRUDENCE

This portion of the Grand Master's address was referred to the Committee on Jurisprudence, consisting of Past Grand Masters R W Woodbury, Chairman, James II Peabody and William D Todd, which committee reported as follows:

DENVER, COLO , September 20, 1893

To the Most Worshipful Grand Lodge

The Standing Committee on Jurisprudence, to which was referred the suggestions and recommendations of the Most Worshipful Grand Master, respectfully reports that it has considered that part relating to a proper memorial observance of the centennial of the death of Worshipful Brother George Washington, which took place on the 14th day of December, 1799. The committee believes that public recognition of the services and characters of the great and good has a salutary influence upon the lives of others, particularly the young, stimulating them to emulation, exalting their own efforts, and ennobling their characters A due observance of the centennial of Washington's death would revive public interest in, and disseminate knowledge of, his virtues, and in the pioneer work of the fathers of the Republic who laid the foundations of our national government

We are taught, as Masons, to be true to the government of the country under which we live, and in a broader sense than mere loyalty, we should be true to the principles which underlie its system   These principles were instilled into the American heart by fortitude, prudence, justice, hardship, adversity, perseverance, unselfishness and toil, and the best manhood to-day comes from the same sources of strength   As citizens, we cannot too often present this truth to those who are striving for fame and influence through paths which are less noble, and we cannot present it through a grander character than that Master Mason on whom was bestowed the loving title of "First in War, First in Peace, and First in the Hearts of His Countrymen."

Tens of thousands of good men have had their favorable attention directed to Masonry because it embraced principles and truths which were deemed worthy of the loyalty of George Washington, and we are proud that it was so in his day, and is so still

We believe the Grand Lodges of the United States will like to unite for the purpose of doing honor to his memory and that the proposition thereto will be especially appropriate from the Grand Lodge of the State which was admitted to the American Union on the hundredth anniversary of the independence of the colonies, which Washington did so much to secure

We therefore approve the Grand Master's suggestion, and recommend the following, viz

That a committee of three be appointed to present the subject to the several Grand Masters and Grand Lodges of the United States and request.

First   The appointment of a committee of one from each Grand Jurisdiction, with one alternate, to serve through all the arrangements, in order to save confusion by annual changes

Second   That the committee from this Grand Lodge arrange by correspondence with the committees from sister Grand Lodges for a place of meeting of said committee at some early date subsequent to the next annual Grand Communication of each of said Grand Lodges

Third   That the committee from this Grand Lodge be recommended to suggest memorial services and suitable addresses at the tomb of Washington at Mount Vernon, at which all the Grand Masters of the United States be present, with their subordinate officers and other members

Fourth.   That the committee representing the Grand Lodges report in detail their recommendations for the memorial to their respective Grand Lodges for approval before the same be actually undertaken

Because of the number of Grand Lodges and the irregular periods of their annual Communications, this process will consume three or four years at least, which will leave barely two years in which to perfect the final arrangements.

Fraternally submitted,

R. W WOODBURY,
J H. PEABODY,
W D TODD,
Committee on Jurisprudence

The report of the committee was unanimously adopted and Past Grand Masters R W Woodbury, W D Wright and W D Todd were appointed on behalf of the Grand Lodge of Colorado to present the matter to other Grand Lodges and Grand Masters of other Grand Jurisdictions

FIRST CIRCULAR

The foregoing report, with the action of the Grand Lodge of Colorado thereon, was subsequently printed in circular form, certified by the Grand Secretary and forwarded to all Grand Masters and Grand Secretaries in the United States, accompanied by the following introductory circular

DENVER, COLO , September 30, 1893

Dear Sir and Most Worshipful Brother

In accordance with the instructions contained in the foregoing extracts from the proceedings of the Most Worshipful Grand Lodge, A F and A M , of Colorado, at the annual Grand Communication held in this city the present month, we have the honor and the pleasure to make official presentation of the same to you   We entertain the hope that the subject matter will be deemed worthy of your approval, and that your Most Worshipful Grand Lodge will join by ordering a committee in accordance with the plan proposed   To facilitate a meeting of the General Committee, which would ordinarily be difficult because of the uncertainty as to when it will be filled by the several Grand Lodges, the committee from Colorado has thought it would be satisfactory if appointments should be made known to them; and when all Grand Lodges shall have acted, they will communicate with all the members, and call a meeting at a central point for organization   Will you please request your Grand Secretary to advise the chairman of this committee of the action of your Grand Lodge hereon, with the name and postoffice address of the appointee named thereby, should such an appointment be made

Fraternally yours,

R W WOODBURY.
W D WRIGHT
WM. D TODD

SECOND CIRCULAR.

Over a year elapsed, devoted to personal and official correspondence, when, under date of March 15, 1895, another circular was issued, copying the first and closing with the following:

Since the adoption of the foregoing report, a sufficient number of the Grand Lodges of America have taken favorable action thereon to warrant the committee appointed by the Grand Lodge of Colorado taking the second step. No information has been received by this committee or by the Grand Secretary of Colorado, of adverse action by any Grand Lodge. It is therefore presumable that all will in time gladly join in suitable memorial observances of that Mason, who was "first in war, first in peace, and first in the hearts of his countrymen."

As foreseen upon the initiation of the project, the irregular periods of meeting of the several Grand Lodges necessarily consumes much time in preliminary arrangements, and at least a couple of years more will be required for the several Grand Lodges to consider and approve the plans to be presented by the General Committee. Prior to calling a meeting of that committee, the members from Colorado have thought that an expression of opinion upon various details would be desirable, and they will therefore thank you, as a member of said committee, to forward to Ed C Parmelee, Grand Secretary, Denver, Colorado, your opinions upon the specific points hereinafter mentioned, together with such others as you may have, relating to the general subject.

The Grand Lodge of Colorado will cause these opinions to be published in full, and a copy forwarded to each member of the committee, in order that all may be wisely considered and the best adopted.

1   Please state if in your opinion any other day than the 14th of December, in 1899, should be considered for the memorial observances.

2   Do you favor a general rendezvous at the City of Washington?

3   Would you favor chartering of transportation to Mount Vernon for Masons alone, to be paid from a general fund to be provided, or for the boat on which the Masons travel to be for the accommodation of the public also, each Mason or other person paying his own fare?

4.   Please state if in your opinion other addresses should be given than one upon the life and character of Washington, and another upon his Masonic career

5   Please state if in your opinion it would be well for every Grand Master to prepare and read an address of two or three minutes' duration, suitable to the occasion

6   Please express your opinion whether or not the President of the United States should be invited to be present

7   Please express your opinion on the advisability of requesting the President of the United States, whether a Mason or otherwise, to give an address

8   Please express your opinion whether or not the Vice-President, Cabinet, Justices of the Supreme Court, or any of them, or others, should be invited to be present in case of an affirmative opinion as to the presence of the President

9.   Please express your opinion if the Grand Master of Virginia should not by virtue of the circumstances, preside at the observances

10.   Please express your opinion if a Lodge of Master Masons should be opened prior to the public observances

11   Please express your opinion if the General Grand Chapter of Royal Arch Masons of the United States, or the Grand Encampment of Knights Templar of the United States, should be invited to participate

12   Please name several eminent Masons, in the order of your preference, who should be selected to give the addresses that may be determined upon

13.   Please express your opinion upon the question of music, its character, whether vocal or instrumental, or both, and the pieces to be selected

14.   Please express your opinion upon the time and place for the committee to be called to formulate the report for presentation to the respective Grand Lodges.

15   Please state your opinion, if the order of procession in Washington, and from the river to the mansion, should place the youngest Grand Lodge at the head, to be followed by others according to juniority, with Virginia at the rear

16   Please state, if, in your opinion, the Grand Lodge of Virginia, or the Grand Lodges of Virginia and the District of Columbia, should be requested to appoint special committees to make local arrangements for carrying out the programme that may be adopted

17   Please make suggestions for observances at Mount Vernon other than those suggested herein.

18   State if in your opinion the respective Grand Lodges should recommend their constituent Lodges to hold memorial services in their respective Lodge rooms on the anniversary of Washington's death.

Respectfully and fraternally yours,

R W Woodbury,
W. D Todd,
W D Wright,
Committee from the Grand Lodge of Colorado

REPORT IN 1896

In 1896 the committee reported progress to the Grand Lodge, again reciting from the original report of the Committee on Jurisprudence, and closed as follows:

A number of Grand Lodges have appointed committees to serve with that from this Grand Lodge, * * * and your committee think there is ample time to complete all arrangements, and that every Grand Lodge will gladly take part in the Memorial Exercises

The only serious difficulty in the original suggestions was the cumbersome manner of arriving at a plan which required committees from all over the United States to meet somewhere and agree, and then report back to their respective Grand Lodges for approval, and when that had been done, to proceed with the arrangements approved In discussing the propositions that should be submitted by this committee to the committees of other Grand Lodges, the latter were invited to express their opinion upon the advisability of the Grand Lodge of Virginia taking the leadership, and the opinions expressed by other committees were in the affirmative

This committee is now further of the opinion that the Grand Lodge of Virginia should now be formally requested to take the leadership, adopt such plans as to it may seem best, and the committee from this Grand Lodge co-operate with the Grand Lodge of Virginia in carrying out those plans As a matter of fact, the Memorial Exercises originally proposed would necessarily be under the auspices of the Grand Lodge of Virginia, if a national gathering of Grand Lodges, or their Representatives, should be undertaken, for such a gathering and the memorial addresses should be held only at Mount Vernon

We therefore recommend that this Grand Lodge authorize this committee to present the matter to the Grand Lodge of Virginia, and make the formal request suggested, providing it first meets the approval of the committees from other Grand Lodges who have notified us of their appointment to act in conjunction with your committee

We further advise that your committee be directed to recommend to its associate committees from other Grand Lodges that each Grand Lodge recommend every Subordinate Lodge in its jurisdiction to hold memorial exercises on the 14th day of December, 1899, simultaneously with the national exercises at Mount Vernon

Fraternally submitted,

R. W. Woodbury
Wm. D. Todd
W. D. Wright.

CIRCULAR OF 1896

Immediately after the approval of the foregoing report by the Grand Lodge of Colorado another formal circular was issued, which after reciting the report in full, and its adoption by the Grand Lodge, proceeded to say

In a great measure the above report explains itself It is often the case that a matter which seems clear at its first inception develops complications after acquaintance, and it has been found in this case difficult to perfect details, or even generals, because of the large number of representatives of Grand Lodges to be consulted, the irregularity of Communications of the various Grand Lodges and the difficulty of conveniently holding a meeting of Grand Lodge committees It was, therefore, thought here that it would be better, all things considered, for the committees that have been appointed by the Grand Lodges to request the Grand Lodge of Virginia to continue plans, as to it may seem best, for such recognition of the 14th of December, 1899 In any event, the Grand Lodge of Virginia would, by right and courtesy, have charge of whatever Memorial Exercises might be provided for at Mount Vernon, and it is probable that every Grand Lodge in the United States would be glad to lend its presence and influence on that occasion upon invitation from the Grand Lodge of Virginia This arrangement would eliminate the difficulties which have developed in the progress of this committee's work, and we will ask you to notify this committee or the Grand Secretary of the Grand Lodge of Colo-receipt of the approval of the majority of the committees heretofore ap-proval could be conveyed without waiting to submit it to your own Grand Lodge, for the reason that it requires no expenditure from your Grand Lodge, and there can be no question of its meeting the approval of all   On receipt of the approval of the majority of the committees heretofore ap-pointed, this committee will communicate and make formal invitation in behalf of these committees, using their names in said invitation, to the Grand Lodge of Virginia, in accordance with the foregoing report

We conceive that the suggestion that each Grand Lodge should advise its Subordinates to arrange for memorial exercises in each of their Lodge rooms on the date of the anniversary, need not necessarily depend upon the adoption or rejection of the invitation to the Grand Lodge of Virginia, but that, should the latter accede to our invitation, the proposition will there-after fittingly emanate from that Grand Lodge, if not, that the several committees should recommend such action to their respective Grand Lodges

Fraternally yours,

R W WOODBURY
W D WRIGHT
W D TODD

LETTER TO GRAND MASTER OF VIRGINIA

DENVER, COLO, May 18, 1897

HON A R COURTNEY, Most Worshipful Grand Master, Richmond, Va

Dear Sir and Most Worshipful Brother—It gives me pleasure to for-ward to you, as the honored Grand Master of Masons of Virginia, the enclosed invitation to your Most Worshipful Grand Lodge, in accordance with the action of the Grand Lodge of Colorado, at its last annual Grand Communication, to assume the leadership in devising suitable Memorial

Services and carrying out the same, on the one-hundredth anniversary of the death of Brother George Washington. It has consumed much time in getting replies from the respective committees of other Grand Lodges, a difficulty that was early impressed upon this committee, and which aroused it to the necessity of your Grand Lodge taking the interesting subject into its own hands, and acting arbitrarily and without consultation with any other.

At the beginning, the Grand Lodge of Colorado felt that as it was admitted into the Union of States on the one-hundredth anniversary of the promulgation of the Declaration of Independence (which Brother George Washington made an effective instrument by his success in the field and in State-craft), the suggestion of holding Memorial Exercises on the anniversary of his death would emanate from Colorado with as much propriety as a child may suggest and arrange to observe the anniversary of a parent's loss with due solemnity and reverence.

I have seen but one unkind reference to the proposition, and that was by some foreign correspondent, whose name and State remains not in memory, and who wrote it somewhat flippantly as a 'celebration," rather conveying the idea of a gala day. This committee has uniformly referred to the exercises as "Memorial" Services, yet it is not inappropriate to speak of "celebrating" it. The church uses the word for its most solemn occasions, but I need not enlarge upon that point. The brother to whose comment I have referred had evidently sought to make a sharp and sparkling report in correspondence, as some occasionally do, and had not permitted his mind to dwell long enough upon this subject to perceive its magnitude. No person of intelligence can think of it carefully without its importance beginning to unfold to him.

Our committee sends you by this mail, under separate cover, copies of our circular letters, and a copy of our last Grand Lodge proceedings, with various references marked in the report of the Committee on Foreign Correspondence relative to the action of other Grand Lodges upon this general subject

You will, of course, understand that the irregular periods at which the Grand Lodges of the United States assemble, and the time required to print all their proceedings and then have them reviewed by a foreign correspondence committee, and that committee to report to its own Grand Lodge, and the latter have it put in type with its own proceedings, precludes the possibility of a single year's proceedings covering the action of all Grand Lodges   Some have been reported by our former proceedings, and some have committees still considering the subject, so far as we know   The various committees have different tenures of office.   Some were appointed to serve until after the proposed Memorial Services   We conceive, however, that if your Grand Lodge now approves the general wish, it should take the initiative as if nothing had been done by us   By your personal sympathy all the Grand Lodges of the United States will become enthusiasts in the support of old Virginia   Our committee thinks that much depends upon you personally, for if your heart is in harmony with the movement, as we believe it to be, you will appoint an exceptionally able committee from your Grand Lodge, broad enough, and great enough to grasp the national scope of this enterprise.

Our committee thinks that as your Grand Lodge does not meet until December, it would serve to increase the interest in the various Grand Jurisdictions were we to report to the several committees and embody a copy of our official invitation to your Grand Lodge, but we realize the impropriety of our furnishing a copy of a paper addressed to your Grand Lodge, to any one except our own Grand Lodge in our official report to that body, which will meet in September   We will, however, issue a circular to the other committees and Grand Lodges, and if it meets your approval, suggest that you write us a letter, to be incorporated in that circular, acknowledging the receipt of the official invitation to your Grand Lodge, and expressing your favorable sentiments upon the general subject All the committees and Grand Lodges would thereupon look with increasing interest for the next Grand Communication of your Grand Lodge

If there be any service this committee can perform to aid you or your Grand Lodge, I beg you to feel that it will be a pleasure to respond, and in behalf of the committee from Colorado I beg you to present our letter of invitation to your Grand Lodge, and accept, Most Worshipful Brother, this profession of our fraternal esteem

Sincerely yours,

R W. WOODBURY,
Chairman

In due time Brother Kemper of the original Virginia committee, appointed to co-operate with the Grand Lodge of Colorado, reported to this Grand Lodge all the Colorado circulars and correspondence, together with the following·

BROTHER KEMPER'S REPORT TO VIRGINIA

To the Most Worshipful Grand Master of the Grand Lodge of Virginia

I have the honor to submit a report of the inception, progress and present status of the proposed observance of the centennial anniversary of the death of Worshipful Brother George Washington

By reference to the Proceedings of the Grand Lodge of Virginia for the year 1893, it will be seen that the Grand Master, in his annual address, made mention of the receipt by him of a letter from a committee of the Grand Lodge of Colorado, proposing to mark the notable anniversary referred to by suitable Masonic observances at Mount Vernon

The committee to whom the Grand Master's address was referred, in their report, among other things, recommended the following action:

"Resolved, 2 That this Grand Lodge accepts the patriotic suggestion of the Grand Lodge of Colorado with regard to the centennial anniversary of the death of Washington on the 14th day of December, 1899, and the Grand Master is authorized to appoint a committee as therein recommended"

This recommendation was adopted, and the Grand Master appointed as the committee Right Worshipful Francis A Reed, principal, and Worshipful K Kemper, alternate

Your committee promptly informed the committee of the Grand Lodge of Colorado of their appointment and their readiness to co-operate, and in due time received from the latter a circular letter dated March 15, 1895, a copy of which is annexed marked exhibit "A," and made a part of this report

Suitable answers to the propositions and suggestions contained in the circular letter were made by the undersigned, the death of our lamented Brother Reed, principal, having devolved the work on the alternate

It resulted from the answers received by the committee of the Grand Lodge of Colorado to the above mentioned circular that your committee received another communication dated September 19, 1896, formally "requesting the Grand Lodge of Virginia to take the leadership in this matter and adopt such plans as to it may seem best" for a successful consummation, in co-operation with the other Grand Lodges in the United States

In evidence of the alacrity with which the other Grand Lodges acceded to the suggestion of the committee of the Grand Lodge of Colorado, that primacy in these interesting ceremonies should be assigned to the Grand Lodge of Virginia, the Colorado committee sent me copies of many of the answers above referred to

No further action was taken until some time in last August, when, in response to an urgent request from the Colorado committee to be informed as to the likelihood of the Grand Lodge of Virginia being willing to assume the proposed leadership, I sent to the chairman of that committee a letter, of which the following is a copy.

Alexandria, Va, August 25, 1897

Right Worshipful Roger W Woodbury, Chairman, etc

Dear Sir and Brother—Acknowledging the receipt of your valued letter, with accompanying papers, concerning the proposed Memorial Exercises in honor of Brother George Washington, in 1899, and suggesting that the Grand Lodge of Virginia should assume the leadership of the same, I have the honor to make answer that I have seized the first opportunity presenting itself to confer person-ally with the Most Worshipful Grand Master of the Grand Lodge of Virginia, and as the result of that conference I am authorized to accept for the present committee of our Grand Lodge the primacy in this interesting matter so gracefully tendered by the Grand Lodge of Colorado, and to say that a full report of the proposition will be made to our Grand Lodge at its annual communication in December next, at which time I have no doubt a committee will be appointed to take charge of the matter, who will in due time formulate a programme, and take all other steps need ful to carry to a successful completion these exercises naturally so full of interest to all Americans, especially to ' the household of the Faithful "

This committee will, when appointed, I am sure, gladly avail themselves of your kind offers of assistance

Reciprocating your kind expressions, I remain,

Yours fraternally,
K KEMPER,
Committee Grand Lodge of Virginia

Immediately following the receipt by the Colorado committee of the foregoing letter, that committee issued a circular note to each of the Grand Lodges in the United States, informing them of the status of the corre-spondence with your committee, and concluding with the suggestion that each committee of the several Grand Lodges "at once forward to Brother Kemper, at Alexandria, their names and addresses, in order to facilitate correspondence from that office "

Following in due time the issuance of this circular from the Colorado committee, letters in furtherance of its concluding suggestion began to be received by your committee, and at this writing I have to report the receipt of these, viz :   *   *   *   *

From the zeal displayed in these letters, and, indeed, in every incident of the correspondence as set forth in this report, it is evident that the proposed commemorative exercises, if carried out to the successful conclusion so plainly assured by the hearty co-operation of our brethren all over the country, will, without doubt, be the grandest Masonic event of the century.

In conclusion, I beg to thank the Grand Lodge for their kindness in imposing upon me this labor of love, as in its performance I have enjoyed the privilege of pleasant correspondence with so many of the brethren of the Mystic tie in different sections of our land, and have the honor to close this report with the recommendation that the Grand Master be authorized and requested to appoint a committee consisting of not less than three nor more than five members to take charge of these proposed commemorative observances, with plenary powers to make all needful arrangements, financial, social, and literary, and to suggest tentatively the following programme   *   *   *   *

All of which is respectfully submitted

K KEMPER,
Chairman.

ACTION OF GRAND LODGE OF VIRGINIA

The foregoing report of Brother Kemper was referred by the Grand Lodge of Virginia to its Standing Committee on Propositions, which reported as follows, and the same was formally adopted by that Grand Lodge.

That they have given careful consideration to the said report and its accompanying exhibits, and that they find that this Grand Lodge at its annual Communication in the year 1893, resolved to accept the patriotic suggestion of the Grand Lodge of Colorado with regard to the centennial anniversary of the death of Worshipful Brother George Washington on the 14th day of December, 1799, and they further find that Right Worshipful Brother K Kemper did, on the 25th of August, 1897, in a letter to Right Worshipful Roger W Woodbury, Chairman of the Committee of the Grand Lodge of Colorado, write him that he had consulted with the Most Worshipful Grand Master of Masons in Virginia, and that as a result of that conference had accepted from the then committee of that Grand Lodge primacy in the matter of the proper observance of the 14th day of December 1899, and that he had no doubt that a committee would be appointed at this annual Communication to take charge of the matter, and would, in due time, formulate a programme and take all other steps needful to carry to a successful completion the exercises naturally so full of interest to all Americans, and especially to "the household of the faithful"

So that the committee, at the outset, ascertained that this Grand Lodge is fully committed to the work of the proper observance of the day indicated

That the matter has received thoughtful attention in the admirable address of the retiring Grand Master, Courtney, who says that the crowning glory of this old Commonwealth is the honor of having furnished a Washington to the cause of liberty and constitutional government, and that every son of hers, whether he be adopted or to the manor born, should join most heartily in the work to be done   In view of these facts, and what your committee believes will be regarded by this Grand Lodge as properly the most illustrious and conspicuous undertaking it has ever been called upon to take part in, we recommend that the suggestion contained in Right Worshipful Brother Kemper's report be adopted, and that the Grand Master, at this session of the Grand Lodge, be requested to appoint a committee consisting of five Master Masons to take charge of these proposed commemorative ceremonies with power to make all needful arrangements, financial, social, literary and otherwise and that in so doing they act under and at all times subject to the direction of the Most Worshipful Grand Master of Masons in Virginia during the recess of this Grand Body, and that the programme tentatively mapped out by Right Worshipful Brother Kemper be referred to this committee, when appointed, with these directions

That, if practicable, Fredericksburg Lodge No 4, of Virginia, in which Worshipful Brother George Washington was entered, passed, and raised to the sublime degree of Master Mason, be included in the ceremonies which it may deem proper to have in pursuance of the object of this report, and that the Board of Lady Regents at Mount Vernon, Virginia, be respectfully and earnestly requested, through this committee, to lend their consent and cordial co-operation in the exercises that may be deemed pertinent and appropriate to an observance of the anniversary of Worshipful Brother George Washington's death on December 14, 1899, and that, as soon as practicable after the closing of this Grand Lodge, a copy of this report be addressed to the Grand Master of every Grand Lodge of Masons in correspondence with this Grand Lodge, and that each and every Grand Lodge be invited to be present (at the proposed services or ceremonies) in the person of its Grand Master, or, in his absence, such alternate as such Grand Master may appoint That the Grand Lodge of Colorado be fraternally thanked for inaugurating this matter, and that some duty in the programme be especially assigned to the Grand Master of the Grand Lodge of that jurisdiction That Fredericksburg Lodge No 4 and Alexandria-Washington Lodge No 22, of the latter of which Worshipful Brother General George Washington was the Master named in its charter, be especially invited to aid in the furtherance of the object of this report, and that, if practicable, each of those Lodges, because of its history and connection with Worshipful Brother George Washington, be given prominent parts in the exercises it may be deemed proper to arrange for in the programme

That the committee hereinbefore provided for be allowed, with the approbation of the Grand Master, to draw on the Treasurer of the Grand Lodge for reasonable sums to be expended in furtherance of the object of this undertaking, and that they be requested in their report to the next Grand Lodge to devise a plan for raising the money necessary to defray the expenses incident to the observance hereinbefore sought to be provided for

That the Grand Secretary in his communications to the several Grand Masters be requested to ask these Grand Masters respectively, to send their replies as soon as possible to the invitations extended, and that the Grand Secretary, as soon as these replies are received, shall furnish the committee, hereinbefore provided for, with copies of the same That this committee be requested to make full report of its acts and doings, and especially as to the programme for a proper observance of December 14, 1899, on the first day of the next Grand Annual Communication of this Grand Lodge And that the committee, hereinbefore provided for, shall be considered as a Committee of Arrangements, and shall exist as such until after the completion of the services at Mount Vernon on December 14, 1899, and that they shall have charge of all the arrangements incident thereto And that further, in view of the magnitude and importance of this work, and that the matter may be disseminated as widely as possible, that a copy of this report be furnished for publication before the publication of the proceedings of this Grand Annual Communication

Respectfully submitted

W B McChesney,	J E Sibbitt
James B Sype,	Jas D Bondurant
J T Lr Snyder	Wm Dean
J H Fisher	Frank E Conrad

A copy teste
     Geo W Carrington,
       Grand Secretary

REPORT OF THE COLORADO COMMITTEE 1897

To the Most Worshipful Grand Lodge

Your committee appointed in 1893 to inaugurate a movement for suitable National Masonic Memorial Services upon the one-hundredth anniversary of the death of our Illustrious Brother George Washington, respectfully and fraternally report

That in accordance with your action at your last Annual Grand Communication they duly communicated through the representative of the Grand Lodge of Virginia and its Most Worshipful Grand Master, with the Most Worshipful Grand Lodge of Virginia, inviting that Grand Jurisdiction to assume and take full control of the proposed Memorial Services, and all arrangements connected therewith   Our Communication was necessarily a review of all that had been done by this committee, so that a clear understanding would be had of the situation, and as a part of the history of this Grand Lodge, we herewith quote the same in full, as follows

To the Most Worshipful Grand Lodge, A F and A M , of Virginia

In accordance with the recommendation made by the Most Worshipful Grand Master in 1893, the Grand Lodge of Colorado, A F and A M , appointed the undersigned as a committee to inaugurate a movement for suitable National Masonic Memorial Services upon the one hundredth anniversary of the death of Worshipful Brother George Washington   As an undertaking so important should be entered upon only after reasonable assurances that it could be carried out in a manner befitting the character and dignity of the occasion, the first duty of the committee was to submit the recommendation to the several Grand Masters, and through them to the Grand Lodges of the United States for their approval

As the result of such preliminary correspondence a sufficient number of Grand Lodges expressly approved the recommendation, and no information of adverse action was conveyed to the committee   The latter, therefore, felt warranted in assuming that in due time all the Grand bodies, representing the great body of American Freemasonry, would loyally unite to appropriately honor the memory of him to whom it was said in the original recommendation of the Grand Master of Colorado, that by "universal consent of civilized men he is the largest figure in all merely human history, and his name stands first upon the roll of Masonry s illustrious dead "

The correspondence of this committee with committees appointed by other Grand Lodges invited expressions of opinion by way of suggestions as to various specific details of the proposed ceremonies   One of these questions was as to the advisability of the Most Worshipful Grand Lodge of Virginia taking the leadership in, and having charge of, the exercises, and that said exercises should most appropriately be held at Mount Vernon   In reply to these questions the co-operating committees expressed opinions in the affirmative

At the Annual Grand Communication of the Most Worshipful Grand Lodge of Colorado in 1896, this committee made a report upon the subject, which was unanimously adopted by the Grand Lodge * * * *

Subsequently, and under date of September 19, 1896, a circular letter was by this committee sent to all committees appointed by other Grand Lodges   It embodied the whole of the report adopted by the Grand Lodge of Colorado, above referred to, together with some additional suggestions on the part of the committee   To this last circular letter this committee is in receipt of replies from the several committees representing other Grand Lodges   Though in some instances modestly disclaiming to speak officially, the distinguished Masons serving on these committees, and from whom these replies were received, may well be regarded as expressing the sentiments of their respective Grand Lodges   And as indicating approval of the recommendation generally, and the kindly sentiment in favor of the Grand Lodge of Virginia formulating and taking full charge of the exercises, this committee takes the liberty of quoting in part only, from a few of these communications, as follows

The representative of the Grand Lodge of West Virginia thus expresses himself "I heartily agree in the suggestions in the foregoing letters   The grand old Lodge of dear old Virginia ought to have the lead in this matter "

The Grand Lodge of Maryland, through its committee, says "We concur in the suggestion that the Grand Lodge of Virginia be requested to assume the lead in the matter   This is especially appropriate in view of the proposition to hold the services upon the soil of that State "

From Vermont on the north, the duly appointed committee of its Grand Lodge says "The suggestions made in the circular recently received from you in relation to the formulation of plans by the Grand Lodge of Virginia for the observance of the centennial of Washington's death, meets with my hearty concurrence   I am joined in this by our Most Worshipful Grand Master, who approves fully of your suggestions "

From Texas in the extreme south, we have the following "I most heartily concur with the committee on the part of our Grand Lodge, wherein they recommend that the Grand Lodge of Virginia be requested to formulate plans for the proper observance of the centennial of the death of Brother George Washington, and that it take active charge and control of the matter "

Indiana, through the proper representative of its Grand Lodge, thus warmly gives encouragement 'I most heartily approve the action of the Grand Lodge of Colorado, and am satisfied that when the time comes the Grand Lodge of Indiana will be found in line, and her Subordinate Lodges in no manner lacking "

The Grand Lodge of Michigan, through its representative, speaks in the following manner "Acting as a special committee to represent the Grand Lodge of Michigan on this memorial occasion, I am in full sympathy with the suggestions of your committee, in requesting the Grand Lodge of Virginia, which was the Masonic home of the illustrious dead, to formulate the plans for this memorial occasion "

The Grand Lodge of Arkansas gives its approval in the following manner ' This Grand Lodge approves the suggestion to invite the Grand Lodge of Virginia to formulate the particular exercises to be held, and will gladly co operate in what ever may be indicated therefor "

From Kansas, the Grand Lodge, through its appointed committee, promises co-operation as follows ' We heartily coincide with the committee of your Grand Lodge in its suggestion that the Grand Lodge of Virginia adopt such plans as it seems best, for the proposed Memorial Services on the one hundredth anniversary of the death of Brother George Washington, and that the several Grand Lodges throughout the United States co-operate with the Grand Lodge of Virginia in carrying out such plans "

In behalf of all the Grand Lodges whose Committees we are in correspondence with, we now feel warranted in assuring you of the strength and support of all The distinguished Masons whose names are attached to many such approving letters may be regarded as speaking on this subject the voice of Masonry in their several States It is, therefore, the great body of the Craft, which, through them, now invites the Most Worshipful Grand Lodge of the State, which was the "Mother of Presidents," to assume its proper leadership in honoring the memory of the first and greatest President, and Virginia's most illustrious son Under such honored leadership, with the interest sure to be taken by the several Grand Lodges and the Craft generally, the Memorial should result in a great National Assemblage of leading Masons, sure to be representative citizens from their several sections It would be a most notable assemblage, held under circumstances which would make it one of the greatest events in the Masonic history of the world It would call attention anew to the remarkable array of great men, who in the "days that tried men's souls," were distinguished alike for love of country and of Masonry It would add to the accepted belief of American Masons that the absorption and ardent advocacy of Masonic principles by so many of the founders of the Republic, happily did much to strengthen the cause of Liberty The many modern fraternities, following as to their main teachings in the footsteps of Masonry, and thereby conserving the best interests of society in the perilous changes so rapidly going on in social and political conditions, it will be remembered were not then in existence The field was occupied almost exclusively by Masonry, then, as now, and at all times, attracting to its ranks the higher grade of men, naturally fitted to mould the destinies of States Under such circumstances, the common fatherhood of God, as taught by Masonry, expanded into the religious toleration and the total separation of Church and State, which the Fathers so wisely embodied in the laws of the Republic, and the Masonic teaching of the common brotherhood of man grew and unfolded into the abolition of the Old-World titles of distinction, and the civil equality of all men before the Law, under a government of the people And thus by the evolution and expansive force of great ideas under favoring conditions the fundamental teachings of Masonry became the foundation principles of the Republic The thoughts and memories suggested by such an occasion should strengthen the sentiment of Patriotism among all our people, and promote the honor and glory of Masonry

In conclusion we assure you that the Most Worshipful Grand Lodge of Colorado, which we have the honor to represent, will do all in its power to assist you in the important work we now fraternally invite you to assume the full control of

Fraternally yours,

ROGER WILLIAMS WOODBURY,
WILLIAM D WRIGHT,
WILLIAM DAVID TODD,
Committee of the Grand Lodge of Colorado

The Grand Lodge of Virginia will meet in Annual Communication next December, but your committee has the extreme pleasure of reporting that your invitation has been received in a spirit worthy of the occasion, as appears from the letter furnished us in advance of the Virginia Annual Grand Communication, in order that their sentiments might be now reported to you (See letter of Worshipful Brother K Kemper, on page 30)

The Grand Lodge of Colorado may therefore rely upon receiving in due time an official request and invitation from the Grand Lodge of Virginia to co-operate with, and join with it, in suitable Memorial Exercises, and we deem further action by your committee, until then, unnecessary, except to communicate to our associate committees appointed by other Grand Lodges the contents of the foregoing letter from the representative of Virginia

We are pleased to advise you of the favorable result of our negotiations, and feel that the Masonic patriotism and statesmanship which has caused your proposition to be so happily received by our distinguished brothers of ' Old Virginia" is a cause for profound congratulation

Respectfully and fraternally submitted,

ROGER WILLIAMS WOODBURY,

WILLIAM D WRIGHT,

WILLIAM DAVID TODD,

Committee of the Grand Lodge of Colorado

FROM ADDRESS OF THE GRAND MASTER OF COLORADO 1898

On February 2, 1898, I received the following letter from the Right Worshipful Grand Secretary of Virginia

Richmond, Va , January 29 1898

Most Worshipful Cromwell Tucker, Grand Master of Masons in Colorado

Most Worshipful Brother—In compliance with the mandate of the Grand Lodge of Virginia, as contained in the enclosed report it affords me great pleasure to extend to your Grand Lodge Virginia s cordial invitation to be present at, and participate in, the Memorial Ceremonies incident to the observance of the death of Worshipful Brother George Washington, to be held at Mount Vernon on December 14, 1899, either in the person of the Grand Master, or such alternate as he may appoint

Full information as to the details of the ceremonies on that occasion will, in due time, be forwarded to your Grand Lodge by the Special Committee of Arrangements appointed by the Grand Lodge of Virginia

Hoping to be notified at an early day of your acceptance of this invitation, I have the honor to be,

Yours fraternally,

GEO W CARRINGTON,

Grand Secretary

To which reply was made as follows:

Denver, Colo., February 9, 1898

Right Worshipful Geo W Carrington, Grand Secretary, Richmond, Va

Right Worshipful Brother—It affords me much pleasure to acknowledge receipt of your letter of January 29, in which you convey the cordial invitation of the Grand Lodge of Virginia to the Grand Lodge of Colorado, requesting our participation in the Memorial Ceremonies incident to the observance of the death of Worshipful Brother George Washington, which are to be held at Mount Vernon on December 14, 1899, either in the person of our then Grand Master, or such alternate as he may appoint, and in reply thereto, I beg to say that without doubt our Grand Lodge will be so represented

The patriotic sentiments contained in the proposed Commemorative Ceremonies appeal so strongly to every member of our Craft throughout the United States of America, that it does not require a prophetic eye to foresee that the gathering of Masons on that occasion will be the largest in our history, and be pregnant with the most important results

We fully agree with the sentiments, so admirably expressed by Most Worshipful Brother Courtney, that the crowning glory of your old Commonwealth is the honor of having furnished a Washington to the cause of liberty and constitutional government, yet we, while not to the manor born," claim almost, if not an equal honor, in the same crowning glory, the effects of which are felt and always will be felt by all civilized nations throughout the world

It is my further duty and extreme pleasure to fraternally acknowledge the courteous action of your Grand Lodge in extending its thanks for our inauguration of this matter, and for the special assignment of some duty in the programme to the Grand Master of Colorado

Permit me to express the hope that the success of the undertaking may be commensurate with the wishes and desires of your own people, and of all Masons wheresoever dispersed, and assuring you of the cordial and hearty co-operation of this Grand Lodge, I beg to remain,

Most fraternally yours,

CROMWELL TUCKER,
Grand Master

On August 29, 1898, the following circular letter was received

To the Most Worshipful Grand Master, Officers and Members of the Grand Lodge A F and A M of Colorado

Most Worshipful Sir and Brethren—At the instance of the Grand Lodge of Colorado, and subsequently at the request of her sister Grand Lodges, the Grand

Lodge of Virginia assumed the conduct of the proper commemoration of the one hundredth anniversary of the death of Brother George Washington, the services incident to the occasion to take place at Mount Vernon, on December 14, 1899 The undersigned, in pursuance of a resolution of the Most Worshipful Grand Lodge of Virginia, have been appointed a committee to prepare a suitable programme, and to devise the ways and means for carrying out the same with credit to those who have undertaken it, and honor to our ancient and honorable Fraternity

After repeated meetings of our committee and most careful consideration of the subject, we have found that it will require an outlay of money which will be equal to a per capita assessment of one cent per member in each Grand Jurisdiction

As the commemoration is to be a national one, and Virginia has undertaken its management at the request of her sister Grand Lodges, this committee deems it proper that these Grand Lodges shall have the opportunity—if they so desire— to contribute to its proper observance

To that end, if your Grand Jurisdiction deem the proposed observance worthy of the expenditure named, they can forward any amount they feel disposed to contribute to R W Fred Pleasants, Grand Treasurer of the Grand Lodge of Virginia, Masonic Temple, Richmond, Va , who has kindly consented to act as treasurer for the committee, and who will receipt for same

K KEMPER,
Chairman
J B SENER,
JNO W DANIEL,
MICAJAH WOODS,
A R COURTNEY,
Committee

Alexandria, Va , August 22, 1898

In regard to the opportunity offered for our financial participation of the expenses incident to the occasion, I would fraternally recommend that as the event is to be a national one, and the management of the same has been undertaken by the Grand Lodge of Virginia at the request and suggestion of other Grand Lodges, we should contribute our per capita proportion and even more if necessary, to protect the Grand Lodge of Virginia against undue expense

Any other matters of importance in connection with this great Masonic ceremony will doubtless be communicated to you by the standing com-

mittee, which consists of Most Worshipful Brothers Roger W Woodbury,
William D Wright and William D Todd, to whom I would respectfully
suggest that the correspondence submitted herewith be referred

This portion of the Grand Master's address being referred to the Memorial Committee, report was made thereon, and unanimously adopted, as
follows

REPORT OF THE COLORADO COMMITTEE 1898

To the Most Worshipful Grand Lodge

Your Committee on Memorial Exercises upon the centennial anniversary of the death of Worshipful Brother General George Washington, respectfully report

That they have had under consideration the references and recommendations made in the address of Most Worshipful Grand Master Tucker,
and during the past year have continued in official correspondence with
the Committee of Arrangements appointed by the Most Worshipful Grand
Lodge of Virginia

The committee of the Grand Lodge of Virginia which was originally
appointed to consider and report upon the invitation of this Grand Lodge to
take general charge of the Memorial Exercises, referred to it in their report
as "properly the most illustrious and conspicuous undertaking" that the
Grand Lodge of Virginia had ever been called upon to take part in   Their
report, which was adopted, also contained the following

"That the Grand Lodge of Colorado be fraternally thanked for inaugurating
this matter, and that some duty in the programme be especially assigned to the
Grand Master of the Grand Lodge of that Jurisdiction "

The Committee of Arrangements of the Grand Lodge of Virginia has forwarded to your Grand Master and to this committee the following proposed order of exercises

PROGRAMME, MASONIC SERVICES, DECEMBER 14, 1899, AT THE TOMB OF BROTHER GENERAL GEORGE WASHINGTON

The Grand Lodge of Virginia, Fredericksburg Lodge No 4, Alexandria-Washington Lodge No 22, delegates and representatives from other Grand Jurisdictions, and invited guests, will proceed from Alexandria to Mount Vernon by electric cars, leaving Alexandria at 9 30 a m

At Mount Vernon the bodies will form on the east side of the house, and proceed to the old vault by the same path and in the same order in which the procession was formed, and moved, on the day of General Washington's funeral, December 18, 1799   At the old vault the services will commence and be conducted as follows

Solemn dirge by the band

Prayer by Brother the Right Reverend A M Randolph, Bishop of the diocese of Southern Virginia

Music by an octette

Address by the Grand Master of Colorado

Procession will then move to the vault, within which the earthly remains of General Washington and his wife now lie, encased in marble tombs   The Grand Lodge will form in a circle around the vault, Grand Officers and Representatives of other Jurisdictions in front, Lodge No 4 on the right and Lodge No 22 on the left

Masonic services at the tomb, conducted by the Grand Lodge of Virginia, aided by the Representatives of other Grand Jurisdictions

Prayer by the Grand Chaplain of the Grand Lodge of Virginia

Vocal music

Benediction

The procession will then return to the east front of the mansion, where the Grand Master of Masons in Virginia will introduce the President of the United States, who will make an address to Masons and the general public, who will then be admitted to full participation in the ceremonies

Hymn "America," sung by all present, the band leading the music. During the ceremonies minute guns will be fired from Fort Washington, and from a United States war vessel, to be stationed in the Potomac opposite Mount Vernon, in case permission can be obtained from the proper officials

K. KEMPER,
Chairman
J B SENER,
JNO W DANIEL,
MICAJAH WOODS,
A B COURTNEY,
Committee

The Virginia committee has also furnished us with a printed account of the ceremonies which took place at Mount Vernon upon the death of Washington, and which we summarize as follows.

Washington died at twenty minutes past 10, on Saturday night, December 14, 1799

On the succeeding Monday a funeral Lodge was held to make arrangements for the interment

At an early hour on Wednesday, the 18th, the Masonic fraternity, under escort of the military and citizens of Alexandria, started for Mount Vernon, where they arrived about one o'clock in the afternoon, and at three the funeral procession moved in the following order

The troops, horse and foot

The clergy

The General's horse (with saddle, holsters and pistols), led by two colored grooms

Music

Guard

The body of Washington, which was borne on a bier by a detail of four Virginian lieutenants

The pallbearers, consisting of officers of the Revolution, all members of Alexandria Lodge, except one

The principal mourners

The corporation of Alexandria

Alexandria Lodge No 22

Brooke Lodge No 47, of Alexandria

Federal Lodge No 15, of Washington

Upon arriving at the grave the services of the Episcopal Church were conducted by the Rector of Christ Church of Alexandria, and the Masonic ceremonies by Dr Elisha Cullen Dick, Worshipful Master of Alexandria Lodge No 22, and Rev James Muir, Chaplain of the same Lodge

During the exercises general discharges were fired by the infantry, cavalry and eleven pieces of artillery on the banks of the Potomac, back of the vault, and minute guns from a vessel in the stream

From the programme arranged for the Centennial Memorial, it will be observed that the procession, salutes and exercises are to follow as closely as practicable the original obsequies

Your committee thinks it would verge upon a Masonic crime for any Grand Lodge in the United States to be unrepresented at the Memorial Ceremonies in honor of the Father of his Country, and whose Masonic influence, through the hundred years since his death, has recommended tens of thousands of good men to become Masons

The presence of the several Grand Masters will be an official act, testifying to the love and affection of all the Freemasons of their respective Grand Jurisdictions, and as such it should be done at the expense of the Grand Lodges themselves

The fame of Washington as a patriot and a Mason belongs to all the States in the Union, and not alone to Virginia, and so each Grand Lodge should feel it a duty as well as a pleasure to contribute from its means towards defraying the expense of the tribute of love and affection which Virginia is called upon to carry through

Your committee therefore recommends the adoption of the following resolutions:

Resolved, That there is hereby appropriated from the Grand Treasury the sum of seventy-five dollars toward the expenses of the Washington Centennial Memorial exercises under the auspices of the Most Worshipful Grand Lodge of Virginia, and the Grand Secretary is hereby authorized and directed to draw a warrant for the amount, and forward the same to Right Worshipful Fred Pleasants, Grand Treasurer of the Grand Lodge of Virginia, for the purpose herein stated

Resolved, That the Grand Secretary be, and hereby is, authorized and directed to inform the chairman of the committee of the Grand Lodge of Virginia, having the Washington Centennial Memorial exercises in charge, that should that committee's estimate of expenses be exceeded, this Grand Lodge will cheerfully contribute such additional pro rata as may be necessary

Resolved, That there is hereby appropriated from the Grand Treasury such sum of money as may be required to pay the necessary expenses of the Most Worshipful Grand Master or his Representative in attending the Washington Centennial Memorial exercises in behalf of this Grand Lodge, and the brethren of this Grand Jurisdiction, and that the Grand Secretary is hereby authorized and directed to draw a warrant for such sum as shall be certified to him for such purpose

Resolved, That each Lodge in this Jurisdiction be and hereby is recommended to make such independent arrangements as to it may seem most appropriate for the observance of the 14th day of December, 1899, in their respective Lodge rooms, in memory of the exalted virtues and public and Masonic services of that brother who was "first in war, first in peace, and first in the hearts of his countrymen"

Fraternally submitted,
ROGER W WOODBURY
WILLIAM D WRIGHT
WILLIAM D TODD

FINANCIAL AID TO THE VIRGINIA COMMITTEE.

FREDERICKSBURG, VA , January 14, 1899

To ROGER W WOODBURY, W D WRIGHT AND WM D TODD, Committee:

Dear Sirs and Brothers—At a meeting of the Executive Committee held yesterday, after most patient consideration of the whole question of the December 14 1899, Centennial, in which your primacy as to its suggestion, and our primacy in its conduct, was fully considered, the necessity of raising means to make it a Masonic success was fully considered, and I was deputed, my brethren, to say these things unto you   As you will see from the papers which I enclose, the Grand Lodge of Virginia has already arranged to raise $3,000 to insure its success, but this will be a long ways from making it a success If you have followed the action of the Grand Lodges of Ohio, Illinois and Texas, no provision has so far been made to extend us any financial assistance It is all-important that at the very latest this committee should know by June 1st what means it can control in order to make the Centennial a success So far the only Grand Lodges that have voted appropriations are Colorado, Delaware, Maryland, Idaho, Montana and South Carolina In all not over $200, on the one-cent per capita basis Now more than this amount was expended in preliminary meetings, printing, travel and postage last year No salaries are being paid Of course, printing, postage and typewriting are inevitable expenses The statistics show that your Grand Lodge has more than seven-twelfths of the membership of our Grand Lodge We recognize, however, that the expense of your committee in attending, and of your Grand Master and Grand Secretary, will cost several hundred dollars, and after maturest consideration it has occurred to us that as we deem it a necessity, you will esteem it a pleasure to raise for the expenses of this occasion at least $1,000 The Centennial occasion will no doubt evoke not only the highest sentiment, but the most practical results for its accomplishment from the Centennial State It does not occur to us that anything more than this simple presentation will be necessary to secure the amount asked for, and we write at this time because we are calling upon our own Subordinate Lodges, as you will see by circular enclosed, to raise their amount if practicable, by the 22nd of February, and advised as you now are, we have no doubt that after conference with your Grand Master and Grand Secretary the necessary steps can be taken to do this My own mother Lodge of Washington of this place, which has contributed $100, did so by calling on its members for personal contributions, and these were promptly made In this connection permit me to ask you to have prepared a short sketch of your Grand Lodge and of your Centennial Grand Master and Grand Secretary, so that we may have the same for the memorial volume I especially invite your attention to the tentative order of observance at the new tomb at Mount Vernon, and ask that you will give it patient thought, and make any and every suggestion that you may deem pertinent, in order that its appropriateness may challenge the admiration of the present generation, and serve as an admirable precedent for another centennial There is a large amount of work to be done and a large amount of correspondence ahead, and I especially rely upon your promptness in correspondence and your cordial co-operation in all of our plans

Fraternally,

James B Sexer,
Chairman Executive Committee.

Grand Junction, Colo, January 24, 1899

R W Woodbury, Chairman, Denver, Colorado.

Dear Sir and Right Worshipful Brother—Your favor of the 19th inst with enclosures as stated, came to hand Saturday evening, and I have given the same careful consideration

I feel anxious that Colorado should do her part and do it generously in providing funds to assist in defraying the expenses of the Washington Memorial Service Believing that brethren so well versed in Masonic law as the members of your committee, would do nothing that could possibly bring any criticism upon their actions, I take pleasure in enclosing you herewith a commission of authority to raise the necessary funds in such a manner, as, in the wisdom of your committee, may seem best.

Permit me to request, however, that you kindly report to me the plan adopted, and the line of action which the committee will pursue in this matter * * *

With kindest personal regards and wishing you abundant success in your undertaking, I am,

Very fraternally,

HORACE T DeLONG,

Grand Master

Grand Junction, Colorado, January 24, 1899

To All to Whom These Presents May Come, Greeting

Know ye, that I, Horace T DeLong, Grand Master of Masons of the State of Colorado, reposing special trust and confidence in the fidelity, skill and Masonic ability of our Worshipful Brothers Roger W Woodbury, William D Wright and William D Todd, do hereby constitute and appoint them a committee to raise, in the name and on behalf of the Most Worshipful Grand Lodge of Colorado, funds to assist in defraying the expense assumed by the Grand Lodge of Virginia in connection with the commemoration ceremonies on the centennial anniversary of the death of Worshipful Brother George Washington

I do hereby authorize and empower them to solicit funds for this purpose from the Masons of Colorado, and from any and all Lodges throughout our Grand Jurisdiction, and for so doing this shall be their sufficient warrant

Given under my hand and private seal this 23d day of January, A L 5899, A D 1899, at Grand Junction, Colorado

HORACE T DE LONG,

Grand Master

By Authority of the Most Worshipful Grand Master of Colorado, A F and A M

DENVER, COLO, February 1, 1899

Dear Sir and Brother·

Six years ago (1893) the Grand Master of Masons of Colorado recommended the Grand Lodge to consider the initiation of a movement for the holding of national Masonic memorial exercises upon the one-hundredth anniversary of the death of Worshipful Brother George Washington, which took place on the 14th of December, 1799

The committee of the Grand Lodge which reported upon the recommendation of the Grand Master said　*　*　*　*

The report was unanimously adopted by the Grand Lodge, and the undersigned were appointed a committee to initiate the movement among the Grand Lodges of the United States　After three years of correspondence, taking it to 1896, so many Grand Lodges had signified their approval and co-operation that the Grand Lodge of Virginia was then formally requested by the Grand Lodge of Colorado to take charge of all further arrangements, which request was formally acceded to at the next meeting of the Grand Lodge of Virginia　Its committee is composed of a number of the ablest men in Masonic, professional and political life in that State, and they expect not only that all the Grand Lodges of the United States will be represented at the Memorial, but also a considerable number of foreign jurisdictions　It is not improbable that the Grand Master of England, His Royal Highness the Prince of Wales, will also be present　In any event, it will be the most general gathering of Grand Masters and representative Masons that the world has ever seen

The Grand Lodge of Virginia will assemble on the 13th at Alexandria, from there and from Washington, the next morning, they will escort by river and rail all their visitors to Mount Vernon, where the Memorial Exercises will be held　The procession and details of the exercises will follow as closely as circumstances will permit, the original funeral exercises of 1799, with two formal addresses, one by Brother William McKinley, President of the United States, and the other by the Grand Master of Colorado—the latter in recognition of the origination and carrying forward by Colorado of the Memorial proposition until it could be successfully turned over to the Grand Lodge within whose jurisdictional limits repose Washington's remains

The brethren of Virginia comprise but a few thousand more than those of our own State, and the financial obligation resting upon them will prove greater than they should be permitted to bear without generous support from the Centennial State, which requested them to assume the responsibility Recognizing fully our duty, due largely to our primal responsibility, and at the request of the Executive Committee from Virginia, we have been officially authorized by the Most Worshipful Grand Master of Colorado to raise not less than $1,000 towards the expenses of our brethren in Virginia, which expenses will be several times that amount

"The Grand Lodge of the State which was admitted to the American Union on the hundredth anniversary of the independence of the colonies which Washington did so much to secure," wishes to stand shoulder to shoulder with old Virginia, not niggardly as it it were an ordinary event, but grandly and nobly, commensurate with self respect, and reverence for the moral, patriotic and Masonic virtues and services of the Father of Our Country It can be expected that the action of our Grand Lodge in initiating this first Memorial will result in the permanent observance of the anniversary upon each centennial recurrence, not only by the Masonic fraternity of our own country, but in time by the whole world The early Masonic Lodge, which inculcated the brotherhood of man, schooled the colonial leaders to build a nation founded on equal rights, and it is indeed probable that when the Memorial Volume of this Centennial shall be perused by the brethren in formulating their exercises at the second centennial observance, there will then be no part of the world uncivilized, and the American and Masonic ideas of our colonial Masons will have become so general that all will deem it a privilege to do Masonic honor to the glory of the first American

With confidence that your sentiments will be in harmony with the desire of our Grand Lodge, and by authority of our Grand Master, we fraternally solicit such contribution as you may be willing to make toward maintaining Colorado's recognized reputation for doing well whatever it undertakes

Subscriptions should be forwarded to either member of this committee, by whom report will be made to the Grand Master and the Grand Lodge, but checks should be made payable to the order of Ed C. Parmelee, Grand Secretary.

Fraternally yours,

R. W. WOODBURY, Chairman,
                P O Box 1344

W D WRIGHT,
                615 E & C Building

W D TODD,
                P O Box 440, Denver, Colo

Past Grand Masters, Committee of the Grand Lodge of
Colorado on the Washington Centennial Memorial.

DENVER, COLO , September 19, 1899

HON. A R COURTNEY, Chairman Committee of Arrangements Washington Centennial Memorial Exercises, Richmond, Virginia:

Dear Sir and Most Worshipful Brother—I take pleasure in informing you that in accordance with my anticipations, the Grand Lodge of Colorado in Annual Grand Communication to-day unanimously voted an appropriation from the Grand Treasury of $1,000 for the uses of your committee, and ordered the immediate drawing of the warrant on our Grand Treasurer, and the sending of a draft in favor of your Grand Treasurer

Our committee reported the names of one hundred Masons who had made personal subscriptions of ten dollars each, but this appropriation of the Grand Lodge relieves those individual subscribers The Grand Lodge believed it to be its duty, which it was glad to make effective by this appropriation There was not a word against it, but the vote was unanimous in the midst of not a little enthusiasm

As heretofore advised you and your committee, the Grand Lodge of Colorado is enlisted heart and soul in the work which you are doing

Fraternally yours,

R W WOODBURY,
Chairman

RICHMOND, VA , September 23, 1899

MOST WORSHIPFUL R W WOODBURY, Chairman Centennial Committee of Colorado

Dear Sir and Brother—Your favor of the 19th inst to hand this forenoon, containing the good news of your success in securing the endorsement of your Grand Lodge for the $1,000 I have just returned from Washington, where I have negotiated for the banquet and the illustrated programme, and the action of Colorado will greatly strengthen the committee * * *

Yours fraternally,

A R COURTNEY,
Chairman Executive Committee

An appendix to the report of the committee to the Grand Lodge of Colorado, 1899, was as follows

Herewith we report a copy of the subscription paper heretofore mentioned in this report, and the names of one hundred brethren subscribing ten dollars each, as follows

Whereas, The Most Worshipful Grand Lodge of Masons of Colorado suggested and initiated proceedings for National Masonic Memorial Exercises to be held on this one hundredth anniversary of the death of Worshipful Brother George Washington, at Mount Vernon, and which movement has been approved by some fifty Masonic Grand Lodges throughout the world, and at the request of the Grand Lodge of Colorado the Most Worshipful Grand Lodge of Virginia has undertaken full control of all the arrangements therefor, and the movement having assumed such proportions that it will be actively participated in by the President of the United States and many other prominent representative Freemasons from the Old, as well as the New World, and will likely be one of, if not the greatest of events in Masonic history, and the Grand Lodge of Colorado being desirous that its brethren should generously aid in contributing to the expense of carrying out this important undertaking with credit to the Masonic name of the State and the general honor of Masonry,

Therefore, We, the undersigned, hereby subscribe the sums set opposite our respective names to be used for the purposes above set forth, and will pay the same at the call of the committee representing the Grand Lodge of Colorado, to-wit Roger W Woodbury, William D Wright and William D Todd

Names	Amount
Wolfe Londoner	$ 10 00
W G Brown	10 00
James H Blood	10 00
B L James	10 00
W H Kistler	10 00
Adolph Schinner	10 00
Cromwell Tucker	10 00
Edmund L Scholtz	10 00
W F Robinson	10 00
Arthur E Jones	10 00
W S Cheesman	10 00
Wm D Peirce	10 00
Henry Bohm	10 00
George Stidger	10 00
Cooper & Powell	10 00

Names	Amount
Julius A Myers	$ 10 00
Geo S Van Law	10 00
W A Marean	10 00
Ed C Parmelee	10 00
L N Greenleaf	10 00
John Chase	10 00
Hubert L Shattuck	10 00
Horace T DeLong	10 00
Wm Smedley	10 00
Philip Feldhausen	10 00
I N Stevens	10 00
Wm H Sanford	10 00
F Dillingham	10 00
P J Sours	10 00
Geo J Besser	10 00
William Geddes	10 00
Ralph Talbot	10 00
E C Shumway	10 00
Melvin Edwards	10 00
Jos N Stephens	10 00
J C Helm	10 00
F J Chamberlin	10 00
Cass L Herrington	10 00
George C Norris	10 00
Harry B Martin	10 00
Jason P LaBelle	10 00
Benj F Harrington	10 00
C D Cobb	10 00
C M Day	10 00
Earl M Cranston	10 00
Chas M Ford	10 00
Jos H Smith	10 00
A B McGaffey	10 00
R W Steele	10 00
W W Dale	10 00
D K Lee	10 00
William G Evans	10 00
Rodney Curtis	10 00
W W Booth	10 00
R A Kincaid	10 00
A L Doud	10 00
Frank Kratzer	10 00
H C Woodworth & Son	10 00

Names	Amount
H M Orahood	$ 10 00
Ernest LeNeve Foster	10 00
Luther H Wygant, Jr	10 00
Henry Apple	10 00
Frank C Goudy	10 00
Durand C Packard	10 00
Andrew W Gillette	10 00
O B Scobey	10 00
C T Linton	10 00
J P Hall	10 00
E M Ashley	10 00
R P Rollins	10 00
J J Walley	10 00
Peter Winne	10 00
J H Montgomery	10 00
Henry P Steele	10 00
Geo L Sites	10 00
James H Brown	10 00
H M Teller	10 00
William E Greenlee	10 00
Robert S Roe	10 00
Wm K Burchinell	10 00
O S Storrs	10 00
Benton Canon	10 00
C M Kellogg	10 00
Booth M Malone	10 00
M S Appel	10 00
H J Hersey	10 00
Wm J Miles	10 00
H A Beard	10 00
J R Saville	10 00
Frank L Bishop	10 00
John Gregor	10 00
Llewellyn Rees	10 00
Lewis B France	10 00
Geo F Dunklee	10 00
J C Johnston	10 00
H J Hernage	1 00
J C Dresser	10 00
Frederick H Randall	10 00
W D Wright	10 00
Roger W Woodbury	10 00
	$1 000 00

After appropriation by the Grand Lodge of Colorado, a postal was mailed to each subscriber in the following terms

DENVER, COLO, September 28, 1899

Dear Sir and Brother—The committee of the Grand Lodge of Masons of Colorado take pleasure in informing you that the Grand Lodge on the 19th instant unanimously appropriated from the Grand Treasury the amount desired for the Washington Memorial Exercises, and especially thanked the brethren who had made up the subscription list, and whose names were duly reported to the Grand Lodge You are therefore relieved from any liability under said subscription

Fraternally yours,

R W WOODBURY,
Chairman

REPORT OF THE COLORADO COMMITTEE 1899

To the Most Worshipful Grand Lodge

In 1893 the Grand Master recommended this Grand Lodge to consider the initiation of a movement for the holding of national Masonic Memorial Exercises upon the one hundredth anniversary of the death of Worshipful Brother George Washington, which took place on the 14th of December, 1799

The committee of the Grand Lodge which reported upon the recommendation of the Grand Master, said

'The committee believes that public recognition of the services and character of the great and good has a salutary influence upon the lives of others particularly the young, stimulating them to emulation, exalting their own efforts, and ennobling their characters A due observance of the centennial of Washington's death would revive public interest in and disseminate knowledge of. his virtues, and in the pioneer work of the fathers of the Republic who laid the foundations of our national government We are taught, as Masons, to be true to the government of the country under which we live, and, in a broader sense than mere loyalty, we should be true to the principles which underlie its system   These principles were instilled into the American heart by fortitude, prudence, justice, hardship, adversity, perseverance, unselfishness and toil, and the best manhood today comes from the same source of strength   As citizens we can not too often present this truth to those who are striving for fame and influence through paths which are less noble, and we can not present it through a grander character than that Master Mason, on whom was bestowed the loving title of 'First in war, first in peace, and first in the hearts of his countrymen'   Tens of thousands of good men have had their favorable attention directed to Masonry because it embraces principles and truths which were deemed worthy of the loyalty of George Washington, and we are proud that it was so in his day, and is so still   We believe the Grand Lodges of the United States will like to unite for the purpose of doing honor to his memory, and that the proposition thereto will be especially appropriate from the Grand Lodge of the State which was admitted to the American Union on the hundredth anniversary of the independence of the colonies which Washington did so much to secure "

The report was unanimously adopted by the Grand Lodge and a committee was appointed to initiate the movement among the Grand Lodges of the United States   After three years of correspondence, taking it to 1896, so many Grand Lodges had signified their approval and co-operation, that the Grand Lodge of Virginia was then formally requested by this Grand Lodge to take charge of all arrangements, which request was formally acceded to at the next meeting of that Grand Lodge   Its committee is composed of a number of the ablest men in Masonic, professional and political life in that State, and they expect not only that all the Grand Lodges of the United States will be represented at the Memorial, but also a number of foreign jurisdictions   It is expected to be the most general gathering of Grand Masters and Representative Masons that the world has ever seen

General Washington died at Mount Vernon at twenty minutes past ten o'clock on Saturday, December 14, 1799

A Lodge to make arrangements for the funeral was held on the 16th at Alexandria

On the 18th, the Masonic fraternity, under escort of the military and citizens of Alexandria, proceeded to Mount Vernon, and formed funeral procession as follows

The troops, consisting of infantry, cavalry and artillery, clergy, three of whom were members of the Lodge, the General's horse, with saddle, holsters and pistols, led by two grooms, music, guard, the body, borne on a bier by four Virginia lieutenants, pallbearers, all officers of the Revolution, and all members of the Lodge No 22 but one, the principal mourners, the corporation of Alexandria, Alexandria Lodge No 22, Brooks Lodge No 47 of Alexandria, Federal Lodge No 15 of Washington

At the grave the services of the Episcopal Church were rendered by the clergy and followed by Masonic services by Washington's own Lodge No 22

Three general volleys were discharged by the infantry, cavalry and eleven pieces of artillery, which lined the banks of the Potomac back of the vault

The order of exercises for the Centennial Memorial is as follows: (Here followed the programme as published later in this volume)

In the early part of the present year, our brethren in Virginia were somewhat discouraged over the contribution of funds to carry out the Memorial Exercises in a manner commensurate with national dignity, and as our Grand Lodge initiated the movement and placed the responsibility upon Virginia, they requested that we should contribute one thousand dollars so as to ensure complete success   As the brethren of Virginia number but a few thousand more than those of our own State, and as the expenses will be several times the amount requested of us, it was at once conceded that they should not be permitted to be unduly burdened by having accepted a responsibility placed upon them by us   We quote from our reply to the Virginia committee as follows·

"The committee representing the Grand Lodge of Colorado desires to assure you, as they have heretofore done, that anything deemed necessary from us will be undertaken with cheerfulness and love Our Grand Master resides several hundred miles from Denver, and we shall immediately communicate with him and request his permission to our raising the sum requested of us * * * We anticipate his willing consent, and have no doubt of our ability to comply with your request "

Your Grand Master entered most heartily into the task which was placed upon us, and gave us much needed encouragement from time to time We also consulted with leading brethren relative to the raising of the desired amount by subscription, and the consensus of opinion was that the Grand Lodge would consider it a duty, as well as a pleasure and honor, to pay the same from its treasury, that having originated and carried on the great enterprise for three years, and having requested Virginia to take on itself the further labor and responsibility, and the latter having solicited our financial support, in excess of the pro rata requested of other Grand Jurisdictions because of our initiation of the Memorial, our Grand Lodge would not hesitate a moment in complying, and would not permit individual brethren to pay the money There being, however, no authority to so employ our Grand Lodge funds, the committee proceeded to obtain individual subscriptions, so that in the event of the Grand Lodge's refusal, the honor of this Grand Jurisdiction should still be maintained The committee first sent out by mail requests for contributions, as a test of the efficiency of that method, but the results demonstrated that a personal canvass was necessary The expense of visiting and canvassing other parts of the State, however, effectually prevented efforts for an equal distribution throughout the jurisdiction, and so the committee felt obliged to confine their canvass to the City of Denver It is well known that soliciting committees are always out, in Denver, on all kinds of missions, and Masons contribute their share to them all, but we could appeal to our Masonic brethren only, and we feel that their response is deserving of more than ordinary commendation from the Grand Lodge which they so graciously served There is no doubt that the brethren of all parts of the State would have responded with equal generosity, but as personal explanation of the facts was always necessary, at greater or less length, it was, as before stated, impracticable to reach them without large expense, to say nothing of the additional time that would have been required for your committee We think it proper to report the names of the subscribers in full, and it is with some pride that we are able to report that we met with no positive refusals in obtaining one hundred subscribers of ten dollars each Most of these were made upon the statement by your committee (after correspondence with the Grand Master), that they would only be called in, in case of the refusal of the Grand Lodge to make the appropriation, and that the committee believed such appropriation would be made

This entire enterprise is in the name of our beloved Grand Lodge. No individual, except he who may become your Grand Master for the ensuing year, and who has been assigned by our Virginia brethren to divide the honors of oratory with the President of the United States, can receive any personal honor It all belongs to the Grand Lodge of the State that was admitted to the American Union on the hundredth anniversary of the Declaration of Independence which Washington made effective And so your committee believes, after conference with many of your members, that it will be entirely foreign to your wishes to use any of the subscriptions that have been made, and that you will prefer to stand shoulder to shoulder with old Virginia, not niggardly as if it was an ordinary event, but grandly, nobly and with generous self-respect, by unanimously appropriating the amount from the general treasury So believing, we recommend the adoption of the following resolution

"Resolved, That the Grand Secretary be, and hereby is, directed to draw a warrant upon the Right Worshipful Grand Treasurer for the sum of $1,000, and that a draft for that amount be immediately forwarded to the Treasurer of the Committee of Arrangements at Richmond, and that such personal subscriptions as have been paid in, be returned by the Grand Secretary to the subscribers, with the thanks of this Grand Lodge for the same."

In a former report by this committee it was recommended and the Grand Lodge voted, that all the Lodges in this Jurisdiction be requested to arrange for local Memorial Exercises on the anniversary of Worshipful Brother Washington's death

During the present year your Grand Master requested this committee to suggest at this annual Grand Communication a suitable programme or order of exercises for use in whole or in part by the Subordinate Lodges In accordance with that report, after availing themselves of valuable suggestions from the Grand Master himself, the committee presents the following to be interspersed with such music as may be arranged by the Lodges:

That where there is more than one Lodge in any town or city, the brethren all unite in the exercises

That they be held on the day or evening of the 14th of December next, the anniversary of General Washington's death

That the Most Worshipful Grand Master be requested to issue general authority to all Lodges that may wish to avail themselves of the same, to hold their exercises in any public hall, to be attended by the public, and to march in procession thereto

That the flag of our country, draped with crape, be displayed in every Lodge room or public hall used by the Lodges during the Memorial Exercises

The reading of an account of Washington's last illness, from the diary of his secretary, published in McClure's Magazine of February, 1898

The reading of a personal letter to the Lodges of Colorado, from the Worshipful Master of Alexandria-Washington Lodge, of which Washington was the first Master under its Virginia charter, which letter includes an account of Washington's Masonic life

An address upon the early influence of Masonry on the development of the American idea of the equality of men, as expressed in the Declaration of Independence, and its culmination in the Independence of the American Colonies

An address on the personal character and public services of Washington

The reading of Washington's "Farewell Address"

We recommend that the foregoing programme be printed in circular form, without unnecessary delay, and copies thereof be forwarded by the Right Worshipful Grand Secretary to each Lodge in this Jurisdiction, and that the letter of the Worshipful Master of Alexandria-Washington Lodge be printed in separate form, and forwarded for reading at each Lodge This letter is of especial interest, first, because coming from a brother who occupies the East, where Washington once presided, it seems to bridge the chasm of time that has elapsed since he sat with his brethren, and second, because it includes an interesting account of the leading events of his Masonic life, of the present condition of the Bible on which he was obligated, the chair in which he presided, and other priceless relics of his connection with Freemasonry This letter was prepared by the Master of that Lodge at our request, for the purpose of being used by our Lodges as herein recommended

We consider that the holding of local Memorial Exercises in all the Lodges of the United States will be of equal or even greater effect, in reviving public interest in the virtues of our great countryman, as the national exercises at Mount Vernon and to foster such exercises in other

Jurisdictions, we recommend that the Grand Secretary be instructed to forward copies of this programme in advance of our regular proceedings, to the Grand Masters and Grand Secretaries of all Grand Lodges with which we are in correspondence

We further recommend that the proceedings of this annual Grand Communication contain a memorial page as a frontispiece, with the following inscription

TO THE MEMORY
of
WORSHIPFUL BROTHER GEORGE WASHINGTON.
Inscribed
on the
Centennial of His Death
by the
M W Grand Lodge, A F & A M.
of the
State of Colorado,
Which was admitted to the
Union of States
on the
Centennial of the Declaration
of Independence,
Which was made effective by
WASHINGTON,
Through his practice of the various
MASONIC VIRTUES

This committee has had a copy made of its correspondence, which with the original letters to it, and the reports and circulars that have emanated from Colorado and Virginia, compose an historical account of the movement from its inception in 1893, and all these have been bound into a volume for preservation. This volume, which will develop historical interest and value, we will now deliver to the Grand Secretary.

In conclusion, Most Worshipful Grand Master and brethren, after six years of service upon this most interesting subject, your committee desires to briefly trench upon the realms of prophecy.

The proposed Memorial Exercises at Mount Vernon and in all the Lodges of the United States, will constitute the most prominent feature in all the daily papers of the country upon the succeeding day. Millions of people will be brought into close knowledge and sympathy with the governing principles of our forefathers, and their sentiments will be favorably turned to Masonry, as something which Washington and his patriotic contemporaries loved, and found worthy of their own connection with. Greater than any mere prosperity to the fraternity itself, will develop a popular perception, now scarcely recognized, of the intimate relations existing between Masonry and the progress of the world.

The action of our Grand Lodge in initiating this Memorial will long appear in its history as the most beautiful jewel that sparkles in a crown. It will result in the observance of the anniversary upon each centennial recurrence, not only by the Masonic fraternity of our own country, but in time by the whole world. The early Masonic Lodge which inculcated the brotherhood of man, schooled the colonial leaders to build a nation founded on equal rights, and when the memorial volume of this centennial shall be perused by our brethren in formulating their exercises one hundred

years from now, there will then be no part of the inhabited world uncivilized; and the ideas of our colonial Masons will have become so universal
that men of all nations will deem it a privilege to journey to Mount Vernon to do Masonic honor to the Memory of the First American

Roger W Woodbury,

William D Wright,

William D Todd,

Committee

HENRY M. TELLER,
Past Grand Master of Colorado.
Special Representative to Washington Centennial Memorial Exercises,
Mount Vernon, December 14th, 1899.

Exercises at
Mount Vernon

ALPHONSE A. BURNAND,
Grand Master of Colorado, 1899,
Who Delivered One of the Three Addresses at Mount Vernon,
December 14, 1899.

Exercises at Mount Vernon.

GRAND MASTER'S ADDRESS AT ALEXANDRIA.

At the annual Grand Communication of the Grand Lodge of Virginia, held at Alexandria, Va, December 13, 1899, the evening preceding the exercises at Mount Vernon, officers from all Grand Jurisdictions were called upon for remarks   Grand Master A A Burnand of Colorado was introduced, received with grand honors, and spoke as follows

Most Worshipful Grand Master and Brethren of the Grand Lodge of Virginia

It gives me great pleasure to meet with you upon this occasion, because of the joy one must feel in visiting a sister Grand Jurisdiction, engaged in the great work of spreading the cement of brotherly love, and because of the opportunity it affords me to thank you on behalf of the Grand Lodge of Colorado for the special mark of honor assigned to our Jurisdiction in to-morrow's Memorial Exercises   In accepting the kind and fraternal distinction, I said to your Grand Master that I fully appreciate the reason why we were selected for special honors, that I was also mindful of the fact that, had the idea not originated with Colorado, it would have presented itself to your own or some other Jurisdiction long before December 14, 1899

Above all things, Masons love constancy and fidelity of purpose, inflexible courage, tempered with charity, sacrifices made in the interest of a common humanity   In all these virtues, who pointed the way like unto Washington? It is for these reasons that I said that had the idea not been presented by Colorado, it would have been by some other Grand Lodge for Masons do not forget their dead, especially those who like our brother willingly ventured their all for the common good when duty called   And this at a time when failure meant the loss of all real and personal property, civil rights and life itself   I can not conceive that the centenary of his death would have passed without national observance for, though childless himself, the country loves to call him father The honor which your kindness conferred upon our Jurisdiction is doubly appreciated, inasmuch as it was entirely unexpected, for I assure you that the brother who first spoke the word which has resulted in this great patriotic gathering of Freemasons from the East, the West, the North and South, did it purely out of love for country and its greatest man

Realizing that you are all desirous of seeing and hearing from this brother, I trust your Most Worshipful Grand Master will at some time during the evening call upon Most Worshipful Brother Roger W Woodbury, and I gladly resign to him such further time as may be allotted to Colorado Let me again assure you that I feel greatly honored in visiting the Grand Lodge of that great Commonwealth which nurtured, maintained and honored our Washington

GENERAL ORDERS.

HEADQUARTERS OF GRAND MARSHAL EBBITT HOUSE,

WASHINGTON, D C, December 8, 1899

I   The undersigned, having been appointed by the Grand Master of Virginia as Grand Marshal, to conduct the ceremonies commemorating the one hundredth anniversary of the death of Worshipful George Washington December 14, 1899, assumes command and announces, for the information of all concerned, the following appointments

AIDES

James Parke Corbin, Fredericksburg Va

S R Donohoe, Fairfax County, Va

Harry Hodges, Norfolk, Va

Edgar Warfield Alexandria, Va

Edward S Conrad, Harrisonburg, Va

William H Sands, Richmond Va

II   The following are the orders for the organization, movement, and dismissal of Masonic bodies participating in these ceremonies·

III   Master Masons of the District of Columbia, except Federal Lodge No 1, will form line on the west side of Fourteenth street, facing east, between Pennsylvania avenue and F street N W, right resting on Pennsylvania avenue

IV   All visiting Master Masons in the District of Columbia will assemble at 8 o'clock a m, and form line on the east side of Fourteenth street, facing west, between Pennsylvania avenue and F street N W, right resting on F street

V   Federal Lodge No 1, of Washington, D C, will form line on the south side of F street, facing north, between Fourteenth and Fifteenth streets N W, right of line resting on Fourteenth street, and will be reported to the Grand Marshal for assignment to position

VI   Grand Masters and Representatives of Grand Lodges of jurisdictions outside of the District of Columbia will be ready to take carriages at 8 o'clock a m at the F street entrance of the Ebbitt House carriages will be formed in columns of twos on Fourteenth street facing south, between F street and Pennsylvania avenue, head of column resting on Pennsylvania avenue

VII   Officers of the Grand Lodge of the District of Columbia, under charge of the Grand Marshal will assemble at Masonic Temple, prepared to take carriages at 8 o'clock a m, and follow in rear of the carriages of the visiting Grand Masters and Representatives of Grand Lodges of Jurisdictions outside of the District of Columbia

VIII   As thus organized, this column, in the order above mentioned, will proceed by way of Fourteenth street to Pennsylvania avenue to Seventh street, thence to the wharf of the Mount Vernon and Marshall Hall Steamboat Company, where they will go aboard the steamer for conveyance to Mount Vernon

IX   The Grand Lodge of Virginia will form on King street, in the city of Alexandria, Thursday, December 14, 1899, at 9 o'clock a m, the head of the column at the opera house, and in order, from front to rear, as follows

Master Masons

Alexandria-Washington Lodge No 22

Fredericksburg Lodge No 4

Officers of the Grand Lodge of the State of Virginia

Grand Master of Virginia

The column will proceed to the landing of the Mount Vernon and Marshall Hall Steamboat Company, where they will go aboard the steamer for conveyance to Mount Vernon

X   In order that the column at Mount Vernon may be organized as indicated below, it will be necessary that the steamer conveying Masons from the District of Columbia make the first landing at Mount Vernon wharf   The steamer conveying the Masons from Virginia will remain at the wharf to embark the Grand Lodge of Virginia which will be the first to take steamer at the close of the ceremonies

XI   On disembarking at Mount Vernon wharf, the procession will be formed in the following order

Third United States Cavalry Band

Grand Tiler of the Grand Lodge of Virginia

Master Masons of the District of Columbia

Visiting Master Masons

Master Masons of Virginia

Federal Lodge No 1 of Washington, D C

Fredericksburg Lodge No 4, of Fredericksburg, Va

Alexandria Washington Lodge No 22 of Alexandria, Va

Grand Masters

Grand Officers

Grand Representatives of Jurisdictions outside of the District of
 Columbia

Officers of the Grand Lodge of the District of Columbia

Officers of the Grand Lodge of Virginia

Grand Master of Virginia

XII The procession as thus formed will then move by way of the
Mansion, where the President of the United States will enter the column,
when the line of the funeral procession of one hundred years ago will be
followed On arriving at the old vault, the ranks will be opened, facing
inward, and the Grand Master of Virginia and invited guests—Alexandria-
Washington Lodge No 22, Fredericksburg Lodge No 4 and Federal Lodge
No 1—will pass between the ranks which will then be closed The
Grand Master of Colorado will make his address from a platform at the old
vault, after which the procession will again form, with the Grand Master
of Virginia, Grand Officers, and invited guests, together with the three
Lodges named, leading, and proceed to the present tomb—the Grand Master of Virginia and other Grand Officers taking a position in front of the
tomb as assigned by programme of Grand Lodge of Virginia, Alexandria-
Washington Lodge No 22 on right, Fredericksburg Lodge No 4 on left,
and Federal Lodge No 1 in rear of Grand Master of Virginia Ranks will
again be opened, facing inward, and the Master Masons in rear will then
move forward between these ranks, thus reversing the column, and will
thence move in circle to the right around the tomb enclosing the Masonic
bodies above mentioned

After the ceremonies at the present tomb the procession will again be
formed and proceed in the original order to the Mansion, where the President of the United States will make an address, after introduction by the
Grand Master of Virginia

XIII   At the conclusion of the President's address the column will again be formed and will proceed in the original order to the wharf   When the head of the column arrives near the wharf the column will be halted, ranks opened facing inward, and the Grand Master of Virginia, officers of the Grand Lodge of Virginia, Alexandria-Washington Lodge No 22 of Alexandria, Va, Fredericksburg Lodge No 4, of Fredericksburg, Va, and the Master Masons of Virginia, in the order named, will pass through the ranks and proceed aboard the steamer for conveyance to and dismissal at the original place of assembly

XIV   The above embarkation having been accomplished, the corresponding bodies from the District of Columbia, beginning from the rear, will pass between the remaining open ranks and take steamer for Washington D C, where the column will be formed in its original order and proceed through the same streets to original place of assembly, where it will be dismissed without formal orders

1   At Fort Washington a gun will be fired every half hour beginning at sunrise and ending at sunset

2   As the procession moves into Mount Vernon grounds a platoon of Light Battery M, 7th U S Artillery, from Washington Barracks will fire twenty-one minute guns

3   At the conclusion of ceremonies at the new tomb the firing party, composed of a detachment from Battery A, 4th U S Artillery, Fort Hunt, Va will fire three volleys

4   At the conclusion of the President's address, twenty-one guns will be fired by the U S S Sylph, anchored in the river

5   Taps will be sounded

Grand Masters officers of Grand Lodges and Representatives of Grand Lodges will wear their official clothing and jewels

Master Masons must be properly clothed—black clothes, black hat, white apron and white gloves. The apron to be worn outside the coat.

Grand Masters, Grand Officers and Grand Representatives of Grand Lodges outside of the State of Virginia and the District of Columbia will report to the Grand Marshal at the Ebbitt House, Washington, D C, upon their arrival in the city, to register and report the number of Master Masons accompanying them, and to receive information and instructions.

Aides and Assistant Aides assigned for duty in Alexandria, Va, will report to Grand Marshal at headquarters in Alexandria, at 8 30 a m, December 14.

Aides and Assistant Aides assigned for duty in Washington, D C, will report to the Grand Marshal at headquarters, Ebbitt House, at 7 30 a m, December 14.

Space has been reserved, during the ceremonies, on the grounds at Mount Vernon for the wives and daughters of Master Masons. Admission to same by card to be obtained only of the Grand Marshal at Ebbitt House, December 12 and 13.

Arrangements have been made for the accommodation of the press and cards of admission within the lines will be issued by the Grand Marshal, at the Ebbitt House, December 12 and 13.

Master Masons (and ladies accompanying them) must secure transportation to Mount Vernon prior to the morning of the 14th, at the following places Grand Opera House, Alexandria, Va, Masonic Temple, Washington, D C, Headquarters Grand Marshal, Ebbitt House, Washington, D C

ROBT WHITE,
Grand Marshal

Official

HARRY STANDIFORD,
Assistant Grand Marshal

PROGRAMME.

The Grand Masters and representatives of the several jurisdictions attending the Centennial Ceremonies, and all other Masons desiring to participate will, on December 14, 1899, leave Washington, D C, for Mount Vernon, at 9.30 a m, in steamers engaged by the committee for that purpose and touch at Alexandria, for the Grand Lodge of Virginia and their families, arriving at Mount Vernon about 11 o'clock a m The procession and entire ceremonies will be in charge of the following officers Colonel Robert White, of Wheeling, W Va, Grand Marshal, Harry Standiford, of Washington, D C, Assistant Grand Marshal Aides—James Parke Corbin, of Fredericksburg, Va, S R Donohoe, of Fairfax County, Va, Edgar Warfield, Sr, of Alexandria, Va, Edward S Conrad, of Harrisonburg, Va, William H. Sands, of Richmond, Va, Harry Hodges, of Norfolk, Va

At Mount Vernon the Masonic bodies will form together with the invited guests on the east side of the Mansion and proceed to the old vault, by the same path and in the same order in which the procession was formed and moved on the day of General Washington's funeral, December 18, 1799 At the old vault the services will be conducted as follows:

Solemn dirge by the band

Prayer by Brother, the Right Rev A M Randolph, Bishop of the Southern Episcopal Diocese of Virginia

Music by an octette from the Grand Lodge of the District of Columbia

Address by the Grand Master of Masons of Colorado

After the address of the Grand Master of Colorado, at the old vault, the procession will march to the tomb in which are now deposited the remains of Washington

The Grand Masters of the thirteen original States (or their representatives) will then stand in a line in front of the tomb facing out. The

Grand Masters of other States and Foreign Jurisdictions (or their representatives) in a half circle facing them   The Grand Lodge and other brethren in a circle around the tomb, joining hands

After prayer by the Grand Chaplain the Grand Master of Virginia will then say.

My brethren, one hundred years ago the Supreme Architect of the Universe removed from the terrestrial to the celestial Lodge our brother, George Washington   About his tomb we assemble to-day in our character as Masons to testify that time has not weakened our veneration for his memory, nor years brought forgetfulness of his virtues   From the East and West, from the North and South, from the Isles of the Sea, Masons have come to-day to mark the first century of his departure from earth to Heaven

My brother, the Grand Master of Massachusetts, what message do you bring us to-day?

Grand Master of Massachusetts: From the Commonwealth where Lexington and Concord and Bunker Hill were fought, from the Cradle of American Freedom, I bring greetings of veneration and respect, and a wreath of leaves from the elm under which he took command of the armies of freedom   Washington and Adams and Warren sleep, but liberty is yet awake

Grand Master of Virginia· My brother, the Grand Master of Rhode Island, have you a message for us?

Grand Master of Rhode Island   From the Old Plantations I bring you a greeting to the immortal memory of our greatest dead   Great men die, but great principles are eternal

Grand Master of Virginia   My brother, the Grand Master of Connecticut, what is your message?

Grand Master of Connecticut. The same blood runs in the veins of those who made the oak the treasure house of their charter. The spirits of Roger Sherman and Israel Putnam hail that of their great compatriot. Hail—never to say farewell!

Grand Master of Virginia. My brother, the Grand Master of New Hampshire, we await your message.

Grand Master of New Hampshire. Of old sat Freedom on the heights, her dwelling place is with us yet. The land of Stark greets these ashes as the Temple in which once dwelt the Father of American Freedom.

Grand Master of Virginia. My brother, the Grand Master of New York, what greeting do you give us?

Grand Master of New York· The Empire State hails the memory of him who might have been king, and would not. The land of Hamilton, his councillor, of Jay, his Chief Justice, brings to his memory love and veneration.

Grand Master of Virginia: My brother, the Grand Master of New Jersey, have you a message?

Grand Master of New Jersey. Monmouth and Trenton and Princeton knew him. Valley Forge yet remembers his prayers, and the endurance of the heroes whom he led. The soul-stirring peals of the bell which proclaimed Liberty from its tower in Philadelphia, the birthplace of Independence, are still sounding through our land testimonials that the memory of Washington is imperishable. No Commonwealth cherishes more faithfully his illustrious name.

Grand Master of Virginia. My brother, the Grand Master of Delaware, have you a message?

Grand Master of Delaware. Where is the Commonwealth in whose borders he is not reverenced? I bring you to-day the love and veneration of my people, as true now as in 1776.

Grand Master of Virginia My brother, the Grand Master of Maryland, your greeting?

Grand Master of Maryland. From the mountains to the Chesapeake his fame dwells secure But a river divides his birthplace and his tomb from our Commonwealth All the seas could not divide us from our love and admiration of his memory

Grand Master of Virginia My brother, the Grand Master of North Carolina, what testimonial do you bring?

Grand Master of North Carolina: His memory is as green to-day as the verdure of our pine trees His fame as enduring as our everlasting hills Cowpens, and King's Mountain and Guilford We brought him these We bring him to-day the love of sons as faithful as their sires

Grand Master of Virginia My brother, the Grand Master of South Carolina, what say you?

Grand Master of South Carolina Sumter and Jasper and Marion were ours Washington was no less ours, for he made their victories complete I bring you this palmetto for your wreath

Grand Master of Virginia My brother, the Grand Master of Georgia, your message?

Grand Master of Georgia Last, but not least of the thirteen! Pulaski's blood enriched our soil! Washington was ours as he was yours Peace to these ashes and peace to the land he loved

All of the Grand Masters: Enlighten us with Thy Light everlasting, Oh, Father; and grant unto us perpetual peace

The Craft· So mote it be Amen

Grand Master of Virginia My brother, the Grand Master of Maine, what say you?

Grand Master of Maine The granite hills shall perish before the memory of his greatness shall pass away. We yield to no Commonwealth in our love for Washington

Grand Master of Virginia: What says the South?

The Grand Masters of Florida, Mississippi, Louisiana, Texas, Alabama and Tennessee in union: Pine trees and palms; broad prairies and savannahs; the Mighty Father of Waters. All these knew of his greatness; all these claim him as the Father of their Liberties.

Grand Master of Virginia: What say the States once part of old Virginia—Ohio, Illinois, Indiana, Kentucky and West Virginia?

Grand Masters in union: Masons throughout our mountains, valleys and prairies honor and revere the memory of George Washington, and bow around his tomb in gratitude for his services to the land he loved, and to the cause of Masonry to which he devoted his earliest and latest manhood.

Grand Master of Virginia: What says the West?

The Grand Masters from all the Western States, in union: We, too, are children of the Father of His Country. Here we proclaim our love for his memory and thankfulness for his life.

Grand Master of Virginia: The North, the South, the East, and the West have spoken. But Washington belongs not to any one clime or people. What say you, my brethren of other lands? Lands foreign the cowan may call you, but in the name of Masonry, I hail you as our own.

Grand Master of England (or his representative) here makes such response as he may deem best, followed by responses from other Jurisdictions outside of the United States.

The Grand Masters (or their representatives) and the Craft then repeat in alternate verse the following:

Grand Masters: Lord, Thou hast been our dwelling-place from one generation to another.

The Craft: Before the mountains were brought forth or ever Thou hadst formed the earth and the world even from everlasting to everlasting, Thou art God.

Grand Masters For a thousand years in Thy sight are but as yesterday when it is past and as a watch in the night

The Craft For we are consumed by Thy anger, and by Thy wrath are we troubled

Grand Masters The Lord is merciful and gracious, slow to anger and plenteous in mercy

The Craft He hath not dealt with us after our sins, nor rewarded us according to our iniquities

Grand Masters As far as the East is from the West so far hath He removed our transgressions from us

The Craft As for man, his days are as grass, as the flower of the field, so he flourisheth

Grand Masters For the wind passeth over it, and it is gone, and the place thereof shall know it no more

The Craft: But the mercy of the Lord is from Everlasting to Everlasting upon them that fear Him and His righteousness unto children's children

Grand Masters The faithful are minished from the earth

The Craft But the righteous shall be had in everlasting remembrance

Grand Masters Precious in the sight of the Lord is the death of His saints

The Craft The Lord knoweth the days of the upright, and their inheritance shall be forever

Grand Masters Who hath raised up the righteous man from the East, called him to His foot, gave the nations before him and made him rule over kings? Who gave them as dust to his sword and as driven stubble to his bow?

The Craft The Lord strong and mighty, the Lord mighty in battle

Grand Masters So teach us to number our days that we may apply our hearts unto wisdom

The Craft Oh satisfy us early with Thy mercy that we may rejoice and be glad all our days

Grand Masters   Let Thy work appear unto Thy servants and Thy glory unto their children

The Craft And let the beauty of the Lord our God be upon us, and establish Thou the work of our hands upon us; yea, the work of our hands establish Thou it.

The Grand Master of the District of Columbia (representing the Atlantic States) This lambskin or white leather apron is an emblem of innocence and the time-honored badge of a Free and Accepted Mason   Kings have not disdained it, princes have been proud to wear it. Washington wore it, and its spotless form lay upon his coffin a century ago   I deposit it here in remembrance of this beloved brother—a workman who in no respect was ever unworthy of his work

The Grand Master of Missouri (representing the Central States). This glove is a token of friendship   I deposit it here as an evidence that death only breaks the handclasp   The tie which binds the heart of man to the heart of man remains unbroken forever and forever

The Grand Master of California (representing the Western States) This evergreen is an emblem of the Masonic faith in the resurrection of the body and the immortality of the soul   I deposit it here in the confidence of a certain faith, in the reasonable religious and holy hope that the dead body encoffined here will at the last day rise a glorious form to meet our God   To whom be glory and honor and power and majesty and might and dominion now and for evermore

The Craft   Amen'

All of the Grand Masters Oh Death where is thy sting?

The Craft Oh, Grave, where is thy victory?

M. W. BROTHER ALPHONSE A. BURNAND,
Grand Master of Colorado, 1899,
Addressing the Assemblage from the Stand in Front of the "Old Tomb" at Mount Vernon,
December 14, 1899.

The Grand Masters then deposit their wreaths or evergreens and the Craft slowly march past the tomb, depositing the evergreens

After which the brethren will proceed to the Mansion, where Brother William McKinley, after being appropriately introduced by the Grand Master of Virginia, will deliver an address, and the ceremonies at Mount Vernon will be closed with an appropriate benediction by Brother Ed N Calisch, rabbi of Beth Ahaba Synagogue, Richmond, Va

The Masons and their families will then return to Washington on the steamers, and from 9 to 11 o'clock that night a reception will be held at Willard's Hotel, corner Pennsylvania avenue and Fourteenth street, by the Grand Masters and other distinguished Masons who will be present, including, as we hope, President McKinley   While the reception is going on in the spacious parlors of Old Willard's, on the upper floor, a buffet banquet will be spread in the grand dining room below, of which guests may partake at their pleasure

Upon the retirement of the guests and the receiving party on this occasion will end the ceremonies of the one hundredth anniversary of the death of the grandest man the world has ever produced, and a devoted Mason from his manhood to his grave

GRAND MASTER BURNAND'S ADDRESS AT MOUNT VERNON

Most Worshipful Grand Master, Brother Mr President and Brethren

We have assembled to-day from every part of our great land in the character of Freemasons, not for ostentatious display, but to offer to the memory of our Brother a renewal of that heartfelt homage and sincere tribute of reverance and affection which our brethren and countrymen felt, when one hundred years ago, they laid him to rest in that peace which the world can neither give nor take away   Love and admiration are due from us, not only as Freemasons, but as citizens of this great republic, for whose liberty and life he gave those years which are usually devoted by men to the pursuit of personal interest   The revolution was the development in America of the old spirit of the Commons of England, protesting, resisting, and then fighting for their reasonable rights   From the extreme north to the extreme South, Liberty became the watchword of patriots   Its cradle was rocked at Lexington, and it matured in Philadelphia, when the old bell proclaimed the birth and independence of a nation   Thrilling as are all these memories, they pale at the thought that the embodiment of all Colonial courage, skill, wisdom, hope and resolve lies buried here   Here silently rests that grand personality, that reserved force, that unmatched courage and individuality which made a possibility a reality, and in spite of adversity, defeat, internal dissensions and a cabal, gave a glorious name and honored grave to every officer and soldier of the Continental Army

That our brother would have been a great and good man under any circumstances, the whole world knows, for I believe man is born great   He may see the light of day in an obscure house, in an unknown hamlet, his early life may offer opportunity but for the simplest education, but the unerring hand of destiny will guide him over all obstacles until he reaches the niche of fame intended for him

Thus our brother was one of those rare beings whom God places among his people on occasions as beacons to diffuse His light upon the path of human progress   Our country has had, has now, and will continue to have, great men, but I believe God intended but one Washington, as he intended but one Lincoln   Each was unique in his place and viewed in the light of the present day each seems to have been created for his particular sphere. We know the teachings of our Craft had nevertheless more or less influence upon Washington's life   He was initiated at an age when the mind is easily impressed, when ideas have not become fixed, when youth merges into manhood and young manhood is inspired with noble and beautiful resolves It would indeed be strange if the time honored and tried tenets of Masonry had not left lasting impressions upon his well ordered mind I hold it impossible for a sincere upright man to receive the degrees of Freemasonry and not emerge with a broader view of his purpose upon earth The maxim that all men are created equal is of greater antiquity than the Declaration of Independence, and it was instilled into the hearts of Freemasons for generations before that immortal manifesto was published, and so we may be assured that the beautiful lessons and sublime truths taught by Freemasonry exerted great influence in the development of those qualities which made Washington the friend and counsellor of the people and enabled him during forty years of public life to deal justly and equitably by all They gave him strength during the dark hours of Brandywine and Germantown, and endowed him with fortitude for the awful days of Valley Forge, for the faithful Mason maintains his trust in God and his faith in the ultimate triumph of right over might

There is a shrine in every land from which radiates an infinity of gossamer threads of tenderness, and here at Mount Vernon, the place of Washington's repose, is the Mecca that appeals to Americans It is the cradle of Patriotism, the soul of solemnity, the fountain of inspiration No American education is finished until this tomb has been visited No father who loves his boy and hopes to see his name enrolled among the wise and virtuous of his countrymen, dare forget the priceless resolves that here have birth No man is equipped to do duty as a legislator or even as a voter, who has not bared his head before this tomb, and received the inspiration that thrills the soul Here, too, is the one place above all others for introspection Here the conscience should be no stranger but a familiar friend Here, too, should be reviewed the history of our land—its victories and its errors, from the work laid out by this immortal chief and carried on at his death by his compatriots, and then by sons nurtured of the same stock, each striving for the best interest of the principles annunciated in 1776 to the culmination of the war of humanity in 1898, when the last stains of despotism and oppression were wiped out in the Western Hemisphere with the blood of the Nation's sons.

Unhappily there are many who subvert great principles conceived in the interest of humanity to gratify personal ambition and aggrandizement. Such individual or parties not only lose sight of the lessons taught by the Fathers of American Freedom, that the noblest motive should ever be the public good, but they also advance us one step towards skepticism, which is always fraught with danger, for when men lose faith in God they also lose faith in themselves, and if that time should ever arrive, which God forbid, then farewell thou dear land of liberty, the home of the free and the brave, land of Washington and his confreres, now sepulchre of all their hopes and ambitions. Brethren, I wish we could all carry with us from this place a patriotism, love of country and fellowman, which would enable us to always place our country's interest in the van of our own, a trait which would elevate us upon a plane far above that of wealth, social ambition or political glory. Let us then on the eve of the Twentieth Century, upon this ground sanctified by the memory and ashes of that great man and brother who left his impression upon the world for all time, resolve to imitate his unselfish example and so leave our children that richest of endowments, a life devoted to God, country and home. Let us consider our mortal existence as a probation, a step, a trial for a more perfect one. Just what that is, need not disturb us, for if we follow the teachings of our Great Light and fulfill our duty to God and man we can safely leave the hereafter in the hands of Him who has ever blessed our efforts and prospered us as a nation.

We are born for greater destinies than those of earth, and unlike our ancient brethren, we build not of things material, but spiritual. The house which we are erecting will stand to the end of time, but the two great pillars of our Craft, the one truth, the other brotherly love, must be grounded upon this life, and if we continue as the builders of old, animated by the same spirit which prompted them, no doubt but that the great crowning arch of our fraternity, *Charity,* will be lost in Heaven and the cope stone placed therein by the Heavenly Host

The State I represent lies among the pine-clad hills and snow-capped mountains of our great country, and within the memory of man some of our national legislators offered a prayer of thanksgiving to the Almighty for placing the mountains there, proposed drawing a line along the ridge marking the western limits of the republic, and upon the highest peak thereof wished they to erect a statue to the fabled God Terminus, never to be pulled down And to-day we also thank God for placing the "stony mountains" there, for by the perseverance, pluck and endurance displayed by the pioneers of forty years ago, among the first and foremost of whom were many of our brethren, this uninviting portion of our public domain has been transformed into the chief treasure house of the nation, as well as into a beautiful commonwealth and was admitted to our great Union of States on the one hundredth anniversary of the independence of the colonies, which our brother did so much to foster and secure From there I bring you upon this occasion the greeting and this immortelle, from a Community of our brotherhood whose love for country and our illustrious great brother is as pure and immutable as the eternal snows which envelop their mountains And now let me close with the words of one of our immortals

' Lord of the Universe ' shield us and guide us

Trusting Thee always, through shadow and sun,

Thou hast united us, who shall divide us?

Keep us, oh keep us, the many in one "

ADDRESS OF PRESIDENT BROTHER WILLIAM McKINLEY AT
MOUNT VERNON

We have just participated in a service commemorative of the one hundredth anniversary of the death of George Washington   Here at his old home, which he loved so well, and which the patriotic women of the country have guarded with loving hands, exercises are conducted under the auspices of the great fraternity of Masons, which a century ago planned and executed the solemn ceremonial which attended the Father of His Country to his tomb   The Lodge in which he was initiated and the one over which he afterward presided as Worshipful Master, accorded positions of honor at his obsequies, are to-day represented here in token of profound respect to the memory of their most illustrious member and beloved brother

Masons throughout the United States testify anew their reverence for the name of Washington and the inspiring example of his life   Distinguished representatives are here from all the Grand Lodges of the country to render the ceremonies as dignified and impressive as possible, and most cordial greetings have come from across our borders and from beyond the sea

Not alone in this country, but throughout the world, have Masons taken especial interest in the observance of this Centennial Anniversary   The fraternity justly claims the immortal patriot as one of its members, the whole human family acknowledges him as one of its greatest benefactors   Public bodies, patriotic societies and other organizations, our citizens everywhere, have esteemed it a privilege to-day to pay their tribute to his memory and to the splendor of his achievements in the advancement of justice and liberty among men   "His fair fame, secure in its immortality, shall shine through countless ages with undiminished luster"

The struggling Republic for which Washington was willing to give his life and for which he ever freely spent his fortune, and which at all times

HOSPITAL AT LASI LAM MANASI

was the object of his most earnest solicitude, has steadily and wonderfully developed along the lines which his sagacity and foresight carefully planned It has stood every trial, and at the dawn of a new century is stronger than ever to carry forward its mission of liberty. During all the intervening years it has been true, forever true, to the precepts of the Constitution which he and his illustrious colleagues framed for its guidance and government He was the national architect, says Bancroft, the historian, and but for him the nation could not have achieved its independence, could not have formed its union, could not have put the Federal Government into operation He had neither precedent nor predecessor His work was original and constructive and has successfully stood the severest tests

He selected the site for the capital of the Republic he founded, and gave it the name of the Federal City, but the commission substituted the name of Washington as the more fitting, and to be a perpetual recognition of the services of the Commander-in-Chief of the Continental Army, the president of the convention which framed the Constitution, and the first President of the Republic. More than seventy millions of people acknowledge allegiance to the flag which he made triumphant The nation is his best eulogist and his noblest monument.

I have been deeply interested and touched by the sentiments of his contemporaries, uttered a hundred years ago on the occasion of his death The Rev Walter King of Norwich, Conn , in the course of an eloquent eulogy delivered in that city on January 5, 1800, said in part

"By one mighty effort of manly resolution we were born anew, and declared our independence Now commenced the bloody contest for everything we held dear The same Almighty Being, by whose guidance we were hitherto conducted beheld us with compassion, and saw what we needed—a pilot, a leader in the perilous enterprise we had undertaken He called for Washington, already prepared, annointed him as His servant with regal dignity, and put into his hands the control of all our defensive operations

'But here admiration suppresses utterance   Your own minds must fill out the active character of the man   A description of the warlike skill, the profound wisdom, the prudence, the heroism and integrity which he displayed in the character of the commander-in-chief would suffer materially in hands like mine   But this I may say—the eyes of all our American Israel were placed upon him as their savior, under the direction of heaven, and they were not disappointed."

The Rev Nathan Strong, pastor of the North Presbyterian Church in Hartford, spoke as follows on December 27, 1799

He was as much the angel of peace as of war, as much respected, as deeply reverenced in the political cabinet for a luminous coolness of disposition, whereby party jealousy became enlightened and ashamed of itself as he was for a coolness of command in the dreadful moment when empires hung suspended on the fate of battle   His opinions became the opinions of the public body, and every man was pleased with himself when he found he thought like Washington

'Under the auspices of this great warrior, who was formed by the providence of God to defend his country, the war was ended and America ranked among the nations   He who might have been a monarch retired to his own Vernon unclothed of all authority, to enjoy the bliss of being a free private citizen   This was a strange sight, and gave a new triumph to human virtue—a triumph that hath never been exceeded in the history of the world, except it was by his second recess, which was from the presidency of the United States"

And on the day preceding, December 26, 1799, in the course of his memorable funeral oration before both houses of Congress, Major General Lee, then a representative from the State of Virginia, gave utterance to the noble sentiment as forceful to-day as in those early years of our national life

"To the horrid din of battle sweet peace succeeded, and our virtuous chief, mindful only of the common good, in a moment tempting personal aggrandizement, hushed the discontent of growing sedition, and surrendering his power into the hands from which he had received it, converted his sword into a plowshare, teaching an admiring world that to be truly great you must be truly good"

While strong with his own generation, he is stronger even in the judgment of the generations which have followed   After a lapse of a century he is better appreciated, more perfectly understood, more thoroughly venerated and loved than when he lived   He remains an ever-increasing influence for good in every part and sphere of action of the Republic   He is recognized as not only the most far-sighted statesman of his generation, but as having had almost prophetic vision   He built not alone for his own time, but for the great future, and pointed the rightful solution of many of the problems which were to arise in the years to come

John Adams, the immediate successor of Washington, said of him in an address to the Senate on the 23d of December, 1799

"For himself, he had lived enough to life, and to glory   For his fellow citi zens, if their prayers could have been answered, he would have been immortal * * * His example is now complete, and it will teach wisdom and virtue to magistrates, citizens and men, not only in the present age, but in future genera tions, as long as our history shall be read "

The nation needs at this moment the help of his wise example   In dealing with our vast responsibilities we turn to him   We invoke the coun sel of his life and character and courage   We summon his precepts that we may keep his pledges to maintain justice and law, education and moral ity, and civil and religious liberty in every part of our country the new as well as the old

ADDRESS OF THE GRAND MASTER OF VIRGINIA

My Brethren—The divisions of time are but the mile stones men erect on the highway leading to eternity   In His sight to whom a thousand years are but as yesterday when it is past and as a watch in the night, the centuries are but as the seconds which are gone ere we can reckon them And we who here to-day, gathering in the light of a majestic memory, commemorate the one hundredth anniversary of the death of a great man— bear testimony that the good man never dies

This is the only answer we can make to the question Why these cere monies?

If one hundred years ago, the real George Washington died, then these ceremonies are but vain and idle and mocking mummeries, serving to recall an event whose memory brings with it only a sense of the emptiness of human glory and the end of human greatness

But Washington lives to-day, not only in the minds of men—in the records of fame—not only in the pages of history—but lives in that serene light which emanates from the presence of God—lives a sentient, glorious and glorified being, and we assemble here to-day to thank God that he lived, to thank God that he lives, and to commemorate the one hundredth anniversary of the dawn of a greater life unto the greatest life that was ever lived by a mere mortal We have to-day borne the same light and the same book and jewels borne when his body was laid to rest. We have retraced in solemn procession the route that simple funeral cortege followed a century ago Cannon have thundered from the river—the voices of war calling vainly to the eternal peace—as they thundered when the great warrior rested in peace We have recited from the great poet the inspired words sung to Israel's God—outliving Israel—recognizing in all humanity that it is His voice alone that can say return ye children of men "

And now all set ceremonies are over, and we have heard the head of the nation pay his tribute to the nation's first head And we shall go back to the city's noise and tumult—we shall leave these quiet fields—this unpretentious mansion—yonder silent and sacred tenement of the dead—to hear the sound of joy and gladness, the notes of revelry, of music and of song Vain and empty and useless will this commemoration be—unworthy of the man and of his memory—if it be merely a commemoration, and stir not up our hearts and minds to some useful purpose—some purer impulse The grander days of the fathers should be recalled—and this recurrence should awaken a recurrence of the spirit of that time Men were men, it is true, then, as now Politicians were politicians then, as now This great soul had enemies and slanderers and vilifiers then, as great men have now and will have as long as greatness exists and vileness can crawl and bite its heel His motives were maligned—his self-sacrifices were belittled—his character was aspersed And yet when he died, a wave of grief and of dismay and an awakened sense of gratitude swept over the entire land, and the voice of slander died away

We may not withhold the highest meed of praise from the great minds who conceived and framed the Constitution Every wind that blows from the Virginia hills, every wave that laps her shores and the shores of the great thirteen States, would rebuke the voice that dare belittle the work of Madison and Hamilton, Franklin and Morris But these men were the sculptors, the designers, who with infinite toil and patience, and genius and skill, made the clay model Washington was the workman that cast the figure in the enduring bronze, that now for over a century has stood the rain and the hail and the mist of doubt and distrust, the storm of war the deadly canker of corruption and the hurricane of party strife

And to-day I would invoke that same cessation of party spirit, that same feeling of a common interest in a common country, and pray that the first lesson we shall carry back from this place shall be a lesson of charity and consideration, and kindliness to all in authority, whether our own suffrages placed the men in authority above us or not That public men and public measures should be judged not in the littleness of party prejudice or party passion, but that in things political as well as in things private, charity should govern all who wish the welfare of their country The curse of this age is the personality, the bitterness, the uncharitableness of politics Nothing is sufficiently vile to say of a political opponent no motive too mean to be ascribed to a political measure No man's patriotism is believed sincere unless his opinion coincides with our own, and the floodgates of vituperation, abuse and misrepresentation are opened often when hardly the mildest criticism is deserved   These things grow and will continue to increase unless sternly repressed   All purity and honesty and desire for good government is not and has never been anywhere in the world the peculiar property of any set of men, and the sooner we recognize this the better for us all

Sad and bitter is the thought that often it is only death that does justice even as the old superstition that a dead hand's touch could remove blots from the skin   Alas! and alas! for men who live amidst the gray mists of popular distrust and distavor, misjudged, maligned, often cursed, above whose graves flowers bloom in the moisture of regretful tears, and paeans of praise ring unheard and uncared for by the clay to whom addressed

It is not for me here to speak, or for you to listen to aught that savors of politics   I do not speak to you as members of one party or another   I speak to you as Masons, professing to work for the benefit of man—of whom Washington himself has said that your "great object is to promote the happiness of the human race"   I speak to you as men—I speak to you as Americans—whose every pulse beat should throb for your country's welfare, and to whom the honor and integrity and happiness of your country should be the first thought.

It has been with some feeling of amused contempt that I have seen it stated and insisted upon that Washington was never a Mason, or, if ever one ceased to recognize his membership or obligations   Washington never failed to recognize any obligation, from the greatest to the smallest.   This was one of the characteristics of the man, one of the characteristics of every truly great man, one of the characteristics that man derives from God to whom there is nothing great or small, in whose august vision the fall of the sparrow is observed, as well as the wreck of a world   That Washington was made a Mason in Fredericksburg Lodge No. 4, August 4 1753 no man

can deny   I myself have seen the record   That he was a charter member
of Alexandria Lodge (now Alexandria-Washington) No 22, and its first
Worshipful Master, can be proved by as indisputable evidence as that he
was our first President   That Lafayette was made a Mason in his presence is beyond dispute, and to-day we have here the Masonic regalia worked
by Madame Lafayette, presented to Washington by Lafayette himself and
accepted by him as a Mason   And to-day we have borne the Bible, the
jewels and the three lights borne by the Lodge at his funeral as a Mason,
one hundred years ago, and I hold in my hand as I speak the gavel he used
when, clothed as a Mason and acting as Grand Master of Masons, he laid
the corner-stone of the capitol   What he thought of Masonry can be easily
found if one desires to find it in his answers to the addresses of Masonic
Lodges in his Union   Printed in his writings, they are of easy access to
every man, and he it was who summed up the conclusion of the whole matter when he said in answer to the address of the Grand Lodge of Massachusetts to their "illustrious brother, George Washington" on the 27th day of
December, 1797, "the great object of Masonry is to promote the happiness
of the human race"

When he wrote these words there were not over eight thousand Masons
in the United States   To-day there are nearly eight hundred thousand in
this nation alone, and the ancient boast of the institution is to-day an absolute verity, "in every clime a Mason may be found"

Here to-day all voices are hushed save those which speak to the higher
impulses of the immortal soul   Here we gather about the dead with no
tears—with no regrets   What have tears and regrets to do with the death
of the just man?

I know of no shrine to which men can come with holier, purer, more
peaceful thoughts than a grave   Glory is the possession of the few—death
is the property of all, and the grave is the gate opening into the tenderest,

sweetest, purest thoughts of the human soul   As had been well said, of all the pulpits from which human voice is ever sent forth there is none from which it reaches so far as from the grave

And here at this shrine we have come, my brethren, to show that Masonry can never forget her illustrious dead   Can never forget that death is but the birth of immortality, and that nothing that is good in man or worthy of love and admiration can ever die

VERSES

To accompany wreaths of oak and evergreen from Londesborough Park, East Yorkshire, sent by The Right Honorable, the Earl of Londesborough, P M 294, P G Senior Warden of England, and the Worshipful Masters, officers and brethren of the Constitutional Lodge No 294, of Ancient Free and Accepted Masons, of Beverley, East Yorkshire, England, to be placed on Washington's tomb on the occasion of the hundredth anniversary of his death

I

An English wreath we fain would lay
Upon this mighty tomb to-day—
Of laurel, ivy, oak and yew,
Which drank the English sun and dew
On far-off Yorkshire's grassy sod,
Where once—we boast—his fathers trod,
Whom East and West unite to praise
And crown with never-fading bays

II

O Washington, thy symbol be
The oak for strength and constancy,

For grandeur and for grace of form,
For calmness in the stress and storm,
The monarch of the forest thou!
To thee the generations bow,
And under thy great shadow rest,
Forever free, forever blest

III

And thine the laurel, for the fame
Illustrious of a Conqueror's name—
Patient to wait and prompt to strike,
Intrepid, fiery, mild alike
Great, for the greatness of the foe
Which fell by thy repeated blow:
Great, for thy country's greatness, won
By thee, her most beloved son

IV

And as the ivy twines around
Cottage and tower, thy heart was found
Clinging to home, and church and wife,
The sweeter for the finished strife
And so thy memory, like the yew,
Will still be green to mortal view—
"The greatest of good men" confest
By all, "and of great men the best!"

RICHARD WILTON,
Canon of York and Chaplain to the Earl of Londesborough
Londesborough Rectory, East Yorkshire, November, 1899

NOTE—John Washington, the founder of the American family of Washington, and great grandfather of the President, lived at South Cave, not far from Londesborough and Beverley, England

MISCELLANEOUS

Denver, Colo., December 18, 1899

To the Ladies Sewing Guild of Christ Church, Alexandria, Va

It would have been a pleasure for me to have returned you in person the thanks that are due for your gift on the 13th instant, of a cane made from a tree from the churchyard where the Father of Our Country once worshipped—but the circumstances were unfavorable, and you will permit me to thank you by letter. I know of nothing more attractive to a reflective mind than a gift which is associated with a great name, and it is now universally conceded that Washington stands at the head of all that have appeared in human history. Everything that is associated with him, or the scenes of his daily life, bridges the years that have passed, and brings us nearer to his personality, his public services, and the loveliness of his domestic virtues. Your gift possesses a special feature in that it relates to Washington's faith in Divine guidance which we know exerted so great an influence upon his public acts. The modern men of so-called greatness may well dwell upon this virtue of the first of Americans, and perhaps discover wherein they are little, and he was so great and strong.

I shall preserve your gift with more than ordinary care and finally leave it to the Grand Lodge of Colorado, with the request that it be preserved, and when the next Centennial of Washington's death shall be observed by the Freemasons of the United States at his beautiful resting place on the banks of the Potomac, it shall be carried by the Grand Master of Masons of Colorado, and the circumstances of its history be again repeated.

Accept my sincere thanks with my wishes for your prosperity, and a long and useful life.

Respectfully,

Roger Williams Woodbury

DENVER, COLO, December 19, 1899

HON A R COURTNEY, Chairman of the Executive Committee,
Richmond, Va

My Dear Sir and Most Worshipful Brother—Inasmuch as the circumstances prevented my addressing the Grand Lodge of Virginia at its late Annual Grand Communication, preparatory to the National Masonic Memorial Exercises on the death of Worshipful Brother George Washington, I would like now to convey to them my appreciation of their labors, and its effectiveness, with some reflections pertaining to it

When I originally proposed to the Grand Master of Colorado in 1893 that he should give the idea the benefit of official introduction to the Masonic world, in his annual address, I think I had, even at that early day, a very fair comprehension of the labor that would be necessary, and when it was formally turned over to your Grand Lodge three years later, it had so long been considered that the labor you have since been called upon to perform, has been no surprise to me   Personally I should have been glad to have continued at the work, instead of calling on the good brethren of Virginia   There were several reasons against this, but I will here only refer to one

It was right for Colorado to propose the Memorial, but it was not so clear that it should undertake to actually carry through National Exercises, that must of necessity be within the jurisdiction of Virginia, and in order to be successful, must have the active co-operation of certain Subordinate Lodges of Virginia, whose history was especially identified with the Masonic life of Washington   I foresaw the possibility of wounded sensibilities, sooner or later, if Virginia was not awarded the honor of taking full charge of these exercises commemorative of her great son   I knew that as the time approached, and the arrangements began to attract more public attention, some of the brethren in Virginia would naturally feel grieved at any Grand Lodge being at the head of the movement except their own—not in jealousy, but with grief at an invasion of privilege that might very properly be held to be theirs by right   It was something of a self denial for us to "step down and out," but I am sure it was the right thing, and I am glad it was done.   The work has been performed by those brethren who of right ought to have done it, and I am satisfied and rejoice at their success

I conceive that the favorable attention of a great many worthy men will be directed to your Lodges through the publicity given to the fact that the first and last Presidents were brothers of the Fraternity   In a somewhat lesser degree this will be felt all over the United States, and reflected in foreign lands

You have brought together more Grand Lodges, through their Grand Masters or their representatives, than has ever been done during the recorded history of Masonry, and we *know* that it reaches back to 1599, just three hundred years

You have written a great chapter in Masonic history, and at the same time it is an important feature in the secular history of our country.   Like the laying of the corner-stone of the capitol, it is a Masonic performance of a great national duty

You have revived public interest in, and disseminated knowledge of, the virtues and public services of Washington and his contemporaries, which has almost passed away from the minds of these later generations You have, through the means of the public press, caused more information about Washington and the early struggles for the Union to be distributed among the people than they had received during the previous many years.

You have laid out the work for untold generations of brethren in the centuries yet to come, for as certain as that Freemasonry will continue to exist in America, will your steps be closely followed whenever the cycling years shall have brought around the Centennial Day

You have linked your names with that of Washington just as your brethren in 1799 handed down theirs to us when they bore the mortal remains of the immortal chief to his tomb

Either of these achievements is well worthy of the labor you have given, but all combined they make the opportunity of a lifetime Permit me to suggest that the records of this annual Grand Communication of your Grand Lodge should be complete to the smallest detail necessary to a perfect understanding, when read for the guidance of your brethren a hundred years hence You should especially apply to each Grand Master or representative who addressed your Grand Lodge on the evening of the 13th instant, for a copy of his remarks, to be inscribed at length in your proceedings, and the exercises of the 14th should be equally as precise, and include as many names of those who took part as the Grand Master and Masters of Lodges can furnish There is much labor in this, but it is an appropriate winding up of the great and solemn event which you owe to the great body of Masons of the United States whom you have represented on this occasion, to yourselves, and to posterity

When the next Centennial occurs all lands will be under civilized governments and those governments will either have for their foundations those principles of liberty which were put into practical test by Washington and his contemporaries, or they will be in process of assimilating them This name will stand as the founder of the world's liberty as it now does of American liberty, and the representatives of those governments and peoples from every country and clime will then come to participate with your Grand Lodge in honoring the mortal remains of the immortal Washington in his beautiful place of repose on the banks of the Potomac

Personally, I wish to thank you for the kindness which I received at your hands as one of the representatives of the Grand Lodge of Colorado; and I trust that no friction will ever mar the warm relations now existing between our two grand bodies.

Fraternally yours,

R W WOODBURY.

REPORT OF COLORADO COMMITTEE 1900

To the Most Worshipful Grand Lodge

Your Committee on Centennial Memorial Exercises of Worshipful Brother George Washington herewith respectfully and fraternally present their final report.

Grand Master Burnand and all the members of your committee were present at the convening of the Grand Lodge of Virginia at the Opera House in Alexandria, Va, on the evening of the 13th of December last. The premises were very much crowded with perhaps one thousand brethren. The officers and representatives of other Grand Jurisdictions were seated upon the stage, and by States they were severally introduced, received with grand honors and made brief addresses, some of which were very appropriate Just how many Grand Jurisdictions were represented we do not know, but most of them in the United States as well as Canada, and one or more from abroad The response to the call for Colorado was most fittingly made by Grand Master Burnand

The Grand Lodge was in session for several hours, and then attempted to proceed to another building a little distance away, where an elegant banquet had been prepared by the brethren of Alexandria in honor of the Grand Lodge and its guests. For reasons for which the brethren of Alexandria were not responsible the toasts and responses that had been arranged to take place after the banquet were all abandoned

WILLIAM DAVID TODD,
Past Grand Master of Colorado.
Member Colorado Washington Centennial Memorial Committee.

On the morning of the 14th several thousand Masons and as many other persons proceeded to Mount Vernon, a detailed account of which appears in the published extracts incorporated in this volume Most of the brethren and visitors went by steamers, included among which were your Grand Master and Brothers Teller and Todd   The other members of your committee had been assigned to the Presidential train by way of the electric railroad

Parts of the grounds at Mount Vernon were as crowded as was the Grand Lodge and the banquet hall the preceding evening, and some of the solemnity of the occasion was lost through the obliteration of the niceties of the programme

The address of Grand Master Burnand was listened to with respectful attention and deep interest, and it was delivered with self-possession, earnestness and dignity   He was accompanied in the procession, and supported on the stand where he spoke by Past Grand Masters Teller and Todd, while the other members of your committee were lost in the throng of the Presidential party.

At the vault where the remains of Washington now repose, and where the formal Memorial Exercises took place, the crush was tremendous, but at the close Brother Todd succeeded in depositing upon the sarcophagus the wreath procured by Grand Master Burnand, and gave it the most imposing place among the floral offerings.

The exercises at Mount Vernon closed with addresses in front of the mansion by the President of the United States and the Grand Master of Virginia

In the evening at Washington a reception was held by the officers of the Grand Lodge of Virginia, and later a banquet was given at one of the hotels, at which Brother Wright of your committee was one of the speakers

Whatever the general verdict may have been as to the details, your committee feel that the exercises were a great national event, as was fore-

seen by this Grand Lodge when it proposed the Memorial We were proud
to represent this Grand Lodge there, and to feel the fraternal warmth that
was frequently expressed toward it by the brethren from other Jurisdictions We know that at the beginning there was no thought of any special
credit attaching to this Jurisdiction because of originating exercises that
must perforce be repeated on each Centennial recurrence of the anniversary, nor any expectation of the Memorial being used for personal display
Colorado cared only to show that the Masonic heart is warm for all that is
good and noble, that it reveres the name of its Brother Washington, and in
holding Memorial Exercises at his grave it expressed affection and indebted-
ness to all who aided in founding the government under which we live

To one who has long lived "beneath the shadow of the Rocky Mountains" there was a wondrous inspiration in gathering on the centennial of
Washington's death where he lived, loved, worshipped and died.   The human mind venerates age, even when pertaining to inanimate objects   Men
look with awe upon lofty mountains, not so much from their being evidences
of infinite power, but because they stand as representatives of untold centuries, long antedating the supposed advent of man upon earth   But the
ancient works of man himself inspire even greater reverence, and when
these are associated with the memories of such historic deeds as cluster
around Mount Vernon, we who journeyed from Colorado (to reach which
a hundred years ago would have consumed more time than is now taken to
encompass the earth) felt it to be hallowed ground, where the head is in-
voluntarily bared, the voice becomes hushed and gentle, and the heart is
open to all those silent influences which make men better, and fill them with
the resolve of emulation

The report of this committee presented at your last annual Grand
Communication presupposed that nothing later would be expected by the
Grand Lodge, but the sentiment then expressed has caused this committee

to recall from the office of the Grand Secretary the bound report then made, and add to it for historical purposes subsequent correspondence, official circulars and reports, newspaper articles, photographs, badges, maps, and a detailed account of the various local exercises held in this Grand Jurisdiction so far as correspondence and personal effort have been made to gather them   All of these features have been incorporated with the volume reported one year ago, so that the book is now a fairly complete history of the Memorial Exercises, from their inception to their execution

A special effort was made by your committee to procure copies of all the addresses made in our Colorado Lodges   Personal application was made by letter to all from which Lodge reports were made to the Grand Secretary, which reports formed the basis of your committee's information as to where Memorial Exercises had been held   Wherever they heard of addresses having been delivered, they wrote for copies, and in some cases several letters were written for a single address   They only succeeded, however, in obtaining the copy of sixteen, as follows

    James H Peabody, Canon City

    Ernest Le Neve Foster and Flor Ashbaugh, Central City

    R D Graham and W T Miller, Colorado Springs

    Ezra T Elliott, Del Norte

    Aaron Gove and F A Williams, Denver

    N C Miller, Durango

    D R Hatch, Georgetown

    Marshall H Dean, Glenwood Springs

    Frank Madden, Greeley

    W L Bush, Idaho Springs

    J M Maxwell and L M Goddard, Leadville

    M H Fitch, Pueblo

These addresses, together with those made at Mount Vernon, will all be found in this volume, and there are some extracts from newspapers or other addresses made in this State Some of those given in full are of exceptional merit, well worthy of being handed down to generations yet to come

By consent of the Grand Secretary the official reports from Lodges, of their observance of the memorial programme, have been incorporated in this volume, so as to bring together everything pertaining to the subject. It is probable that at some future time some of our Lodges will regret that they are unrepresented

We have also included in this book such memorial circulars from other Grand Lodges as have come into our possession These are of interest to us because some of them closely follow the Colorado programme, republishing and circulating to their Grand Jurisdictions as a part of their local programme, our letters from Brother Treat and the Worshipful Master of Alexandria-Washington Lodge

There are also bound in this volume four photographs of the Mount Vernon exercises—two being different views of your Grand Master while delivering his address, the third being the front of the mansion, and the President of the United States and his audience; and the fourth, Washington's tomb, showing the floral deposits through the gates, conspicuous among which is that of Colorado

Also appearing in the book are the badges worn at Mount Vernon by one of your committee Also a map showing the order of the procession on the grounds, and the places where the respective addresses were delivered

The newspaper clippings occupy fifty pages, with three columns to the page They are mostly from the Washington press, and not only contain much matter of Masonic and general interest, but verify the former prediction of your committee that millions of people would by these exercises be brought into closer knowledge and sympathy with the historic facts and governing principles of our forefathers   These newspaper clippings also have many illustrations of Washington and his home, and other scenes and persons of present interest.   They also include in full the accurate and excellent compilation of Brother Greenleaf in his "Square and Compass"

Your committee are unable to close their final report, at the end of seven years of service in this most interesting field, without directing attention to the fact that every action of this Grand Lodge upon the subject of the Washington Centennial Memorial Exercises, from their inception, has been unanimous, and that no disposition has been manifest from any source not in harmony with the exalted objects of the Memorial   Every member of the Grand Lodge has appreciated the patriotism, and we may add the statesmanship, involved in and underlying this great national proposition, and we repeat what we said last year, that the action of this Grand Lodge in initiating this Memorial will long appear in its history as the most beautiful jewel that sparkles in a crown

To all the brethren who have contributed to lighten the labors of this committee, to the members generally of the Grand Lodge who have so generously supported the recommendations of the committee, to the Grand Secretary, who has co-operated in so much of their clerical work, and to the several Grand Masters who have presided in the Grand East since the appointment of this committee, and some of whom have given invaluable advice and assistance, we return our profound acknowledgements

ROGER WILLIAMS WOODBURY,

WILLIAM DAVID TODD,

WILLIAM D WRIGHT,

Committee

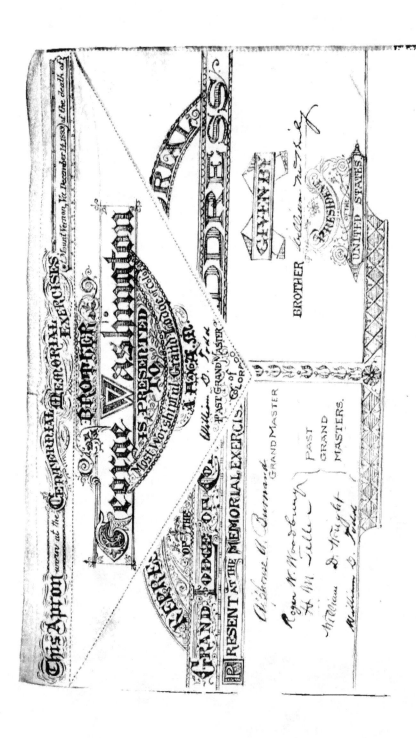

Lamb-skin Apron Worn by Past Grand Master William D. Todd at Mount Vernon December 14, 1899.
The Inscription Partially Concealed by the Flap Reads:
"Representatives"

Exercises in
Colorado

Memorial Exercises in Colorado.

LETTER TO THE MASTER OF WASHINGTON'S LODGE.

To the Worshipful Master of Alexandria-Washington Lodge,
A F & A M , Alexandria, Va .

My Dear Sir and Worshipful Brother—The Grand Lodge of Masons of Colorado is arranging for Memorial Services on the centennial of the death of Brother George Washington, to be held in every Lodge in this Jurisdiction, and in preparing a programme for adoption we desire an official letter from you, as Worshipful Master of the Lodge once presided over by Washington   Your letter we desire to print and furnish to each of our Lodges, to be read on the occasion specified   It seems to us that the reading of a letter from the brother who now presides in the East where Washington once presided, would bring us into closer fraternal union with him and his Masonic life, his personal worth, and his exalted public services Without undertaking to outline what such a sketch should contain, we beg to suggest that it include a sketch of his Masonic life, his connection with your Lodge, and the adoption of his name by your Lodge   We wish to print for our Subordinate Lodges a good account of Washington's Masonic life, and we had rather it should be incorporated in your letter than to be obliged to have recourse to some printed account, which will be much less interesting than one coming from you

Our Grand Lodge meets on the 19th of September, and as our report will be quite long, we would like your letter as early in the month as possible   In the meantime, will you kindly inform me at once if we may rely upon your compliance with our request? You are at liberty to make the letter as long as you desire, and not feel restricted in the least.

Thanking you in advance for your courtesy, and assistance, and with the most kindly sentiments, I beg to remain,

Fraternally yours,

R W WOODBURY,

Chairman.

LETTER FROM THE MASTER OF WASHINGTON'S LODGE.

ALEXANDRIA, VA, September 2, 1899.

To the Brethren of the Grand Jurisdiction of Colorado, Greeting

On the 14th of December, of this year, we meet in Solemn Lodge to celebrate the one hundredth anniversary of the death of our illustrious Masonic Brother George Washington.

He was a man of destiny, sent by the Supreme Architect of the Universe for a specific purpose, and that accomplished, his soul winged its flight to the Heavenly Lodge above, where the King of Glory in all majesty and dominion presides History fails to record a nobler, purer, and more unselfish character Cæsar thrice refused a crown that they would not have dared offer the patriot Washington Napoleon Bonaparte erected statues of bronze and marble to commemorate his achievements, accomplished at the expense of infinite suffering and torrents of blood, but these monuments will crumble to dust, while the fame of our noble, gentle and humane Washington, enshrined in the hearts of a grateful people, will go reverberating down through the ages, gathering greater and greater lustre until time is no more

Washington's advent into the world was co-incident with the establishment of Masonry in this country, for he was born on the 22d day of February, 1732, and the first regular Lodge of Masons in America was instituted in Boston, Mass , in the year 1733, under a charter granted by the Grand Lodge of England

Just before Washington attained his majority a Lodge was established at Fredericksburg, Va , and he immediately, although he was not twenty-one years of age, applied for admission He was duly elected, and received the Entered Apprentice degree on November 24, 1752, the Fellow Craft degree on March 3, 1753, and was raised to the Sublime degree of Master Mason on August 4, 1753

The Bible on which he was obligated was printed at Cambridge, England, in 1688, by John Field, Printer to the University, and is to-day in a splendid state of preservation Its hallowed associations make this book the most valuable and venerated of all Masonic treasures in America

The fact that Washington was initiated into the mysteries of Freemasonry before he became of age, was not an unusual proceeding at that time, for he had already attained the physical, mental and moral developments of a man, and thoroughly understood and appreciated the responsibilities of life Then, too, it was customary in some European countries, to admit into the fraternity men under twenty-one years of age, who were well vouched for, notably the sons of Masons

On the 3rd of February, 1783, the Masons of Alexandria, Va , obtained a warrant from the Grand Lodge of Pennsylvania to hold a Lodge of Ancient Masons, and was numbered thirty-nine Robert Adams was the first Master. It wrought under this warrant until a Grand Lodge was established in Richmond, Va , when it immediately petitioned for a new charter, and asked that "our Brother George Washington, Esq ," should be named as the first Master of the Lodge This prayer was granted at the next communication of the Grand Lodge of Virginia, on April 28, 1788, and the number changed to twenty-two Edmund Randolph, Governor of Virginia, was Grand Master at the time

George Washington was, therefore, first Master of Alexandria Lodge No. 22   In 1805 the members unanimously requested the Grand Lodge to change the name of the Lodge to "Alexandria-Washington Lodge" No. 22, and this was accordingly done   So the name of the immortal Washington is indissolubly linked for all time with the Lodge with which he was so intimately associated for many years

On the 18th of September, 1793, the corner-stone of the capitol in the City of Washington was laid with appropriate Masonic ceremonies, Washington (at that time President of the United States) acting as Worshipful Master of Lodge No 22   The Masonic regalia worn by him on that occasion, and the trowel he used to spread the cement, are preserved as precious relics by this Lodge

The chair he occupied in the East has been in continuous use ever since, and it is the highest ambition of the members of the old Lodge to be elected to the station he once filled with such signal ability.

He died at Mount Vernon, his beloved home, on the banks of the Potomac, six miles below Alexandria, on the 14th day of December, 1799, before nature's decay had begun to impair his wonderful physical and mental vitality

He was laid to rest at Mount Vernon on the 18th day of December, by the brethren of the Order he loved so well, and whose precepts he had so faithfully followed   Well might he have said with the Evangelist: "I have fought a good fight, I have finished my course; I have kept the faith; Henceforth there is laid up for me a crown of righteousness which the Lord, the righteous Judge, shall give me at that day, and not to me only, but unto all them that love His appearing"

With brotherly greetings from your brethren of Alexandria-Washington Lodge No 22, I am,

Cordially and fraternally yours,

BENJ M AITCHESON,

(Seal of Lodge)   Worshipful Master Lodge No 22

SUBSEQUENT CONNECTING CORRESPONDENCE WITH THE MASTER OF WASHINGTON'S LODGE.

DENVER, COLO , September 8, 1899

BENJ. M AITCHESON, ESQ , Worshipful Master Alexandria-Washington Lodge No 22, A F and A M , Alexandria, Va

Dear Sir and Worshipful Brother—I am in receipt of your letter of the 2nd inst , to the brethren of this Grand Jurisdiction, and in their behalf I thank you very much for the same

Its spirit is harmonious with the lofty subject, and its reading to the hundred Lodges of this Grand Jurisdiction at their local Memorial Exercises on the 14th of December, will add immeasurably to the interest of that occasion

I have received by express your gift of the handsome volume, "The Lodge of Washington "

I was most agreeably surprised at the character of its contents, and find it of much more than ordinary interest, even in a historical sense, apart from Masonry. I do not wonder that your members regard No 22 with unusual love and reverence It is like a sturdy oak, whose spreading arms have sheltered generations of worthy men, and have become broader and stronger and more protecting as the years roll on

There are Washington Lodges in name all through our country, but yours alone is the Lodge of Washington I think the hallowed associations that cling around it must excit a lasting and beneficent impression upon the minds of your members—not so solemn as when standing at the tomb of Washington at Mount Vernon, but nevertheless imposing and majestic, and calculated to arouse silent resolutions that make good men and true citizens

I thank you very much for your thoughtful kindness, and after loaning the history to my associates on my committee, it will be used by such as desire to know more of the Masonic life of Washington, and the Lodge over which he presided　　　Yours fraternally,

R W Woodbury, Chairman.

Denver, Colo, October 9, 1899.

Benj M Aitcheson, Esq, Worshipful Master Alexandria-Washington Lodge No 22, Alexandria, Va.:

Dear Sir and Worshipful Brother—Since the meeting of our Grand Lodge on the 19th ultimo, we have sent a copy of the programme for exercises in the Colorado Subordinate Lodges, to all the Grand Lodges of the country, hoping that many of them, if not all, will also arrange for local exercises and be assisted by our programme, of which I enclose a copy. We concluded that we would not send out copies of your letter to our Lodges until just before the memorial exercises, so that its interest would not be reduced by prior reading.

The Grand Secretaries of Kansas and Arkansas have just written, asking for a copy of the letter to be used in their Jurisdictions, and I presume similar requests will be received from other Jurisdictions. We will have copies sent to those which ask for it, feeling certain that it will meet with your approval. To such as we thus send, we will suggest that as the letter is addressed to the brethren of this Jurisdiction, that they might omit the address (to Colorado) or write you for permission to change the name of the State so as to apply to their own Jurisdictions I have thought that it might be more satisfactory to them to have it that way, than to use it as written for another Jurisdiction

Fraternally yours,

R W Woodbury, Chairman.

ALEXANDRIA, VA , October 21, 1899

MR. R W WOODBURY, Chairman, Denver, Colo :

Dear Sir and Brother—I have your letter of October 9th, with copy of programme of exercises for the Colorado Subordinate Lodges, for which please accept my thanks   I regret very much that I was unable to answer your letter sooner, which was caused by my taking a good deal of interest and time in the sesqui-centennial of Alexandria, and hope my delay in answering the same will not cause you any inconvenience   I enclose you three copies of the letter which I sent you some time ago, addressed to Colorado, Kansas and Arkansas, on which I have put the seal of our Lodge, as I was unable, as I wrote you before, owing to the seal having been burned, to have it put on the letter I wrote at first   I thought you would like to have one with the seal of the Lodge as a matter of record   I am very much obliged to you if you will forward the letters to the Kansas and Arkansas Grand Secretaries, so that they may use them as they desire   I have written the Grand Secretary of Kansas that I have forwarded this copy, and that you would, no doubt, send it as soon as received.

Fraternally yours,

BENJ M AITCHESON,

Worshipful Master Alexandria-Washington Lodge No 22.

RICHMOND, VA , October 21, 1899

HON. R W WOODBURY:

Dear Sir and Brother—Yours of the 10th inst came duly to hand with a copy of Worshipful Brother Aitcheson's letter   Please accept my thanks.

It would be a great help to me if you were here or in Washington to assist us in mapping out and conducting the exercises, and if you are a man of leisure, which I hope you are, I would be glad for you to come on at once to the Ebbitt House, which has been selected as our headquarters, and remain there until the ceremonies are over, as one of the committee, wo paying your expenses. I think it would be but a just compliment to the brother who originated this movement, that he should have an active part in carrying it through, and I know our whole committee agree with me in this

I am just about concluding a contract for printing the booklet, which I have frequently mentioned in our correspondence, and the first pages of this work should contain an account of the origin of the movement, and pictures of the originators. Please furnish me with this at your earliest convenience.

Awaiting your reply, which I hope will be immediate, I remain,

Yours fraternally,

A R. COURTNEY,
Chairman Executive Committee.

LETTER TO BROTHER ADNA ADAMS TREAT, A CENTENARIAN.

DENVER, COLO, September 19, 1899

MR ADNA ADAMS TREAT, Denver, Colorado

Dear Sir and Brother—In 1893 the Grand Lodge of Masons of Colorado initiated a movement for the holding of Centennial Memorial Exercises upon the anniversary of the death of Worshipful Brother George Washington, at Mount Vernon, Virginia, on the 14th of December, 1899 Those exercises at Mount Vernon will be participated in by between fifty and sixty Grand Lodges of the United States, and some foreign Jurisdictions, and the Subordinate Lodges in this Jurisdiction and others, will at the same time hold exercises of a similar nature in their respective Lodge rooms The programme which has been prepared for the use of the Subordinate Lodges of Colorado includes the reading of a letter addressed to the brethren of Colorado from the present Worshipful Master of Alexandria-Washington Lodge No 22, of Alexandria, Va , of which Lodge Washington was the first Master. In the report of the special committee to the Grand Lodge of Colorado made to-day, covering their conveyance of respect and reverance to you in your one hundred and third year, it was stated that you had, many years ago, personally met Brother Marquis de La Fayette, the friend, compatriot and Masonic brother of Washington The request was made that this committee, representing the Grand Lodge of Colorado, in the arrangements for the Washington Centennial Memorial Exercises, should request of you a letter to be read to all the Lodges in this Jurisdiction at those Memorial Exercises, particularly relating to your recollection relative to this great friend of Washington, and such other matters as it may be your pleasure to write for use upon that occasion In accordance with the wishes of the Grand Lodge, I now formally invite you to prepare such a letter and forward to me at Denver, Colorado, and the same will be thankfully received and used as designated

Fraternally yours,

R W Woodbury,
Chairman

LETTER TO COLORADO MASONS BY BROTHER ADNA ADAMS TREAT, CENTENARIAN

Denver, Colo , November 23, 1899.

To the Most Worshipful Grand Master, Grand Secretary, Officers and Members of the Grand Lodge of Colorado, Greeting

The request of the chairman of your committee to briefly outline some events in the early history of my Masonic career has been received.

I was born April 8, 1797, hence was nearly three years of age at the time of General George Washington's death

I was one of a committee from Apollo Lodge, Troy, N Y , to receive and entertain General Marquis de Lafayette, who had been a warm personal friend of General Washington, at a reception tendered him by the city of Troy on September 18, 1824, and took part in the Masonic division of the grand procession on that day.

Our committee escorted him to and from the Lodge where a reception was held

As I recall the impressions made upon my mind of his appearance and address, he was of medium height, erect of figure, with faultless dress   In manner and appearance a French gentleman.

It would give me great pleasure were it not for my infirmities, to be present upon so memorable an occasion to do honor to an event that holds in memory one of the most illustrious characters in modern history, occurring within the span of my life, one hundred years ago.

As we are disposed to honor the good deeds and acts of the living, it is also right to honor the important events that have crowned the lives of the dead, "For their works do follow them," as we bow in silent adoration to the behests of our Creator.

Fraternally yours,

ADNA ADAMS TREAT.

OFFICIAL PROGRAMME OF MEMORIAL EXERCISES IN COLORADO

The M W Grand Lodge of Colorado, A F & A M

OFFICE OF THE GRAND SECRETARY

Denver, Colo , October 1, 1899

At the Annual Grand Communication of the Most Worshipful Grand Lodge of Colorado, A F and A M , held on the 19th of September, 1899, the committee on the Washington Centennial Memorial Exercises made report, which included a general order of exercises for the use of the Subordinate Lodges of the Jurisdiction on their local observance of the occasion. The report expressed the opinion that local exercises by Masonic Lodges throughout the country would be of at least equal effect as the national exercises at Mount Vernon, in attracting the attention of the present generation to the virtues, patriotism and Masonic and public services of Washington and his compeers The report of the committee was unanimously adopted, and in accordance with the action of the Grand Lodge, you are hereby furnished with a copy of that part of the report which relates to said local exercises, which is as follows

That where there is more than one Lodge in any town or city, the brethren all unite in the exercises

That they be held on the day or evening of the 14th of December next, the anniversary of General Washington's death

That the Most Worshipful Grand Master be requested to issue general authority to all Lodges that may wish to avail themselves of the same, to hold their exercises in any public hall, to be attended by the public, and to march in procession thereto

That the flag of our country, draped with crape, be displayed in every Lodge room or public hall used by the Lodges during the Memorial Exercises.

The reading of an account of Washington's last illness from the diary f his secretary, published in McClure's Magazine of February, 1898

The reading of a personal letter to the Lodges of Colorado, from the Vorshipful Master of Alexandria-Washington Lodge, of which Washing-n was the first Master under its Virginia charter, which letter includes n account of Washington's Masonic life

An address upon the early influence of Masonry on the development f the American idea of the equality of men, as expressed in the Declara-on of Independence, and its culmination in the independence of the Amer-an Colonies.

An address on the personal character and public services of Wash-gton.

The reading of Washington's "Farewell Address"

To be interspersed with such music as may be arranged by the Lodges

A copy of the personal letter from the Master of Alexandria-Washing-n Lodge, addressed to the Lodges of this Jurisdiction, will be furnished u shortly before the time for its use

I will also state that the committee has requested of Brother A. A. reat of Denver, now in the one hundred and third year of his age, a letter scriptive of his personal meeting with Washington's personal, military d Masonic friend, Marquis de Lafayette, to be read on the memorable casion, and, if received, a copy of same will be furnished you.

The magazine article, the Farewell Address, etc, will not be sent out om this office, but each Lodge will easily be able to supply itself.

The authority of the Most Worshipful Grand Master, covering the ird paragraph in the above order of exercises, will be forwarded later

Please acknowledge receipt.

Fraternally yours,

ED C PARMELEE, Grand Secretary

DISPENSATION FROM THE GRAND MASTER.

THE M W GRAND LODGE OF COLORADO, A F. & A M

GRAND MASTER'S OFFICE

A. A BURNAND, Grand Master   LEADVILLE, COLO

The Most Worshipful Grand Lodge of Colorado, A F and A M., having recommended a general local observance of the centennial of the death of Worshipful Brother,

GEORGE WASHINGTON,

which took place on the 14th of December, 1799,

Now, Therefore, Authority is hereby granted Subordinate Lodges of this Jurisdiction, to appear in public procession, hold their Memorial Exercises in a public hall, or invite the public to their own halls if they so prefer, on the day or evening of the 14th day of December, 1899, A L. 5899

It is to be hoped that every Lodge in this Jurisdiction, no matter how small the membership, will in some way observe the day, which should be dear to the heart of every Mason.   Let all unite to do honor to the memory of him, of whom it was said, "Providence left him childless that his country might call him father"

I am informed by the committee that the programme outlined by them and published by the Grand Secretary under date of October 1, 1899, is not mandatory in its intent, but advisory   Lodges are requested, however, to conform to the same as closely as possible.   Washington's "Farewell Address" will be found in "Great Words from Great Americans," published by G P Putnam's Sons

Given under our hand and seal this 23d day of October, 1899, A L 5899

ALPHONSE A BURNAND, Grand Master.

Attest

ED C PARMELEE, Grand Secretary

ALAMOSA.

Masonic Hall, Alamosa, Colo , December 14, 1899

Alamosa Lodge No 44, A. F and A M , met as a Lodge of sorrow to commomorate the one hundredth anniversary of the death of Brother George Washington of Alexandria-Washington Lodge No 22, of Alexandria, Va , with the following named officers:

Brother George Booth, Worshipful Master.

A C Cole, Senior Warden

Henry Bachus, Junior Warden.

W H. Hirst, Secretary

The great lights being draped, as well as the American flag in the East, the Lodge was opened on the third degree in due form. Lodge was then called from labor to refreshment and the public was admitted Brother H H. Dubendorff was called to act as Master of Ceremonies, which he did by first stating the object of the meeting and the reading of the Grand Secretary's circular under date of October 1, 1899, after which prayer was offered by Brother W Taylor Douglas

Duet	Mr and Mrs Bullock
Address on Masonry	Brother C C Holbrook
Solo	Miss Louise Gertensen
Recitation	Miss Stella Van Fleet
Solo	Mrs Brunson
Reading letter from Adna Adams Treat, and comments	
	Brother W Taylor Douglas
Song	Misses Louise Gertensen. Minnie Bucher and Maud Watson
Washington's Farewell Address	W H Hirst

The public was then dismissed, Lodge called on, and closed in due form

Fraternally,

W H. Hirst,

(Seal of Lodge)

Secretary

ASPEN

Aspen, Colo , December 28, 1899.

Washington Centennial Memorial Exercises were held by Spar Lodge No 60, A F and A M , and Hiram Lodge No. 98, A F and A M., at the Presbyterian Church, Aspen, Colorado, on the evening of December 14, 1899, A. L 5899, when the following programme was rendered:

     I   Music
    II   Prayer
    III   Introductory remarks by chairman and reading of letter from the Worshipful Master of Alexandria-Washington Lodge No 22, of Alexandria, Va
    IV   Music
    V   Reading of Washington's farewell address by Brother Mark C Kobey
    VI   Music
    VII   Reading of extracts from newspaper printed in 1800, bearing upon the obsequies of Worshipful Brother Washington, also letter from President John Adams, by Brother Branscombe
    VIII   Reading of Brother Adna Adams Treat's letter, followed by address by Brother Percival
    IX   Music
    X   Benediction

L T Tenscher,
Secretary Spar Lodge No 60, A F. and A M.

T N Gillespie,
Secretary Hiram Lodge No 98, A F and A M

BERTHOUD.

BERTHOUD, COLO , December 28, 1899.

ED C PARMELEE, Grand Secretary .

Dear Sir and Brother—Berthoud Lodge No 83, A F and A M , accepted an invitation from Fort Collins Lodge No. 19 to be present with them on December 14, and participate in the Washington Memorial Exercises held on that date.   A very enjoyable time was had and the exercises were very appropriate

Yours fraternally,

F. M WRIGHT,
Secretary.

BRECKENRIDGE.

BRECKENRIDGE, COLO , February 22, 1900

A A BURNAND, Grand Master, A F and A M , Denver, Colo .

Dear Sir and Most Worshipful Brother—On the one hundredth anniversary of the death of Worshipful Brother George Washington, Breckenridge Lodge No 47, A. F. and A M., held appropriate services at G A R Hall, and the I O R M participated with us in giving the prescribed programme, to a large and appreciative audience.

Very fraternally,

B A ARBOGAST,
Secretary

BUENA VISTA.

MOUNT PRINCETON LODGE No 49, A F & A M

Your committee appointed to draft resolutions in commemoration of the life and character of our esteemed patron, friend and brother, George Washington, upon this the one hundredth anniversary of his death, beg leave to submit the following

Whereas, We esteem the nation happy indeed which can claim Washington as its most illustrious soldier, its wisest statesman and most distinguished and honored citizen, of whom it has been truly said he was "first in war, first in peace, and first in the hearts of his countrymen" In the language of Charles Phillips "A conqueror, he was untainted with the crime of blood, a revolutionist, he was free from the stain of treason—for aggression commenced the contest, and his country called him to the command Liberty unsheathed his sword, Necessity stained it, and Victory returned it If he had paused here, history might have doubted what station to assign him, whether at the head of her citizens or her soldiers But the last glorious act crowns his career and banishes all hesitation Who like Washington, after having emancipated a hemisphere, resigned its crown, and preferred the retirement of domestic life, to the adoration of a land he might almost be said to have created!"

The lapse of time and the wear of ages, monuments crumble and return to dust The greatest statesmen, soldiers and orators fill the public mind for a brief period, and then fade from sight and memory A few, it is true, have lived longer in the hearts of their own countrymen, but to Washington alone it has been given to command and receive the respect and veneration of the world

But it is as a Mason that we would give honor to his memory to-night, and we deem ourselves fortunate to be able to claim him among the great brotherhood of the mystic tie His name and character have given dignity to our order, and inspired with enthusiasm all true lovers and patrons of Masonry

Therefore, be it Resolved, That we admire his record as a soldier, honor him as a statesman, venerate his memory as a pure patriot, and love him as a brother

Resolved, That a copy of these resolutions be spread upon the minutes of the Lodge

T J BRISCOE,

H JEAN WETERING,

Committee

BUENA VISTA, COLO, December 14, 1899

CANON CITY.

CIRCULAR TO MEMBERS

CANON CITY, COLO, December 11, 1899

Dear Brother.

In accordance with arrangements made for the proper observance of the Washington Centennial Memorial, the following particulars are hereby promulgated for your guidance

Assemble at the Lodge room promptly at 7·30 Thursday evening, December 14, 1899. From the Lodge room procession will move to the M E Church, where suitable seats will be reserved for Masons

Members of the Craft will wear white gloves and aprons, which will be furnished at the Lodge room and collected at the close of the exercises.

A programme is enclosed herewith, which should be preserved as a memento Others will be furnished at the church

It is confidently expected that every member of Mount Moriah Lodge will assist in making this event one long to be remembered, and, that this may be accomplished, all should be in prompt attendance at the Lodge room and join in the ceremonies.

Sojourning brethren are urgently requested to participate with us

By order of

A R FRISBIE,
Worshipful Master

Attest

H. L PRICE,
Secretary

PROGRAMME WASHINGTON CENTENNIAL MEMORIAL EXERCISES

1799   (Picture of Washington)   1899

Under the Auspices of Mount Moriah Lodge No 15, A F and A M

M E Church, Canon City, Colorado,

December 14, 1899

Officers of Mt Moriah Lodge No 15, A F and A M, for the year 1900

Arthur R Frisbie	Worshipful Master
Frank N Carrier	Senior Warden
George E Trout	Junior Warden
James H Peabody	Treasurer
Henry L Price	Secretary
Wilbur T Little	Senior Deacon
William J Davis	Junior Deacon
Henry T Gravestock	Senior Steward
Charles H Gravestock	Junior Steward
Joseph T Little	Tiler

Piano solo—"Star Spangled Banner," Concert Paraphrase (Troyer)

       Miss Grace Dale

Prayer   Rev B E Harl, Trilumnia Lodge No 85

Reading of a personal letter to the Lodges of Colorado, from the Worshipful Master of Alexandria Washington Lodge of Virginia

       Worshipful Master A R Frisbie, Mt Moriah Lodge No 15

Quartet—"Soldier's Farewell" (Kinkel)   .

       Messrs Armstrong, Brighton, McClintock, Chemberlin

Reading of an account of Washington's last illness, from the diary of his private secretary

       Rev W J Fisher, Pastor Cumberland Presbyterian Church

Address—"Personal Character and Public Services of Washington"

       Most Worshipful James H Peabody, Past Grand Master of Colorado

Quartet   "Tenting on the Old Camp Ground"

Address—"The Early Influence of Masonry on the Development of the American Idea, as Expressed in the Declaration of Independence"

       Rev R A Chase, Mt Moriah Lodge No 15

Reading of Washington's farewell address

       Right Worshipful Jos W Milsom, Deputy Grand Master of Colorado

"America"   Audience requested to join in singing

Benediction

PAST MASTERS OF MOUNT MORIAH LODGE NO 15, A F AND A M

G B Frazier	1867 68 69-70
Thomas H Craven	1871-76-78
B F Smith	1872
B F Shaffer	1873
W H Thompson	1874-75
A L Rudolph	1877
W T Bridwell	1879
James H Peabody	1880 81 82 83-84-94-95
Henry Earle	1885
George W Roe	1886-87
J T Little	1888 89 98
D A Bradbury	1890 91 92
Joseph W Milson	1893
E C Stewart	1896
F N Carrier	1897
A R Frisbie	1899

Dispensation issued December 11, 1867
Charter issued October 6, 1868

ADDRESS OF J H PEABODY, PAST GRAND MASTER

Worshipful Master and Brethren, Ladies and Gentlemen

A story is told somewhere in ancient history of an unlettered youth of foreign tongue, who sought admission into one of the institutions of learning in Athens As an only means of communicating to this ignorant boy the necessary refusal, a glass filled with water was submitted to him as a token of the impossibility of his admission, whereupon the undaunted child plucked a rose leaf and floated it upon the sparkling surface, in humble but beautiful demonstration of his willingness, but inability to add to the crowded halls of science In like humble manner, my honored brethren and friends, I ask your attention for a few moments while I add my feeble "pen leaf" to the brimming catalogue of orations, speeches and addresses delivered this day throughout the length and breadth of this glorious Republic, commemorative of the "personal character and public services" of our beloved countryman and brother, the peerless Washington

One hundred years ago this day the Supreme Architect of the Universe removed from the terrestrial to the celestial Lodge our Brother George Washington, and about his tomb on the brow of beautiful Mount Vernon, overlooking the placid and peaceful Potomac, our brethren are assembled to-day in the character of Masons, to testify that time has not weakened their veneration for his memory, nor years brought forgetfulness of his countless virtues From the East and the West, from the North and the South, yea, even from the isles of the sea, Masons have come to day to mark the first century of his departure from earth to heaven

In like manner are we, and are thousands of Lodges and tens of thousands of Masons, assembled this evening to proclaim our love for his memory and to congratulate ourselves that by and through his noble heroism and patriotic actions, liberty still lives, and America is free

You ask why we, as Masons, assemble to do honor to his memory? I will answer you

Masons have everywhere been benefactors of their race, they have championed every cause dear to the poor, the ignorant, and the oppressed, and have many times fought the battles of human liberty against the votaries of tyranny and superstition, they have always borne aloft the banner of religious liberty

From age to age the light of divine truth has been shining upon our altars, and we have guarded the Word of God as closely, and we have followed its traditions, preserving its golden pages in our hands, and hiding its teachings in our hearts We are, therefore, holding these ceremonies in honor of Washington, who, when this nation struggled for its rights among the greater powers around it, stood among the other Masons surrounding the open Bible with their uplifted swords, renewing their vows to set free the captives of power, to make the life of the poor a less burden to them, to teach men their rights, and to enlighten those whom ignorance and error held in bondage, and to help make the world a better place for men to live in Washington was bound by these same sacred ties that bind us, and he lived and died the noblest type of American manhood in this or any other age

In the arena of public affairs, in science, literature, statesmanship and politics, the life of Washington has been told over and over again, till such words seem familiar and are half meaningless, that his writings and words spoken, serve to this day to mould public opinions and national affairs, no one with authority dare deny

He was a splendid type of the Divine Master's handiwork—tall, erect, compactly built, polite, courteous, loving but not demonstrative, firm in his purpose, but never overbearing, strong in his convictions, but ever mindful of the wishes of others, sincere in his love for his country and his countrymen, no labor was ever too great for him to undertake, no danger too threatening to deter him from espousing the cause of justice and right A devout churchman for years a steady worker in that body, manifesting by his words as well as by his deeds, the nobleness of his character and his duty, and his love for both God and man In fact, the sum of his good deeds passes human comprehension, and his reward is the limitless and deathless gratitude of every dweller in his matchless land

Washington's home life was an ideal of domestic happiness, born in a humble cottage, less than thirty feet square, upon a farm of a thousand acres, lying along the banks of the Potomac river, he possessed a complete reflection of the loving disposition and grace of manners of his mother His youth was spent in farming, a vocation but little more profitable then than now, and in studying books whenever he had an opportunity At the age of twenty-seven he married the young and handsome widow of Daniel P Custis Speaking of his marriage, one historian writes "The dark eyes of the comely little bride were brighter and handsomer than ever, and her usual dignity was softened by the characteristic Southern graciousness, to please those about her, while Washington was the handsomest man of that handsome assemblage "

From the date of his marriage, in 1759, to 1779, Washington was a farmer, vestryman in the Episcopal church, sportsman, and member of the Legislature, as well as being twice elected to the Continental Congress at Philadelphia

He was extraordinarily prominent in those days for his lavish hospitality, made possible through his great wealth, and for his military successes Both Washington and his wife were exceedingly fond of company, their "At Home" days being every day in the week and every week and month in the year Guests from every portion of the land filled his house, relatives and friends, the aristocracy and the nobleman, the politician and the clergy, all found a ready welcome within his household

An exquisite horseman and fearless rider, many were the hunts indulged in by both Washington and his guests The chief quality in a horse, he often asserted, was to "go ahead," consequently, he usually outstripped his companions, and was always "in at the death "

Washington left Mount Vernon in 1775 to attend the Continental Congress, a colonel of militia He returned after an absence of eight years, a conqueror, of whom Louis XVI of France, Carlos IV of Spain, Frederick the Great, and the powers of Great Britain, were outspoken in proclaiming his greatness

The wisdom and foresight of Washington were clearly manifested in his selection of Alexander Hamilton and Thomas Jefferson for two of his Cabinet ministers, their great minds being honestly fired with radically opposite ideas—one of "anarchy," and the other with "monarchy " Washington was enabled to discern clearly the middle course, and to follow it, thus perpetuating a government free from "centralized power" or "state rights," and founding a nation "that shall never perish from the earth "

The personal character of Washington stands forth as pure and clear as a Greek statue, which has lain serene and white in the bosom of mother earth for centuries. Probably no man ever lived who was so little understood as Washington. The historian has exhausted every source of knowledge to tell the minutest details of his life. Every house in which he lived has been fully described. His private letters have been searched out and given to the world until they are familiar. Yet, despite all these things, and the thorough knowledge of his great fame, the character of Washington is not understood by posterity, which to-day reverences his memory. The sternness of his character is shown by the silent and thorough manner in which he crushed out the slights, the sneers, and intrigues of his jealous enemies at home, notably such men of high rank as President Mifflin of the Continental Congress, and Generals Gates, Wilkinson and Conway, who were continually plotting against him, and hoping for his failure and final overthrow, almost as eagerly as was Cornwallis himself. General Conway, in writing to General Gates, said that "heaven was determined to save our country, else a weak general and bad counselors would have ruined it."

The sincerity of his actions in the noble cause he had espoused, is made most clear in rebuking his brother for having furnished the British army with provisions in order to save Mount Vernon from damage, using these words: "It would have been less painful to me to have heard that in consequence of your non-compliance with their request, they had burnt my house and laid my plantation in ruins."

His persistency is manifested by the fact that while Congress was considering the reduction of the army, Washington was laying his plans to move down the Chesapeake, which resulted in the surrender of Cornwallis and his entire army at Yorktown.

His fearless bravery was established by his reply to an officer, who, anxious for his safety at a time of extreme peril and danger, reminded him of his perilous position. "If you think I am in danger," said Washington, "you are at liberty to go back."

The nobility of his character has been too lightly referred to by the historian in relating the tempting offer made him to establish a monarchy in America, with himself as king. No other man in that day could have resolutely declined such an offer. None other than Washington would have done so, and a French orator, in describing the scene of Washington resigning his commission as Commander-in-Chief of the Continental army, says: "A crown, decked with jewels lay upon the book of the constitution. Suddenly Washington seizes it, breaks it, and flings the pieces at the assembled people. How small ambitious Cæsar seems beside the hero of America."

Washington s statesmanship and marvelous judgment are shown most conclusively in his words, both before and after the final adoption of the Constitution of the United States, saying in opposition to the half hearted measures proposed by some members of the convention "If to please the people we offer them what we ourselves disapprove, how can we afterwards defend our work? Let us raise a standard to which the wise and honest can repair The event is in the hand of God" And on September 17th, 1797, the date on which Washington affixed his handsome signature to our Constitution, he said, as he stood at the table, pen in hand 'Should the States reject this excellent Constitution the next one will be drawn in blood "

And thus in Washington we see a famous soldier, who conducted a long and trying war to a successful end, a fact wholly impossible without him

We see a great statesman who did more than all other men to shape and lay the foundations of our government, which has continued in prosperity for more than a century

We see in him a man of great intellectual force and will of iron, a pure and high-minded gentleman, of dauntless courage, stainless honor, stately of manner, kind and generous of heart

Such was George Washington, and he will always receive, as years increase in number, the admiration and reverence of mankind, because they see embodied in his character the noblest possibilities of humanity

CENTRAL CITY.

CENTRAL CITY, COLO, December 16, 1899

ED C PARMELEE, Grand Secretary, Denver, Colo :

Dear Sir and Brother—The Washington Centennial Memorial Exercises were appropriately observed on the evening of December 14, 1899, by the Lodges of Gilpin County The Lodges met at Masonic Hall, Central City, and proceeded to the Opera House as a body, where the following programme was held

An Address Upon the Early Influence of Masonry on the Development
     of the American Idea of the Equality of Men, as Expressed in the
     Declaration of Independence and Its Culmination in the Independ-
     ence of the American Colonies   F LeNeve Foster .
Selection   Orchestra

Reading of Letters from the Master of Alexandria-Washington Lodge
    and Brother A A Treat   P A Kline

Duet   Brothers Bate and Tippett

An Address on the Personal Character and Public Services of Wash-
    ington   Flor Ashbaugh

Selection   Orchestra

Reading of an Account of Washington's Last Illness   Thomas Bate

Solo   William Tippett

Reading, "Washington s Farewell Address"   H G Thurman

Song, "My Country, 'Tis of Thee'"   Audience

The above named speakers and singers were Master Masons The public were admitted to the Opera House, and a fairly good audience was present, considering the weather.

Fraternally yours,

F H Owen,
Secretary No 6, A F and A M

ADDRESS OF PAST GRAND MASTER ERNEST LE NEVE FOSTER

Just a century ago there was transpiring at Mount Vernon an event fraught with the greatest moment and interest to the young American Republic, and ere the clock struck the midnight hour, the news went forth that the spirit of George Washington had taken its flight, and that he had gone to the undiscovered country from whose bourn no traveler returns

It was not with the rapidity of the electric spark, which to-day would in a moment have flashed the important intelligence to the whole civilized world, but with the slow processes of communication then existing, that the American people learned of the great loss they had sustained That George Washington, the Father of his Country, was dead, that he who had been immortalized as "First in war, first in peace and first in the hearts of his countrymen," he—whose master mind history informs us, did so much toward laying broad and wide the solid foundation for the upbuilding of the grand fabric that to day has taken its place as the Great American Republic, and dominates the land, an illustration of a free people, who not only enjoy privileges of self-government, equality and freedom, but are desirous of extending the same boon to all people, and to do so are ready to defend the weak against the strong, and to seal with their very blood the principles with which they are inculcated—would no longer guide the destinies of the young nation

Yet though it is true that his mortal frame would no longer tread the paths of earth, or his commanding voice be heard to stir the air with the grand inspirations which filled his brain, he was not dead, for "He is not dead whose glorious mind lifts thine on high, to live in hearts we leave behind, is not to die" He had left behind a record and heritage which it has been the lot of but few to attain, for, notwithstanding the lapse of time, whose ruthless hand in a few short years blots out the memory of almost all of us, one hundred years has not sufficed to even dim the virtues and greatness of this patriot, statesman and Mason, but on the contrary, as time passes on, his greatness becomes more and more apparent, and, like the rolling snow ball, which increases in size, so his admirers, who, though at first were counted only by the thousands, to day number the whole American people, 70,000,000 strong, from the small child who can scarce lisp the name of Washington, to the tottering old man, who had only just entered the world when Washington left it, are ready to proclaim his greatness and enthuse at the mention of the name of him who did so much for the cause of liberty and constitutional government

Washington at an early age imbibed the grand principles of Masonry, for on the 4th day of November, 1752, or before he had reached his majority, he was initiated an E A, not, however, receiving the Master's degree until the August following This, we confidently believe, was the first step in the direction that led him on and on, until he arrived at the noble goal of the first citizen on the American continent, and gave him the position which he holds in history and in the hearts of a grateful people The pure and glorious principles of the institution imparted to him at this impressionable period of his life, were a potent force among the many sources of culture that helped to prepare that active mind, and shape the breadth and strength of his intellect, and so energized the activities of his spirit the wisdom and truth that burned upon the Masonic altar were to him in after life a stimulus and inspiration to perform its duties

Thus it was that the seed sown on that November evening fell on rich soil, and grew and flourished, bringing forth fruit one hundred fold As the years rolled by this knowledge ripened into a love and zeal for the institution, and even amid the trials, struggles, perils and excitements of his life spent in battling for the liberties of his country, and the endeavor to preserve them when once attained, he never lost sight of the principles taught him on the checkered floor

I might mention one instance of his love and veneration for the institution, which was shown during the war of the Revolution In the Forty sixth Regiment of the British army there was a traveling Lodge, with a warrant from the Grand Lodge of Ireland After an engagement between the American and British forces, in which the latter were defeated, the private chest of the Lodge, containing its jewels,

furniture and implements, fell into the hands of Washington's troops When this
was reported to him, he at once ordered the chest to be returned to the Lodge and
the regiment, under a guard of honor The surprise and the feeling of both officers
and men may be imagined when they perceived the flag of truce that announced the
elegant compliment from their noble opponent, but still more noble Brother The
guard of honor, with music playing a sacred march, the chest containing the constitution and implements of the craft borne aloft like another Ark of the Covenant,
equally by Englishmen and Americans, who had but lately engaged in combat, was
carried through the lines of the regiment, who presented arms and colors, hailed
the glorious act by cheers which the sentiment rendered sacred as the hallelujahs
of an angel's song

With a chieftain thus endowed, is it to be wondered at that he should have
been surrounded by others in like manner impressed with the force, wisdom,
strength and beauty of the same institution, and that his personality and love for
these principles should have influenced his association with them?

Beginning at the earliest period of the development of the country and nation,
Masonry is found influencing its growth and institutions The Puritan landed at
Plymouth, and the Cavalier at Jamestown, after which followed the struggle of
those early settlers to get a foothold on the soil of the new continent The natural
difficulties in the new surroundings, the resistance of savage tribes, as well as
the attacks of wild beasts, had to be overcome, and these, together with the necessity for a proper administration of the affairs of the new land, called forth the
four cardinal virtues, Temperance, Fortitude, Prudence and Justice To strengthen
and sustain this civilization as it spread over the new world, it was necessary to
raise the barriers of education and religion, which were conducted in rough and
primitive buildings erected to the service of the Great God, and side by side with
these, cheering and supporting them, appeared the first Masonic altars

Taking these historic spots as a starting point, it is needless to recapitulate
every step in the progress of the people, from that time until the whole continent
was reclaimed from the Atlantic to the Pacific, but it is not too great a claim for
Masonry, to say that it was a potent factor in the great change, and a co worker
with both school house and church in the wonderful achievements that constitute
the warp and woof of our present civilization

Still I hear some of the uninitiated say What is Masonry, and what are its
principles, that you claim so much for it? I say to the inquiring mind, read the
life of George Washington, and you can learn from his character and actions what
its principles are They will teach you what real Masonry is, or, to state it
briefly Masonry is a human expression of the human needs for liberty, order and
justice

The instructions given to the novitiate, when he is first received into the fraternity, are that he should be true to the government under which he lives, and just to that country, that he must conform with cheerfulness to the government, and do all he can to uphold the authority of the rulers whose laws afford him protection, further, that he is to be loyal and discountenance disloyalty

From the Sacred Book we learn that in the construction of the Temple of Solomon, this idea was exemplified by the vast host of men employed in different capacities to gather and place in position the material of which it was built, not only were they found upon the hilltop, where that majestic fabric based on earth rose unto the skies, but also in the shadows of the mountains of Lebanon, upon the sea and in the quarries, and following these principles they so wrought together in harmony, that neither confusion nor discord interrupted the work

The Masonic doctrine of the equality of man teaches the two fundamental principles of all just government, the Fatherhood of God and the Brotherhood of Man Even before the Netherlands rose from amidst the endyked waves, before the Commonwealth of England had formulated its Magna Charta, before this Republic had risen with its declaration and constitution and set on fire the beacon light of liberty that should be reflected to all shores, the Masonic Fraternity had taught to a hundred generations of men the undying essentials of growth and freedom and law

Masonry has never aided tyrants, in its light the rich, the poor, the prince and the peasant disappear, and man stands level and equal in natural light It has never allied itself with unjust authority, it could not—the law of its being does not tolerate alliance with oppression, the very essence of its existence is organized justice, in it the weak and many are banded for self protection, for justice and for charity

Masonry has never drawn an unholy sword or sought to hallow an unholy altar, no prisons built by its malice stand along the pathway of man's happiness, no men demand their martyrs of its channels, no nation demands the liberty of its usurping powers Drawing its inspiration from the Holy Bible, in its creed the essentials of human growth, safety and freedom are found Then laying its foundations on no reserved ground of Church or State, but in the affections of the human heart, it there fortifies itself and becomes impregnable, using as its motto, "To Caesar Caesar's and to God God's own" Thus it was that there was infused into the government those ideas which through the ages had been working to produce the love of freedom so attempered as to originate the sublime spectacle of a government administered by the people and for the people, and it was George Washington, the Mason and patriot, who was the herald to proclaim, and the statesman to give, them lasting shape in constitutional liberty and popular government Not only was he the friend of his country, but looking back through the long vistas and the results of his actions, we see that he was just as great a friend of the country whose yoke he threw off. The line of policy and thought in that nation, produced by the loss of its richest colony, has helped to upbuild it, by a more judicious use of its power, and a more just treatment of its other colonies, so that at this time the loyalty of Canada and Australia and its other possessions are like Cæsar's wife. It is shown in the recent readiness of those colonies to join the Mother Country in upholding the very principles which Washington fought for, the right of represen tation and just taxation for the Uitlander living in the land of a so-called Republic but Republic only in name. What, then, is more probable than that when the pro pitious time arrived, Washington and his cotemporaries found themselves in a po sition which made it necessary to formulate a plan of government for the colonies that were about to throw off the yoke of the Mother Country than that they should select as a model the institution to which they were devoted, and found the government upon the same broad principles of equality and liberty?

It has been asserted that of the fifty five signers of the Declaration of Inde pendence all but two were Masons, this, however, is probably an excessive claim as there appears no well authentic record of its having been so, but there is no the slightest doubt that a large number of them were. The Mason, reading between the lines of that historic document, as important to the American as the Magna Charta of King John's time to the Englishman and the whole Anglo-Saxon race, can see there traced out the principles and tenets of the noble institution which have now become a part of the civilization of the country, and helped to illumine the pages of its history

And a hundred years from now it is the earnest hope of every Mason that our posterity may again meet under the auspicious patronage and love of the fraternity whose privilege it has been to organize these Memorial Services throughout the length and breadth of our land, and then again revive the virtue, great deeds and recollections of our departed brother

ADDRESS OF FLOR ASHBAUGH

I fear that I have accepted too thoughtlessly the place I occupy upon this programme to night. When requested by the committee a few days since to essay this task, my casual thought was that a short extemporaneous talk, consisting of historical outlines, varied by a few words of eulogy, would be sufficient. Investi gation showed that I was to exhibit and describe to you to day a jewel so brilliant so pure, that I shrink from the service as one unworthy so high a duty. And yet it is a labor of love The few minutes snatched each day from a very busy week in which to contemplate the beautiful character of Washington, have been seasons of pleasure, and filled my heart with a glow of gratitude that this rare nature, this perfection of American manhood is ours Ours to emulate, ours to hold in loving remembrance, ours to crown with encomiums, ours to hold up before the entire world, challenging it to produce a grander hero I cannot trust my memory in the performance of this service Every sentence descriptive of this "noblest American of them all" should be perfect, rounded to its fullest meaning For each word of adulation will meet an answering glow from every face that looks into mine, and find an echo in each heart

These are days of skepticism as regards human perfection We worship our heroes a little while—but not without a few mental reservations—a sort of proviso attachment We take them on probation, as it were—if they stand the test, we continue our friendship, if not, we forget them But the character of Washington has come to us through the hundred years unscathed, untarnished by a single blemish King, prince, potentate, poet, philosopher, warrior and statesman, have risen, flashed in meteoric brilliancy athwart the great dome of our national sky, and gone down into the darkness and oblivion of the eternal past—but the name of Washington lives on When we turn loose upon other celebrities the shafts of criticism, we breathe his name with reverent attention This is triumph of the personal character—a direct refutation of the favorite dogma of this rapid age, "that it does not pay to live an honorable life" Too often we see an otherwise great character hampered by minor characteristics which mar its equilibrium and prevent its rising to true greatness With our hero this was not the case Thoroughly balanced at all points, he presented to the world an example of such forbearance, self control and benignity as made all men marvel, and forced even the narrow-minded and envious to respect him In the quiet pursuit of his calling—that of surveyor—he moved along through the early years of his life, tranquilly waiting for the illuming hand of destiny It is a beautiful thought that when the Grand Master of the Universe is marking out the future greatness of a nation He is also moulding the men who will be the instruments for accomplishing that benign purpose, history invariably illustrates this, whether he shall lead on to victory for his country, and crown that victory by a life of happiness and peace in the full fruition of his years of sacrifice and privation, as did Washington—or whether he shall steer the ship of state through all the stormy voyage, and, as the morning dawns, with the peaceful harbor just in sight, he shall lay his tired head and great loving heart low in a martyr's grave, as did Lincoln—the Anointing Hand is as surely discernible

Average human nature is marked by many good traits There are many good men and women in the world whose rugged integrity compels our admiration and respect, but when we become cognizant of a character distinguished by all the beautiful attributes that humanity is capable of, we know with reverent knowledge that man is divinely commissioned for the execution of a noble work   Such was Washington   All the traits of a great martyr were his—he was loyal, steadfast, honest, brave, sincere and unselfish   His loyalty manifested itself early in the devotion to his king and the mother country   Not until he was convinced beyond all doubt that they were opposing the colonies, that their main feeling toward America was not one of interest and affection such as a government should have for dependent colonies, but was one of greed, tyranny and avarice, did he consent to declare for independence, but when that allegiance was finally transferred to the struggling weaker power, every energy of his life was devoted to the cause he had espoused   Oh' happy America, to have the love and championship of a man like Washington'

Loyalty was but one of the characteristics of this great man   Of itself, it would scarcely have been remarkable, but to that loyalty was added courage, to courage, patience, to patience, perseverence, to perseverence, benevolence, to benevolence, mercy   All these, supplemented by firmness, clear judgment, self-control, a highly cultivated intelligence, and almost phenomenal power of both physical and mental endurance, and we have in view a crystallization of character as wonderful as it is unusual   What wonder that little children gathered at his approach to scatter flowers in his pathway'   That people came from all parts of the country to shout his praises and do him honor'   What wonder that our Wendell Phillips's almost inspired pen traced of him this glowing tribute   "Were I to tell you the story of Washington, I should take it from your hearts—you, who think no marble white enough on which to carve the name of the Father of his Country'"

Washington's whole life from early manhood might be called a series of public services   Would that I were versed in the ways of older and more eloquent speakers, that I might by command of enthusiasm and versatility of expression, impart upon your minds an appreciation of the many and important services George Washington rendered America   He seemed ever to have a deep sense of responsibility for the welfare and prosperity of his country, even while it was composed of separate colonies   He seemed vividly interested in every measure that came up for their improvement, and deeply anxious over anything that tended to their undoing   It was this solicitude, doubtless, that prompted him to undertake in November, 1753, that important but hazardous expedition to the Canadian post near Lake Erie, to demand, in the name of the king of England, the withdrawal of the French from the territory which was claimed by Virginia   This perilous enterprise had been declined by a number of brave officers, yet Washington accepted the commission, and through many difficulties and many perilous adventures brought it to a successful termination. This was his initial service. Through the years that followed, until difficulties began to arise between the colonies and the mother country, he served his king loyally and with distinguished honor. He served as a soldier, always trusted with the command of bodies of soldiery. He was eminently fitted through his knowledge of the country and its mode of warfare, to conduct military movements, and had his suggestions been adopted, many humiliating defeats would have been avoided. With wonderful forbearance and patience he strove to counteract the effect of the obstinacy that would take no advice, and did much to control and influence affairs for the benefit of his beloved colonies.

Washington's wonderful forbearance was often sorely taxed, but there was one point on which he would not yield, that point was the relative position of his majesty's soldiers and the provincials, as the colonial soldiers were then called. Any attempt to relegate the American soldier to an inferior position met with determined remonstrance from Washington, and at one time for that cause, he indignantly resigned his commission and returned to Mount Vernon. He was eventually induced to again identify himself with military service, and as commander-in chief of Virginian forces accomplished so many heroic deeds that time would fail to enumerate them.

With the cessation of Indian hostilities, and the expulsion of the French from Ohio, he again withdrew from military service for the reason given before, that he would prefer private life to association with men who denied the equality of British and American officers and British and American rank and file, in the same army, and fighting for a common cause. Thus, although deeply attached to military service, he made a final surrender of his commission under British dominion, and again sought his quiet home.

This slight divergence from the subject is to illustrate the true, just nature of the man, and shows that even then, a spirit of independence and universal equality was lurking in the heart of Washington, and doubtless finding an echo in many other American hearts.

We have gone thus far with Washington, through his preparation for the great work that lay before him. We have seen him as the loyal subject of the King accepting tasks that others lacked the courage to accept, and we have seen him as the loyal comrade, retiring from a pursuit he loved rather than compromise the dignity of American soldiers. Now we see him called by a unanimous voice to an arena in which his fame and greatness was to become world wide, for throughout the length and breadth of the land the cry arose, "The cause of Boston is the cause of all." That cry caused the convening of the first Continental Congress, and to this Congress, as delegate, came Washington, drawn there by the appealing voice of his countrymen, and by the promptings of the loftiest patriotism

No need to go into the details of the years that followed, every schoolboy knows the history of the seven years of bloody struggle From Concord to Lexington, from Lexington until the treaty of 1783, it was a time of sorrow, of privation, and sacrifice for the colonists, and of the deepest care for the Commander-in-Chief No dress parade war was that for our patriotic hero and his suffering soldiers In poverty, cold and hunger, oppressed by all forms of dire necessity, they fought their way through those terrible seven years Perhaps in all the colonies not another man could have been found that would have remained steadfast through the besetting discouragements of that time Who but Washington could have cheered that desolate army, till hard pressed, as they were, they were willing to endure yet a little longer?

How unselfish was his love for his country and its defenders' We of the present day would do well to remember, in contemplating the services of this man, that while our favorite warriors of to-day draw comfortable salaries which continue after they retire, and are turned into pensions for their widows after their death, Washington drew no salary, would accept no pay, but gave his services for seven years to America While our armies of to day have all the conveniences of modern warfare, with abundance of food and clothing, Washington and his little band of patriots had nothing but the most primitive accoutrements, and often went hungry Yet the sublime courage of the man, his unselfishness and personal magnetism, held sway over all hearts, and led the way to a triumphant closing of the war What priceless service did he render to America at that time' A man makes no sacrifice to be a friend to America to day—rich, powerful, independent, America can reward her heroes' services abundantly—but to serve a country that could not even provide its defenders with the necessaries of existence, to devote seven years to battling for an uncertain cause, to go through dangers and hardships indescribable in peril from cold, in peril from exposure, in peril from treachery, yet, with the bullets flying thick about him, kneeling to pray the God of Battles for victory' Oh' matchless champion' where shall we find fitting language with which to express our sense of such service?

How sublime must have been the emotion of this man, when, the long war was over, victory crowning his efforts, he listened to the treaty acknowledging the independence of each colony A king might have envied him

Gladly would he have laid aside the habiliments of public service, and rested quietly in his beautiful home, but the people could trust none but the friend who had led them so safely out of their trouble They would take no refusal, they would make him their ruler—their king They gathered about him, eager to display their love by placing a crown upon his head. How deeply did they mistake the nature of the man they delighted to honor, and how clearly did he comprehend their best interests, as he gently but firmly refused their request.

No crown should adorn such a man. The richest gems that glisten in the crown of royalty to-day pale in the brilliancy of the integrity and unparalleled devotion of Washington.

Finding him firm in his refusal, they listened to better counsel, formed themselves into a union, and elected him as their president. And on the 30th day of April, 1789, in New York city, in the presence of an immense concourse of people, were instituted the inaugural ceremonies that made Washington the first President of the United States. His reception was marked by a grandeur never before witnessed in the metropolis. He had intended, hoped, to make the journey quietly, but a grateful, loving people turned it into an ovation. Everywhere on his way he was greeted by thronging crowds, eager to see the man whom they regarded as the defender of their liberty. And everywhere he was hailed with those manifestations of love which spring spontaneously from the hearts of his admiring countrymen.

As a statesman Washington was, if possible, more popular than as a warrior. He was chosen for a second term by the unanimous vote of every electoral college. His administration for the two terms was successful beyond the expectation of his most sanguine friends. His policy brought success in every branch of industry. The finances of the country were no longer in a cramped condition, and the public credit was fully restored. The precedents he established have proven most wise and beneficial to posterity. Three new members were added to the Union, and friends of liberty the world over rejoiced in the demonstrated fact that a republic so established could live and prosper.

Washington decidedly refused to accept a third term, and returned again to Mount Vernon to enjoy the rest he had so richly earned. His universal patriotism was again put to the test, when, in 1799, war with France was threatened, and he was called to take command of the United States forces, with the rank of Lieutenant General. Luckily, a treaty of peace put a stop to the action. But the incident illustrates the love and esteem in which he was still held by his country, and his unselfish devotion in his willingness to again relinquish the peace and joy of domestic life for his country's benefit.

One hundred years ago to-day, Washington, the brave general, the beloved President, the loyal American citizen, the generous friend, the honored Brother Mason, passed into eternal rest. We say of this beloved hero, "he is dead," we pay rich tributes to his memory, we dedicate this day to him with fragrant floral wreaths, with solemn funeral dirge, and embalm him anew within our hearts. Millions to day, all over this wide land, and in other lands across the waves, have signalized this day with grateful remembrances of liberty's most illustrious champion—and it is well All that we can bestow of gratitude, of love, of hero worship, is not too much for such services as he rendered us But there comes to us the better, wider and more glorious conviction—Washington is not dead He lives to-night all over America, from north to south, and from ocean to ocean He is the embodiment of freedom, and he lives wherever freedom's banner waves over freedom's soil He lives in thousands of happy homes—homes that his patriotism and devotion made possible He lives in our almost perfect system of public schools He lives in the songs and shouts of happy little children He lives in all the wonderful reforms and inventions that make the world the delightful abiding place it is to-day He lives in America's universal prosperity and freedom, in her every triumph over land and sea, in every dedicated monument pointing heavenward He lives in the valorous deeds of every boy in blue that served in '61 and '98, in Dewey's brilliant fame and intrepid manhood He lives in Hawaii's happy adoption, and in poor bleeding Cuba's final redemption He lives in the inspired proclamation that gave freedom to 6,000,000 of human beings In every star, stripe and fold of Old Glory

And more vividly than all else, he lives in Masonry Down deep in the heart of every true Mason he exists imperishably, and will exist until the Grand Master of the Universe shall inscribe our names on the roll book of eternity

COLORADO SPRINGS.

Hall of El Paso Lodge No 13, A F and A M

February 23, 1900

To the Worshipful Master, Wardens and Brethren of El Paso Lodge No 13, A F and A M

Your committee on the Memorial Services to be held on the anniversary of the death of Brother George Washington, beg leave to submit the following report:

Lodge was opened on the third degree of Masonry with Past Masters acting as officers, and proceeded to the Christian Church, where the following programme was rendered, following the request of the Most Worshipful Grand Lodge:

Brother Ira Harris, as chairman

First—The reading of an account of Washington's last illness, from the diary of his secretary, by Brother E P Hufferd

Second—The reading of a personal letter to the Lodges of Colorado from the Worshipful Master of Alexandria-Washington Lodge, of which Washington was the first Master, under its Virginia charter, which letter includes an account of Washington's Masonic life, by Brother J P Madden

Third—An address upon the early influence on the development of the American idea of the equality of men, as expressed in the Declaration of Independence, and its culmination in the independence of the American colonies, by Brother Robert D Graham

Fourth—An address on the personal character and public services of Washington, by Brother W T Miller

Fifth—The reading of Washington's Farewell Address, by Brother Isaac S Harris

The able addresses offered by Brothers Robert D Graham and W T Miller accompany this report

(Signed)   Jno Williams,
G D Kennedy,
E J Smith,
A M Holden,
G W. Musser,
Committee

ADDRESS OF R D GRAHAM

Ladies and Gentlemen, and Brethren

The topic that has been assigned to me for the evening is somewhat lengthy I would not ask you to remember that, it is too long   So I have taken the liberty to boil down this topic and express it as I understand its meaning, in these words "The destiny of America, and the part Masonry has played in working up that destiny "   I am very much in favor of public services like this that we are holding at the present time   There seems to be a wrong impression in regard to the Order that we represent   There always have been wrong impressions regarding good things   This is not a secret society, it is a society with secrets   Some years ago I had the privilege of addressing El Paso Lodge No 13, and I emphasized that at the time   There is a vast difference between a secret society and a society with secrets   For instance, if I were to ask you the purpose and plan of the so called Clan Na Gael Society, you could tell me nothing about it   It is a secret society But if I ask you the purpose and the motive of Masonry, any intelligent man or woman can tell at once what its ideas are, and what it stands for, and what its purposes are, even though it has secrets   I say I believe in such a service as this, because it brings prominently before the people, as this Anniversary Service will do, the beauties of the society that we love, and the society that we mean to do all we can to honor   You know it does not always follow that because people are say ing nothing they are "sawing wood"   Why, the Sphinx has not spoken a word for five thousand years, and all it has to show for it is a pile of sand   Masons do not go around parading their virtues, or their goodness, or their ability, or anything of that kind, but you know even Balaam's ass spoke once, and I don't see why we should not, once in a while at least, find our way out into the world, and let people know what we are and what we stand for

I am thoroughly impressed with this fact—that the history of the United States, read by any person of average intelligence, will convey this impression   that it is not ordinary history, such as you will find regarding the nations of Europe Now, speaking of my text—you know I am a preacher and must have a text—if you will turn away back into the Old Testament, you will find a scene in Jacob's time   Jacob was about to depart to be with his fathers   He asked Joseph, the favorite boy, to bring his two sons into his presence that he might bless them The two boys were brought there, and the old man crossed his hands and he put the right hand, which would have the greater blessing, upon the head of the younger boy   Joseph drew the attention of the old man to this fact, and he said, "Let it be"   He knew what he was doing, and in putting off Joseph he informed him that both of the boys would represent great nations, but the younger of the boys would in all respects be greater than the elder

For the purpose of analogy and pointing a moral or drawing an outline, sup pose that we say these two boys represent England and America   Suppose for a moment that the elder is England   You know that a service like this brings very vividly to my mind the scenes of a little over a hundred years ago   There was a man who got things a little mixed the other day when he told me that the Boer has got John Bull by the horns, and a fellow standing by answered, ' No, that is not the way he has him, that he had got John Bull by the lion's tail "   And some way

a service like this is bound to bring to my memory the scenes when the younger
boy in my text had John Bull by the lion s tail, too. We have a great deal of
sympathy for the Boers in this their struggle for independence.

In the providence of God, this hemisphere was reserved for a special purpose,
and that purpose was the exhibition of the highest form of human government
capable among men. See what that means? It means that there is a Supreme
Architect, as Masons love to designate Jehovah, God, and that according to the
plan and purpose of that great beneficent being, there was to be established upon
the American continent the highest ideal of human government. Now you will see
what it means. In the providence of that God, Masonry has been called upon to
play an important part in working out that ideal. Next to a theocracy, which
would be represented by ancient Judaism before the days of the kings, the government under which we live is the highest ideal, a democracy. Of course, I am not
going to enter into a political speech. The time allotted to me for this discussion
is altogether too short, but I want to tell you that within thirty days last past I
took a week in old Boston. A friend of mine up here in Denver, a dear old German
brother, who was a personal friend of my father s asked me one day why I was
going so far away from home. I told him that I was going East to where they
wore blue stockings, wear spectacles and eat beans, and he says 'Don t tell me
that. You know better."

I took a walk down old Hanover street, and walked past that old church
away high up in the steeple of that old church on the famous night the lantern
was hung. A man on a horse across the river saw that lantern, and Paul Revere
started on his ride that brought the battle of Lexington and Concord into being.
Two years and a half ago I attended a celebration, and had the honor to be by
proxy, a member of the Grand Lodge of Massachusetts down in dear old Bridge-
water and they were celebrating the centennial of their Lodge and there was their
oved record—Paul Revere, Grand Master of Masons of Massachusetts. What part
id Masons play at that time? When I came to this country first I always liked to
go to the high places, and so I crossed over to Charlestown and step by step—
there used to be an elevator in Bunker Hill Monument, but the thing did not work
or it did not pay—so if you want to go to the top of it you have to climb. I climbed
to the top of that monument and looked out all over those famous surroundings,
and I thought of the battle of Bunker Hill. Then I remembered the name of the
general who lead the patriots at that battle, and General Joseph Warren, if you
please was the man who fell in the battle of Bunker Hill. Three weeks ago I was
at a visitation of old St Andrew's Lodge in Boston. The Deputy Grand Master
was making his annual visitation and he called for the charter of the lodge. It
was a facsimile of the old charter the original charter having been burned in the

Boston fire, and there was the signature of General Joseph Warren, Grand Master of Masons for Massachusetts

You know that a man who reads much, or tries to, lives, to a very large extent, a solitary life There is to every student a solitariness Once in a while, though I do not begin to pretend to say that I am a student, but I like to read—there would come over me a feeling of peculiar loneliness, and I would go over to Harvard and watch the boys cut up their pranks, and walk over their lawns, and visit their campus, and go into their library, and out to that elm tree, and see the place where General George Washington took charge of the army in the days of the Revolution Talk about the part that Masonry has played in working out this ideal

I think of the testimony that was once given in a court of justice in 1835 There have always been people, you know, that growl at Masons If this was a church service, I would talk to you a little about a certain influence that always poses as good—and there was a time, you know, when it seemed as if Masonry was under a great cloud, the anti Masonry movement Upon the stand there at that time, a man swore that every one of the Presidents of the United States but two were Master Masons, and these two were the Adams That is up to 1835

I think of the days of Madison We have been talking to, or my topic assigns me, something about the Declaration of Independence—these two, Madison and Dolly Madison, saving that valuable document when the British were coming, and preserving it until it could be put into safe keeping

I think of our dear friend, Lafayette, as a Mason You know even in these days they have Lafayette, the French patriot, up as an exhibit of foolishness, because he was a Mason In this same testimony that this fellow gave, he said there was nobody amongst the Masons but great fools When I read that, I was reminded of a little incident that is said to have occurred A dear father has a boy that was wayward, and a friend came to admonish the father to speak to his boy The father said "It's no use, he wouldn't listen to me It makes no difference what I say to him He will only listen to fools Will you go and talk to him?"

And so, if all Masons are fools, what has the world been listening to all this time? But I will tell you something, and it is a consolation to you brethren, like myself, that there are no bald headed fools No, and you will get a great many like those I have named that are capable of being listened to You know they say that sometimes Masons become great men, but no great men become Masons I wonder when a man becomes great? When he is in the President's chair, as McKinley is, a good Mason? Isn't the element of greatness in him long before, and doesn't it just express itself?

I tell you to night, and that is one of the highest honors that can be conferred upon this Order, that that pursuit of happiness, the inalienable right which the

Declaration of Independence says belongs to every man, of life and liberty, these things that are inherent in manhood as such, are the underlying tenets of this Order that we love. It would have been utterly impossible, it will be as long as time shall last and this Order exists, impossible for despotism, tyranny, for wrong or oppression in civil or religious affairs, to exist alongside of this Order. I turn to Old Mexico, and see the priest ridden people liberated from Romanism. I asked the reason why. I asked the secret of it, and I found that in the liberty of that people in Mexico the secret lies in the part of the army. I go a step further, and I found that there is not an officer in the Mexican army that is not a Freemason. I will go a step further, and say that there never will be an officer in that army except he be a Freemason.

I am reminded of a little story in regard to a boy who was leading a large dog along. The dog seemed to be having the best of it. A friend came along and wanted to know where he was going to take the dog. The boy said, "That isn't what's bothering me. What's bothering me is where the dog is going to take me." And so things have changed, and it isn't a question of what is going to become of Masonry, but of what Masonry is going to do for this world of ours. It is not a question of what tyranny or despotism is going to do with us. It is somewhat changed. The question now is, what are we going to do with it? That is the point.

Speaking of the Declaration of Independence. Away back when Thomas Jefferson, who has the credit of drawing up this wonderful instrument, the Declaration of Independence, was engaged in this work, in the community was a little Baptist church, and if you want to have an exhibition of the purest democracy—(not the Democratic party)—you will find it in a well regulated, well organized Baptist church. And do you know that he got his ideas, at least, it is commonly reported that he got his ideas, from that source? And so I find great pleasure to-night in speaking not only as a man and as a Mason, but as a Baptist, in regard to the work that this great Order has done in bringing about the equality of men. I might go on and name a great many more Revolutionary heroes who said in word and in deed, "By the grace of God, and the sacrifice of our blood, we will give vent to the independent wish, and we won't let you make us groan." So, indeed, Masonry has had a wonderful influence in America. It is said that when the war was in progress, that culminated in the Declaration of Independence, that it was almost impossible to tell when the Committee of Public Safety adjourned and the Lodge gathered. It was all one and the same thing.

There was a time, you know, when Boston was famous for one more thing than eating beans. They had a tea party down there once. I have gone down to that old wharf and looked at the place where the ship lay in the offing. A party of red Indians boarded the vessel that night, and, of course, red Indians don't know anything about tea, but these red Indians knew something about taxes, and these red Indians knew something about a certain tavern up Hanover street where the Masonic Lodge used to meet. I would not say to-night that these red Indians were Masons. I would not like to leave, however, the impression in your minds that they were not Masons. They went down, and you have all read about this Boston tea party and the result of that tea party.

I love to think, if you will pardon another reference to a thing that is dear to me, that the rectory across the street from the spot where the first American blood was spilled, is now the Traveler building. There used to be an old church standing there, and in front of that old church was a little lawn, and upon that lawn the people used to be lashed upon their bare backs for certain offenses, and the first blood of American and civil liberty was shed just across the street, and that blood came from the back of a Baptist preacher, who had come up from Rhode Island to give consolation to a certain Baptist who happened to be in Boston. I am not going to name the denomination that had the poor Baptist preacher tried and lashed. They have outgrown all that sort of thing now. The liberty that brought civil rights brought religious freedom, too.

I wish it had not been so cold to-night. I had one or two thoughts in regard to the subject about which I was to speak to-night, but they came pretty near getting frozen up on the road down here. I recommend to you to look for the marks of Masonry from the earliest days in American history up to the present time. You will recognize them anywhere, if you look for them. Away down in Maine there was once a man who expected an express package. Maine is a prohibition state, you know. He expected the package to come there to his name, and he went to the office looking for the bundle. He had been in the habit of writing his name with a mark, a cross. He thought he wouldn't go up to the clerk and ask for the bundle, the clerk might not know him, but he would look around and see if he could see the bundle with his name on it. He got a box in the office with three marks on it, so he reasoned, why, of course, in order that there might be no mistake, the man put his name on it three times, and he took up the box and started home with it. You know what he had in the box? Just like that man, if you and I care to look for the marks, we will find them.

Coming back to my text—for, like the prodigal son, I must return, isn't it a fact that the Great Architect of the Universe has commissioned this country to represent His will concerning man, and that the Declaration of Independence, the epitome of our government, represents His will? You and I are entitled to the unmolested pursuit of all those things that are near and dear to the human heart.

Brethren, they say that Masonry is an irreligious thing, that Masonry takes the place of the church, that Masonry somehow discredits and dishonors the

church   I appeal to all that the history of your beloved land shows, and I ask you
if it is at all likely that the men who worked out the providence of God should be
so diametrically opposed to God   It is not right, it is not reason   There is something upon us, men and brothers   They look to us outside   They say, "He is a
Mason"   They expect something from him   They ought to get it   What about
the generations that are to come?   As we think of Paul Revere, as we think of
General Warren, as we think of Franklin, as we think of Washington, as we think
of Lafayette, as we think of Madison, and all on down   will we pass on to the generations that are yet to come the heritage that we received   torn and soiled, and
stained and injured, or will we pass it on better than when we received it?   May
grace and wisdom be given to us so that in the plan and purpose of God those that
shall follow us may receive from our hands in better shape if possible, that which
we have received from the hands that have preceded us   I tell you, men and
women, to-night, there is something grand in the thought that the liberties, the civil
rights and all that goes to make up this great, grand and glorious people, have been
entrusted to nearly a million men, bonded together for the purpose of seeing that
these things are preserved   Have we done anything like this?   Is the American
ideal of the equality of men helped by this Order?   I ask you to answer

ADDRESS OF BROTHER W T MILLER

Ladies and Gentlemen, and Brethren of the Masonic Fraternity

You may not know it, but I will tell you now that I am not a preacher   I
would not tell you, but I expect to live in your city, and if I live here many years I
know you will find it out   I am sorry, however, that I am not good enough to be a
preacher, because I think they are the happiest, best men in the world   I regret
deeply that the "Old Dominion" has not present on this occasion a preacher, or at
least an abler son to portray the personal character and public services of her
greatest and noblest son, Washington

That old State produced Patrick Henry, whose eloquent words and burning
patriotism did more to thrill the hearts of the people of the American colonies with
the proud and lofty spirit of American liberty, than perhaps any other man   His
immortal words in that church in Richmond, 'Give me liberty or give me death,"
have echoed and re-echoed down through the ages, and to-night may strike a re-
sponsive chord in the hearts of all true American citizens

That grand old State was the birthplace of the illustrious Jefferson, who
penned the Declaration of Independence, a document which no one can read without being impressed with the idea that it was written under the influence of inspi-

ration That document sounded the death knell of all despotic governments, and it struck the keynote of human liberty when it announced that all men are free and equal, and that all governments derive their just powers from the consent of the governed Those sentiments will be echoed and re echoed down through coming ages until all the teeming millions of the earth enjoy the same liberty that we now enjoy

The old State of Virginia has in her galaxy of statesmen, jurists and military heroes, many bright stars, but none of them shine with such refulgent splendor as that of her greatest and noblest son, the immortal George Washington While it is true that he was born in the State of Virginia and that old Commonwealth has received his ashes, it is also true that he was too great to be claimed only by Virginians That star has risen so high in the firmament that it can be seen and admired not only by Virginians, not only by the people of the original thirteen States, or of the United States, but it sheds a brilliant lustre to the whole world, and all appreciate the unselfish life of that great and noble man We are all, to a certain extent, hero worshippers, but our ideas of heroes are many and varied Some admire, perhaps, physical strength, some, genius, others, high intellectual powers, others still, goodness and purity of heart Therefore, for me to assert that Washington was the greatest man that America or the world has ever produced, would be to make an assertion which I could prove only to those whose ideal of greatness corresponds with my own

It has been contended that circumstances or the occasion, make the man To this proposition I cannot accede Circumstances may erect the stage, or the arena, and may select the actors who are to take part in the great dramas of life, and the world is invited to look on Such was the case with Washington

Sometimes the time between the entrance and the exit is very brief, and glory is won in an hour or by a play in one single act Such was the result, perhaps, in the recent wars I would not detract from the glory won by Admiral Dewey, or of the renown won by the gallant Hobson, but I desire to contrast briefly the difference between the honors won in an hour and those won by the sacrifices of the best part of a long life to the public good When you take his acts, see the various parts that he took in the great drama of life, from the time that he first engaged in the French and Indian wars, until his return to his beautiful and pleasant home on the banks of the Potomac, after having served his country in war and in peace, returning there after two terms of service as President of the United States—I say tnat the finger of history fails to point to any man, in my judgment, who acted so well, so nobly, so unselfish, the various parts, as did George Washington

We should be proud of the fact that he was a Mason, though Masonry really needs no such proof of its unselfish purposes, and of the great good that it is doing to humanity. If Freemasonry could produce no further evidence that it is an institution having for its object the promotion of the general good and happiness of mankind, than the tact that an unselfish and patriotic man as Washington was one of its enthusiastic members and great admirers, it would be sufficient proof of its noble purposes and unselfish objects.

Washington received the "lamb skin," or white leathern apron, before his majority, and as he received it without spot or blemish, so he wore it unsullied until the day of his death. He drew his sword only in self defence, or in the defence of his country, which is the same thing. He was not prompted by a desire for conquest, or for renown of an earthly nature, as military heroes have been. He was there in his home, quiet and contented, when the thunders of the Revolution were first heard. He unsheathed his sword at the call of duty. He performed his part nobly and bravely under all circumstances. He was a man of the highest and purest type in public life. He made good use of all the working tools of Freemasonry. He took the Holy Bible as the rule and guide of his faith. By the Square he squared his actions toward all mankind. With the Compass he circumscribed his desires and kept his passions within due bounds. With the common gavel he divested his heart of all the devices and superfluities of life, and thereby prepared his soul, a living stone, for that spiritual building not made with hands, "Eternal and in the heavens," so that when death granted him a final demit from Alexandria Lodge, his pure and immortal soul took its flight to that celestial Lodge above, where the Supreme Architect of the Universe presides.

Men in all ages have sought to erect monuments of an earthly character to perpetuate their greatness, but as yet, in vain. They have daubed with untempered mortar, and admitted into their structures the base and discordant materials of pride and ambition. Hence, their edifices have toppled from their foundations, or been torn assunder by internal violence, and where are they now? The weeping voice of History answers, "Fallen." The durability of the works of this immortal man and the imperishability of his memory do not depend upon the words of the orator, the pen painting of the poet, the brush of the painter, or the chisel of the sculptor, but are firmly engraved upon the hearts of the American people and the lovers of liberty throughout the world.

Now, my brethren and companions, let me say in conclusion that we will all do well to emulate his unselfish example, by using the working tools of Freemasonry for the purpose of fitting ourselves for that spiritual building that will stand when all earthly monuments shall have crumbled to dust. The proud and lofty structure of Freemasonry, sustained and supported by its author, the Great High Priest, will stand until the sun shall cease to rise to gild its cloud-capped towers, or the moon lead on the night to illuminate its starry decked canopy. The tide of time and chance may roll at its base, the heavy waves of calumny may beat about its walls, the gusts and storms of malice may assault its lofty battlements, the fierce rains of persecution may descend upon its precious roof, but all in vain. Thus sustained and supported, it will stand until the pillars of the universe are shaken, and all things have passed away as the baseless fabric of vision. Then, and not till then, will Masonry cease to revel in charity and riot in nobleness of soil

CRIPPLE CREEK

Under the joint auspices of Mount Pisgah Lodge No 96, Victor Lodge No 99 and Goldfield Lodge U D, the Masons of the Cripple Creek District conducted Memorial Services commemorating the one hundredth anniversary of the death of George Washington, at the Opera House. They were well attended, and were marked by sublime and beautiful sentiment. The address of the evening was delivered by Judge E C Stinson of the District Court. His subject was " The Life of Washington "

The officers for the evening were as follows

Worshipful Master—J Knox Burton, Mt Pisgah Lodge No 96

Senior Warden—Harry Hendrie, Victor Lodge No 99

Junior Warden, Luff L Hamilton, Goldfield Lodge, U D

Treasurer—B F Jones, Goldfield Lodge, U D

Secretary—T L Tremayne, Victor Lodge No 99

Senior Deacon—Floyd Thompson, Mt Pisgah Lodge No 96

Junior Deacon—Sol Camp, Victor Lodge No 99

Senior Steward—Wm McKenzie, Goldfield Lodge, U D

Junior Steward—Joe Hamilton, Goldfield Lodge, U D

Grand Marshal—R Burke, Goldfield Lodge, U D

Tilers—M C Barker, Mt Pisgah Lodge No 96, Cade Weaver, Victor Lodge No 99, John Jennings, Goldfield Lodge, U D

PROGRAMME

Music—March	Hospitalier's Orchestra
Reading—By Secretary of Instructions from Most Worshipful Grand Master of Colorado to hold these public Memorial Services	
Prayer	Rev C Y Grimes
Bass Solo—"The Old Sexton"	W H Cole
Address—"The Life of Washington"	Brother E C Stimson
Soprano Solo—"The Holy City" (Adams)	Miss Marie Neilson
Musical Selection	Hospitalier's Orchestra
Public Services in Honor of the Memory of that Great Mason, George Washington	
McKinley's Letter	Brother L H R von Ruecau
Tenor Solo—"For All Eternity" (Mascbereni)	J G Jones
Address—"The Influence of Masonry"	Brother J W Huff
Musical Selection	Hospitalier's Orchestra
"Account of Washington's Last Illness"	T H Thomas
Personal 'Letter from the Master of Alexandria Washington Lodge	
	Brother George E Simonton
Musical Selection	Hospitalier's Orchestra
"Washington's Farewell Address"	Eli Cann
Baritone Solo—"The Palm Trees" (Faure)	C Buechner
Masonic Poem	T L Tremayne
Short Address and Benediction	Brother William Mellen
Musical Selection	Hospitalier's Orchestra

State Grand Masters—Virginia, J Knox Burton, Rhode Island, Luff L Hamilton, Vermont, George E Simonton, New York, M P McArthur, Pennsylvania, W C Morrish, Maryland, John R Williams, South Carolina, Morris Glauber, Maine, C J Stevens, Massachusetts, Harry Hendrie, Connecticut, L C Shaw, New Hampshire, T C Keating, New Jersey, Frank P Mannix, Delaware, Frank P Moulton, North Carolina, Thomas R Jones, Georgia, Leslie W Thayer.

Southern States—Floyd Thompson, Felix A Walter, M Gohen, C M Burke, A L Arnold, A J Davis

Western States—Thomas Livingstone, Walter C Westcott, Henry Moore, Sampson Hore, Charles A Phillips, Norris E Eads

Atlantic States—Eli Cann	England—Ed Nathan
Central States—W B Squires	Germany—John E Rinker
Colorado—Tom A Smith	

DEL NORTE.

Brother Alphonse A Burnand, Most Worshipful Grand Master

Dear Brother—In compliance with your dispensation and request Del Norte Lodge No 105, A F and A M, convened at its hall on the evening of the 14th of December, A D 1899, and there opened Lodge in due form on the third degree

After so doing a live square was formed and marched to the M E Church, where the following programme was carried out in a very impressive manner

1 Song   "America"
2 Opening address   By Master of Del Norte Lodge
3 Invocation   Rev Weir
4 Song   "Hail Columbia"
5 Reading a Personal Letter from Brother Adna Adams Treat, and Reading of a Personal Letter from the Master of Alexandria Washington Lodge   Brother Hill
6 Song   "Star Spangled Banner"
7 Reading of Washington's Farewell Address   Rev Hole
8 Song   Male Quartette
9 Address   Brother Elliott
10 Song   "Auld Lang Syne"
    Benediction   Rev Hole

After the conclusion of the ceremonies the brethren re-formed line of march and returned to the Lodge room, where the Lodge was closed on the third degree, peace and harmony prevailing

Thomas A Good,
Secretary

Del Norte, Colo, February 23, 1900

R W Woodbury, Esq, Chairman

Dear Sir and Brother—Your favor of the 21st to hand, and in reply I have to say that the acting Master at the Memorial Exercises was Brother

Jno B Haffy   His was an oral introductory statement of the object of the meeting   I enclose you Brother Ezra T Elliott's address   I have it copied verbatim in my records

Fraternally yours,

THOMAS A GOOD,
Secretary

ADDRESS OF EZRA T ELLIOTT

This fourteenth day of December, one hundred years ago, there passed from the stage of human action into the infinite hereafter, presided over by an all powerful Supreme Being a man beloved by all citizens of his country, and respected for his mental qualifications and honorable conduct, by all countries throughout the civilized world   Not only was he dear to the hearts of his countrymen as an exponent of all that was good, brave and intelligent but he was doubly dear to thousands of Masons throughout the world who were proud to call him brother   In the time of darkness and adversity when the bitter winter of Valley Forge, which has gone into history, tried men's hearts and souls, and made a nation weep for the unmerited sufferings of her noble supporters. Washington called into his councils, not only men of general good repute and standing for intelligence and patriotism but men who had been tried by the plumb square and level and not found wanting—men that in that dismal time he knew could be depended upon until death

It is a singular thing and worthy of note, that the original suggestion of the observance of this Memorial day should come from the Grand Lodge of Freemasons for the State of Colorado a part of this continent whose existence was known during Washington's lifetime only vaguely as a piece of the great unexplored Spanish Southwest   And it is still more odd that after leading Freemasons in the United States had taken the plan in hand and invited the Craft in other lands to cooperate that the first acceptance should have come with every manifestation of enthusiasm, from far off New Zealand which in Washington's day was a savage dominion, lately discovered and seized by Captain Cook the explorer, in the name of King George of England   Nothing could mark the world's progress in the intervening century more clearly than these circumstances

For him then as an eminent Mason Del Norte Lodge No 105 A F and A M meets this evening to join with thousands of other Lodges throughout the world in

holding these Memorial Services in recognition of his great ability as a man, and
testify to their heartfelt appreciation of his manifold gifts as a worthy brother
Master Mason

It is a well-known and undisputed fact that no man can be a good Mason and
live up to the tenets of our Order, unless, independent of that qualification, he
stands before his fellowmen as a good and exemplary citizen and a model of faith-
fulness to his God, his country and his family   Many a man can be a good man
without being a Mason, but no man can be a good Mason without being a good
man   Every tenet of our Order inculcates the highest morality, the broadest charity and a devoted love to mankind as the children of God   George Washington
probably came as near living up to this lofty ideal of the standard of Masonry as
any other man in this or any other country has ever done, and as such a beautiful
character Masons bow their heads to his memory and offer a fervent prayer to the
Grand Supervising Architect of the Universe that they may in their poor way endeavor to emulate his glorious example

Washington was a man of deep religious feeling, and his every walk in life
as our foremost citizen, and as the plain Virginia planter, was guided by his devotion to the Almighty, his love of his country, and his affection for his family, and
his friends   All loved him, and when he passed from this life to that of the Great
Unknown, countless mourners dropped a tear to his memory and prayed that they,
too, might be uplifted by his worthy example   His "Farewell Address," which you
have just heard, is a masterpiece of literary effort, and it seems that my task this
evening is like unto "painting the lily," or "attempting to refine pure gold," but
there are a few things which I will call your attention to in General Washington as
a Mason which have not been touched upon

The universal brotherhood of man is directly taught and illustrated upon the
floor of every Lodge of Masons throughout the world, and early imbibing the grand
idea so taught, George Washington, although the owner of 124 slaves, became convinced that slaves were human, and as humans must be brothers under and by
virtue of God's law, and hence, by logical reasoning, he became one of the first
Abolitionists in America   The natural grandeur of his character would not endure
that foul blot upon our escutcheon of freedom, a relic of the benighted ages, when
Masonry alone kept alive the theory which he was trying to follow out   In 1786 he
formed and wrote a resolution, never, unless compelled by particular circumstances,
to possess another slave by purchase, and that particular circumstance was to
prevent the severing of families   In writing to Gouverneur Morris on the subject at
the time, he says

"There is not a man living who wishes more sincerely than I do to see a plan
adopted for the abolition of slavery under legislative authority, as far as my suffrage
will go it will never be wanting

This expression shows to any disinterested observer the strong hold the teachings of Masonry had upon him, and his duty as a good Mason to help uplift the men he recognized as brothers under God's law

When the time came for a rupture with the mother country, he deeply deprecated and deplored the occasion, and his habitual respect for lawful authority inculcated by his Masonic oath and teachings, made it a hard measure for him to cast his lot with the Colonies, but an utter disregard of the rights of the citizens of this continent, an oppressive tax to sustain an expensive and dissolute court, with no opportunity to be heard, and no representation as to the making of laws, caused him, after a careful and God fearing study of the situation, to ally himself with, and become the central figure in, that band of patriots who made America a land of freedom, a country of its own, and acknowledging allegiance to none   This revolution, which added a new and brilliant star to the galaxy of nations, and separated the United States from the monarchy of England, also was so far reaching in its effect that it exonerated the American Masonic Lodges from their old allegiance to any and all foreign Grand Lodges   For why? Because the principles of Masonry teach and obligate us to an obedience to the laws of the government under which we live   Then, after the war, and when white winged peace had spread her snowy pinions above us, the Masons, as though approaching an altar erected to God, resorted to the proper and necessary means of forming and establishing independent Grand Lodges for the government of the fraternity in their respective jurisdictions, and since which time the United States of America, as a Masonic power, and the United States of America, as a nation, stands before the wondering eyes of the world pre eminent among them, inferior to none, and with her starry flag respected by all

DENVER

Circular to Brethren

Denver, Colo, November 24, 1899

At the Annual Grand Communication of the Most Worshipful Grand Lodge of Colorado, A F and A M, held on the 19th of September, 1899, the Committee on the Washington Centennial Memorial Exercises made report, which included a general order of exercises for the use of the Subordinate Lodges of this Jurisdiction, on their local observance of the occasion The report expressed the opinion that local exercises by Masonic Lodges throughout the country would be of at least equal effect as the national exercises at Mount Vernon in attracting the attention of the present generation to the virtues, patriotism and Masonic and public services of Washington and his compeers

Pursuant to the above action of the Most Worshipful Grand Lodge, a joint meeting of all the Lodges of Denver has been arranged to be held at the Trinity Methodist Episcopal Church Thursday evening, December 14, 1899, and the following programme has been provided for that occasion:

Reading of the Account of Washington's Last Illness, from the Diary of His Secretary, by Brother Peter L Palmer

Reading of a Personal Letter to the Lodges of Colorado from the Worshipful Master of Alexandria Washington Lodge, of which Washington Was the First Master under Its Virginia Charter, which Letter Includes an Account of Washington's Masonic Life, by Brother George F Dunklee

An Address upon the Early Influence of Masonry on the Development of the America Idea of Equality of Men, as Expressed in the Declaration of Independence, and its Culmination in the Independence of the American Colonies, by Brother Aaron Gove

An Address on the Personal Character and Public Services of Washington, by Brother Frederick A Williams

The Reading of Portions of Washington's Farewell Address, by Brother Robert W Bonynge

The above programme will be interspersed with appropriate music to be furnished by the Apollo Club

Tickets to the exercises will be furnished by the secretary of your Lodge to all members and their families desiring to attend, but as the Committee in charge wishes to know in advance the number of Masons who desire to attend, it is earnestly requested that you immediately notify your secretary whether you desire to attend, and if so, how many tickets you will require The seating capacity will probably not permit of extending the invitation to any but Masons and their families

Fraternally yours,

Frank L. Bishop,
Chairman of the Committee on Arrangements

To All Past Masters of This and Other Jurisdictions

It has been deemed advisable by the Committee on the Washington Centennial Memorial Exercises to open a Lodge and march in procession to Trinity Church, but on account of the large city membership it has been found impossible

The committee has decided to request all Past Masters of this and other Jurisdictions to meet with the Masters and Wardens of the city lodges at 7 15 p m, sharp, at the Masonic Temple, where those present will be formed in procession and march to the church as Denver Lodge No 5 It is estimated that there are one hundred Past Masters in the city, and in order to make a good impression we need just that many. Seats will be reserved for one hundred Make applications for tickets for your family to the secretary of your Lodge

In case you are not affiliated with one of the Lodges in the Jurisdiction, make your application to me Notify me at once if you will meet with us

Fraternally yours,

Frank L. Bishop,
Chairman Committee on Arrangements

TRINITY METHODIST EPISCOPAL CHURCH,
DENVER, COLO, December 14, A L 5899

At the Annual Grand Communication of the Most Worshipful Grand Lodge of Colorado, A F and A M, held the 19th of September, 1899, the Committee on the Washington Centennial Memorial Exercises made report, which included a general order of exercises for the use of the Subordinate Lodges of the Jurisdiction, on their local observance of the occasion The report expressed the opinion that local exercises by Masonic Lodges throughout the country would be of at least equal effect as the national exercises at Mount Vernon in attracting the attention of the present generation to the virtues, patriotism and Masonic and public services of Washington and his compeers

Pursuant to the above action of the Most Worshipful Grand Lodge, the following named Lodges arranged this programme

Denver Lodge No 5
Union Lodge No 7
Schiller Lodge No 41
Harmony Lodge No 61.
Temple Lodge No 84
Highlands Lodge No 86
Oriental Lodge No. 87
Rob Morris Lodge No 92
South Denver Lodge No 93

PROGRAM

Organ	Prof Henry Houseley
Invocation	Brother Thomas A Uzzell
"Sanctus"	Apollo Club
Reading of the Account of Washington's Last Illness, from the Diary of	
His Secretary	Brother Peter L Palmer

Reading of a Personal Letter to the Lodges of Colorado, from the Worshipful Master of Alexandria Washington Lodge, cf which Washington Was the First Master under its Virginia Charter, which Letter Includes an Account of Washington s Masonic Life

            Brother George F Dunklee

'Martyrs of the Arena"   Apollo Club

An Address upon the Early Influence of Masonry on the Development
of the American Idea of Equality of Men, as Expressed in the Declaration of Independence, and Its Culmination in the Independence
of the American Colonies   Brother Aaron Gove

"Finland Love Song"   Apollo Club

An Address on the Personal Character and Public Services of Washington   Brother Frederick A Williams

"The Star Spangled Banner"   Apollo Club

The Reading of Portions of Washington's Farewell Address

            Brother Robert W Bonynge

"America"   Apollo Club

Organ   Prof Henry Houseley

  (The audience is requested to join in singing "America")

The above ceremony was carried out in full by the Denver fraternity
under the auspices of Denver Lodge No 5, A F and A M

          J. C JOHNSTON,

           Secretary

ADDRESS OF BROTHER AARON GOVE

Subject—"The Early Influences of Masonry on the Development of the
American Idea of the Equality of Men as Expressed in the Declaration
of Independence, and Its Culmination in the Freedom of the Colonies "

Mother Nature is, and has been from the beginning, the great teacher of man
In advancement, all science, whether physical or mental seeks for Nature's methods Severe and kind, this mother has pursued her even and constant march from
the foundation of the universe, and to her has man looked for example in thought
and conduct

One great lesson learned from her is that of the power and value of patience
All her momentous achievements have been accomplished, and are accomplishing,

without intimation of violence or confusion The earthquake and the whirlwind are with us, not in obedience to, but in violation of, law, as their primal cause

In the still night men gaze upon the heavens with its millions of matter masses, moving at an almost incredible rate, noiselessly The forest gains size, strength and power little by little, day by day, and no man has seen it grow The farmer looks in the morning upon his acres of growing corn so much taller, thicker and broader than he saw it yesterday, but no eye saw it take upon itself such magnificent proportions

The inhabitants of our planet—ourselves, live in comfort and satisfaction, scarcely thinking that quietly, but surely, we are traveling through space at the incomprehensible speed of twenty-five miles a second And all these results accomplished in silence and secrecy

In the animal creation, as Nature made them, unwarped by the training of men, Nature's silence seems to obtain Only pleasure or pain, joy or sorrow—for anger is the output of pain—draws from the beasts of the forest and plain, notes of voice Even the domesticated ox and horse, so near and dear to man, refrain from giving expression to their contemplations or intentions except in extraordinary circumstances The burdens are borne and services are rendered in sweet, silent, patient methods, contributing to the beauty and glory of their environment solely by the inspiration of the gentle, expressive eye

For the human mind has been reserved the articulate speech, man only, by the vocal organs, is permitted to give to his fellows the product of head and heart Pleasure and joy inexpressible, pain and anguish incomparable, are given and inflicted So true is this, and so great the power, that one may well contemplate relatively the joy and pain of the world bestowed through the instrumentality of the human tongue, and sometimes the sorrow side of the balance appears to be the heavier

It is certain that much, very much, of the sadness, misery and heartache of the world lies directly at the door of too much talk The greatest achievements of the universe accomplished in silence are represented by the greatest human achievements Silent men make up the large class of the world's heroes and saviors It is not true that "still waters run deep," but it is so nearly true as to be worth quoting If the owl is not as wise as he looks, his silence is no hindrance to his success as an owl The garrulous hinder themselves, and contribute to the defeat of undertakings

Next to the greatest of human virtues that of never deserting a friend, stands the other virtue of silence, except when the purpose requires speech In the three great professions, when the lawyer obtains the important and necessary facts of his client's case, silence is the invulnerable shield When the physician, compelled to know the most intimate and secret family relations, ceases to be silent, his profession condemns and ostracizes him When the pastor and priest, confidants of the most holy thoughts as well as wicked actions of their charges, forget to bridle their tongues, the sacred work becomes a devilish activity, carrying with it harm and despair

George Washington, the centennial anniversary of whose death we to-day commemorate, was one of the silent men, ugly in feature, unattractive in voice, but with such a physical personal presence, and such a noble character, as to mark a page in the history of the world never excelled in virtue and integrity In social circles, especially as a host at the dinner table, his powers of conversation were marked, and so he contributed to the pleasure and happiness of his guests, without whom, especially in his later years, he seldom dined He seems to have observed all propriety with regard to subjects of conversation, and never to have allowed his plans, anticipations and intentions to be announced until the time of their execution had arrived

The effect of the power of silence is no interference with agreeable association, even Nature, in its silent methods, sends us the music of the murmuring brook, of the wind through the pine forest, and the rustling of the corn blade, and so the part taken in the social world by the silent man does not preclude beautiful expressions of heart and head

Washington withheld his opinion on important issues except where decision was necessary, one reads that when Mrs Custis, Mrs Washington's daughter-in-law, asked for his advice as to her proposed marriage engagement, Washington replied

A woman very rarely wishes an opinion or requires advice on such an occasion until the resolution is formed, and then it is with the hope and expectation of obtaining a sanction, and not that she means to be governed by your disapprobation, that she applies"

In a word, the plain English of the application may be summed up in these words

I wish you to think as I do, but if, unhappily you differ from me in opinion, my heart, I must confess, is fixed, and I have gone too far to retract

This illustration of Washington's prudence but portrays the heart of woman to have been a hundred years ago much as it is to day

His anger was intense and violent, his silence was characteristic of power, and his passions, in another man less strong, would have wrecked the individual

One of his rules of life he gave to his staff officer "I never judge the propriety of actions by after events "

He lived and worked during that part of our history when the nation was forming and the government making, what part he took is public history, so far as official acts are concerned, what he had to do with affairs as influenced by Freemasonry, will never be written. Washington would have been a Freemason in all but name had he never been placed in the northeast corner of the Lodge. The tenets of Freemasonry were the tenets of his life, the teachings of the brotherhood his daily practice, especially these three emphatic lessons taught by the ritual, viz. "To keep a tongue of good report, maintain secrecy, and practice charity."

The Craft have learned that the last of these—to practice charity—stands well to the top of the lessons inculcated, but the fathers placed next to that, 'to maintain secrecy." These two virtues are so closely related and interwoven as to be inseparable, one cannot practice charity except he maintain secrecy, unless he withholds blame of those who in opinion differ from him, and refrains from condemnation by tongue, of acts and words not in accord with his own opinions.

But the greatest effect, after all, of Freemasonry in Colonial times, must have come from that important teaching of democracy, technically expressed, 'to meet upon the level." Perhaps in no other institution in the world, at that age, was democracy, the equality of men, so aptly taught and inculcated as within the body of Freemasons. Elevated from the lowest to the highest position amongst fellows, with power and authority almost unlimited, then to step down from that position and take a place in the ranks in common with the throng, was a teaching and a practice that had an effect on the organization of our free national government. "To meet upon the level," to stand upon the same plane, to regard each man not for worldly wealth or honor, but for his personal value, and to trust him because of confidence in his integrity, is one of the foundation planks of the Declaration of Independence. Men in our national life have occupied alternately eminent and humble positions, a President of the United States has followed his term of exalted office by a term as Congressman in the lower House, and later, a President of the United States has retired to private life and re-entered his law office and resumed practice in common and alongside of the people from whom he came. These are illustrations of the principles of Freemasonry, as embodied in the formation of our government.

Only members of the Craft can fully appreciate the jealousy dominant in the hearts of men, as taught in the ritual, with regard to personal and equal rights. At the meetings of the fraternity, craftsmen know well of the lectures read and the rituals enacted, all teaching and emphasizing this great cardinal principle of the equality of men, and when one remembers that in isolated and tiled rooms along the Eastern coast, week after week, were gathered groups of men, that in that little room at Alexandria the great man whose career we celebrate, as well as in Massachusetts and South Carolina, teachings were constant, the conviction is deep that the impressions carried from the Lodge room silently to the home, the shop, the market place and the convention, were a factor in the framing of the policy that culminated in the Declaration of Independence The influence of Freemasonry must have been great, it was great, and the more peaceful because so silent

I have not learned of the extent of Freemasonry or the number of Masonic Lodges during Colonial days I am fairly familiar with the teachings of the Craft, in common with the brethren I am sure of the effect and influence of the lectures, the obligations and tenets of the Order in the direction of all that the declaration implies 'We hold these truths to be self evident, that all men are created equal, that they are endowed by their Creator with certain inalienable rights, that among these are life, liberty and the pursuit of happiness," is but an adaptation of one of the Masonic lectures delivered within the tiled Lodge

Jefferson wrote it, Adams amended, when Franklin completed the draft which was originally presented Virginia and Massachusetts peopled with men widely apart in ancestry, breeding and social life, in marked contrast one with the other, and Franklin, with Puritan ancestry and Quaker training the fortunately-appointed arbitrator on the committee to adjust differences

In one direction only, and in complete accordance, was the Puritan and the Cavalier—love of country—patriotism Washington and Adams in the nature of things, could never have been warm social friends nor mutual personal admirers, but the great cause of liberty and democracy inspired and animated them to joint action

The Virginia gentleman and the Massachusetts commoner laid aside all senti ment save the promotion of the principles of the declaration The silent, powerful influence of the Masonic Craft, unconsciously, perhaps, was a force that fluxed the stern, hard, discordant elements resulting in the solid, cohesive mass that stands to day, impregnable as it was formed in 1776 expressive of eternal truth, the instru ment of accomplished democracy, and declaration of the equality of man, a reitera tion of the oft heard words from the Master 'Masonry regards no man for his personal wealth or honor "

The closing century looks upon a generation of people, the legitimate children of the Colonial fathers Doubts have arisen and been dispelled, storms have come and gone, the terrors of war have been about us, but we assemble to night in memory of the eminent man and Mason, who, with his associates, accomplished the birth of the American Republic, and send to them across the unknown gulf, and to our God, without whose assistance and blessing, nothing would have been accom plished the devout thanks of a happy and prosperous, united nation

Evidence of the truth that Masonry largely influenced the spirit that uttered the Declaration of Independence can be conclusive only to members of the Craft With the brethren doubts cannot exist

A complete abiding by the fellowcraft's lecture, "we learn to act upon the square, keep a tongue of good report, maintain secrecy and practice charity," will lead us in the future, as it has caused us in the past, to be one helpful factor in holding to the faith proclaimed by Jefferson, Adams and Franklin, and approved and adopted by their fraters, whose signatures are still read on that instrument

ADDRESS BY F A WILLIAMS

But a few days ago Union Lodge No 7 of this city assembled for the purpose of conferring Masonic burial on the first Master of that Lodge, one of the fore most citizens of the city and State   A Lodge was opened, and brothers' hands bore the remains to their last resting place   The plaintive requiem of the Masonic fraternity was sung, three times the brothers circled about the open grave, hands were lifted as we said   "The spirit of our brother hath ascended on high, his memory we cherish in our hearts, his body we consign to the earth ' the sprig of acacia was deposited in the open grave, last of all, the lambskin, and the earthly career of the distinguished man and citizen was over

One hundred years ago this night, and this hour, another distinguished man and Mason was near his end   He was as self composed in the last hour as in any incident of his life   He felt his own pulse, said to his physician, 'I am dying, sir, but am not afraid to die"   To his wife, "Bring me the two papers in my desk This is my will, preserve this, and destroy the other "   To a friend, "I am going now   See that I have a decent burial, and that my body is kept for three days before being deposited in the vault "   The faithful wife said 'Is he gone?" and the physician raised his hand, indicating that all was over

Then, as now, a Lodge of Masons was opened   Then, as now, brothers' hands bore the remains tenderly to their last resting place   The requiem was sung, hands were lifted to the skies the acacia was deposited, last of all the lamb skin, and the most distinguished man of his time thus received Masonic burial

This ancient ceremony, the most simple and impressive in our Masonic ritual, unites us at once to the past and the future and keeps ever before us the lesson of mortality as an incentive to right living   This is the truth that is brought home to us at each step of life   we are passing away   It is a note that never ceases   Whatever the mood in nature, and whatever our surroundings, its low monotone may be heard It is the sound of the wind among the forests, the sob of the wave upon the seashore, and by this sign and ceremony the departure of Washington is as real to us to-day as if it had occurred but yesterday

In all ages and lands our venerable Order has claimed as its own the most useful and eminent men in every walk of life The qualities which made them conspicuous, the traits of character which in public or private life made them useful and endeared them to friends, are the qualities and traits by which our Order will at all times be judged While to young or old an abstract principle or rule of living can alone furnish but a feeble guide for human conduct still an example in the concrete, a living, breathing example of sterling worth and merit, is to all a personal inspiration

We meet to night to celebrate the virtues of one whose character is an inspiration to all It needed no national organization of the Masonic fraternity to call us together A recommendation from the Grand Lodge of Colorado was sufficient, and as if by common impulse the members of the Order, from the coast which our first general defended to a coast whose border line as the western boundary of our great Republic he may, perhaps, have faintly imagined, but could never have fully conceived, have met in city and hamlet to honor the man, who, as citizen, soldier and statesman, has furnished the theme for more earnest study and reflection than any other man our country has produced

While the principal observances are being held in the capitol of the nation, in every community from ocean to ocean, where a Masonic Lodge exists, the occasion is respected and observed If ever the Masonic family was one in thought, purpose and feeling, it is at the present moment, while thousands are contemplating the character and public services of a good man and Mason

What is Washington to us? What is there in his life of special significance to us as Masons?

Time was, in the history of our land, when membership in this Order, now so vast, but then so limited, was to many the subject of reproach Good, sincere and devout men believed it to be a device of the devil, while others were convinced that obligations assumed by Masons were naught but foolish, reckless and wicked oaths, that secrecy was proof positive of guilty purposes and that membership in the Order was an effective shield for crime

The answer to such charges, when any answer was necessary was found in the character of the men, good and true, who without entering into argument, retained their active membership in the institution and from the days of the first President to the present time no cause has been more potent to attract men to its shelter then the moral and social standing of a large majority of its members Washington was a Mason at heart before ever he was a Mason in form, but once a

Mason he remained such to the end   And while as a soldier we admire, and as a statesman we revere, him, we may be pardoned if to night, in common with the multitudes of others who are bound to us by three fold ties, we claim him as a brother

It should have been a sufficient answer at any time to the calumnies of our enemies to say that such men as George Washington were Masons   His name has added, I will not say respectability, but character to the society, and, on the other hand, it is sure that the ceremonies of his initiation, passing, and raising, sank deeply into his susceptible and thoughtful nature, and aided him materially in the struggle for self mastery

To understand a man living at any time we must understand his surroundings   It is the popular belief that a man is necessarily the creature of his surroundings, that environment makes all of character, and that it is well nigh useless for one to endeavor to resist or rise above the conditions that exist, and that seem to control his life   But this view leaves out of the reckoning the power of human will and the strength of human affections and passions   Dr Jeffrey said a few years ago to the Y M C A of this city, that any young man is successful who rises somewhat, even though but a little, above the average of his associates, and in every-day life, as in national movements, it is certainly true that many men, by their strong force of character, have had much to do with the shaping of human and national events   It is fair to say that, given sufficient strength of purpose and sufficient intelligence and means, men may as well carve their destinies as to submit to destiny, though in most cases the policy of men is a policy of drift

What is it that has endeared Washington to the people of this land, and all lands?   Was it success only?   We read with pleasure the tales of his early life and training, his entry upon public life, his military failures and successes, his distinguished services as a statesman, and his dignified retirement to the peaceful occupation of a wealthy Virginia farmer   His place in human history is forever assured   Proud we are that he was an American, that his sword brought national liberty and independence, and that his wise counsels contributed to the formation of a government which we fondly think is the best on earth   But when all is said we find most delight in regarding him as a great and good man, one who by birth and early training was prepared for great events, and who unconsciously moved forward by the force of his own greatness, his mastery of facts, his knowledge of conditions, and his preconception of what was necessary and inevitable, to the foremost place in American history, and in every place and in every condition displayed the same noble qualities of mind and heart, and the same masterful intellect that distinguished him as well in private life   It is the man Washington that lives in the hearts of the American people

He was no paragon of virtue Like the rest of us, he had his imperfections The perfect ashlar, squared, dressed and finished, is typical only Washington's physical equipment was simply magnificent Six feet two inches in stature, weighing two hundred and twenty pounds in his prime, with long and powerful arms, hands that were simply huge, feet that required number thirteen boots, a figure straight as an arrow, fond of the chase, familiar with all manner of out-door exercises, accustomed to frontier life and exposure, the strongest man in his army, he possessed the first requisite for long and arduous labor in the cause of his country

He was no Puritan in his mode of living, though strictly temperate and self-restrained, liberal in his views on all public questions, he conceded to every man the right of private opinion He could never have shares in the narrowness of many of the New England settlers, of whom it is said, that early in their political growth they passed two resolutions "First The world should be governed by the saints Second We are the saints "

It is said that his clear, strong countenance, his light gray eyes, set widely apart, his massive chin, his firmly set chin, and the wrinkles between his eyes, invariably gave the beholder the impression of the most perfect self control Strong passions were held in check by a stronger will and though at times, under the most exasperating provocations, his temper went beyond bounds reason soon and surely asserted itself, and all was calm again

The lofty spirit of the man is seen in his letter to Governor Sharp, who, having a commission from the king, and desirous of securing the services of Washington, recognized as the best fighting man in Virginia, offered him a company In answer Washington said ' You make mention in your letter of my continuing in the service and retaining my colonel s commission This has filled me with surprise, for if you think me capable of holding a commission that has neither rank nor emolument annexed to it, you must entertain a very contemptible opinion of my weakness, and believe me to be more empty than the commission itself In short, every captain bearing the king's commission, every half pay officer, or others appearing with such a commission, would rank before me * * * yet, my inclinations are strongly bent to arms " Of this incident Mr Lodge says "It was a bitter disappointment to withdraw from military life but Washington had an intense sense of personal dignity not the small vanity of a petty mind but the quality of a proud man, conscious of his own strength and purpose and it was of immense value to the American people at a later day "

Although no martinet, he was a strict disciplinarian, and sometimes lost his temper because of the failure of his subordinates to execute orders On one occasion a messenger being dispatched to obtain information returned, saying he was unable to cross the river because of a storm and the floating ice Washington, then in his tent, seized an ink stand, and, throwing it at the messenger, shouted, 'Begone, sir, and send me a man." The messenger departed and performed his errand

Later, on one occasion while dining, the President received dispatches which were to be delivered only to the Commander-in-Chief, and which announced that the Army of St. Clair had been surprised by the Indians and cut to pieces. Later in the evening, when all were gone but Colonel Lear and General Washington, he broke out suddenly with

"It's all over—St. Clair's defeated, the officers nearly all killed, the rout complete, and a surprise in the bargain. Yes," he said, walking to and fro, with great agitation. "Here on this very spot, I took leave of him, I wished him success and honor. You have your instructions, I said, from the Secretary of War. I had a strict eye to them and will add but one word—beware of a surprise. I repeat it beware of a surprise—you know how the Indians fight us.' He went off with that as my last solemn warning thrown into his ears. And yet to suffer that army to be cut to pieces, hacked by a surprise—the very thing I guarded him against! O God, O God, he's worse than a murderer! How can he answer it to his country?' The blood of the slain is upon him —the curse of widows and orphans—the curse of Heaven!''

'This torrent came out in tone appalling. His very frame shook. It was awful'' said Mr. Lear. More than once he threw his hands up as he hurled imprecations upon St. Clair. Mr. Lear remained speechless, awed into breathless silence.

The roused chief sat down on the sofa once more. He seemed conscious of his passion, and uncomfortable. He was silent. His wrath began to subside, he at length said in an altered voice, 'This must not go beyond this room.'' Another pause followed—a longer one—when he said in a tone quite low. 'General St. Clair shall have justice. I looked hastily through the dispatches, saw the whole disaster, but not all the particulars. I will hear him without prejudice, he shall have full justice.

'He was now, said Mr. Lear, perfectly calm. Half an hour had gone by. The storm was over and no sign of it was afterwards seen in his conduct or heard in his conversation. The result is known. The whole case was investigated by Congress. St. Clair was exculpated and regained the confidence Washington had in him when appointing him to that command.''

Of the personal courage of Washington, everybody knows. To a major, who had exhibited cowardice at Great Meadows, and who had complained at not receiving what he considered his share of public lands, Washington wrote as follows

"Your impertinent letter was delivered to me yesterday. As I am not accustomed to receiving such from any man, nor would I have taken the same language from you personally without letting you feel some marks of my resentment. I would advise you to be cautious in writing a second of the same tenor. * * * All my concern is that I ever engaged in behalf of so ungrateful a fellow."

Being taken ill on the march to Fort Du Quesne, he made Orme promise that he should be brought up before the army reached that place and wrote to his friend that he would not miss the impending battle for five hundred pounds. Arriving at the front, the battle was soon commenced. A disaster it proved for the British. Of this event it is said

Washington at the outset flung himself headlong into the fight. He rode up and down the field carrying orders and striving to rally the dastards as he afterwards called the regular troops. He endeavored to bring up the artillery but the men would not serve the guns although he aimed and discharged one himself. All through that dreadful carnage he rode fiercely about, raging with the excitement of battle and utterly exposed from beginning to end. Even now it makes the heart beat quicker to think of him amid the smoke and slaughter as he dashed hither and thither his face glowing and his eyes shining with the fierce light of battle, leading on his own Virginians and trying to stay the tide of disaster."

It must be confessed that some of his military movements were ill planned, and that serious mistakes were made, but Washington was a man who would learn and did learn by defeat, and the story of his life in public and private affairs is the story of the growth and development of a strong, capable, self-reliant, and conscientious man and soldier

We cite these instances merely to show that he was not perfect. To many he has been pictured as an ideal, incapable of doing wrong. Such characters are impossible and insipid. The man Washington is dearer to us because of his imperfections, and because by the aid of the monitor within, his amazing grasp of existing situations, and his knowledge of men, he overcame difficulties within and without

Grateful as the American people are for his distinguished public services, that for which he is loved and most revered by the common folk, is that he brought to the public service the best qualities of mind and heart that distinguished him as an individual. Because he was a man of growth and development, simple in his tastes, refined in manners, imperious in command, comprehensive and far reaching in his judgment, and fearless in the discharge of duty. He endeavored to square his life in public and in private with the rule of justice to all men, and with the compass he swept a circle beyond which impulse and passion were not permitted to go

No one imputed selfishness to Washington. Every call to the public service found him reluctant, but obedient. Each time he returned from service in the British army, from the houses of burgesses of the native colony, from the command of the American army, from the presidency of the constitutional convention, and from the presidency of the Republic, to private life at Mount Vernon, grateful for the privilege, earnest in the hope of being able to lead a private life, and devoting his energies to the improvement of his property and the betterment of agricultural conditions in his community

Time would fail to tell the dangers which beset the ship of state in his time. But who shall say that equal dangers are not at hand at the present day? To what excesses and dangers may the acquisition of foreign territory by this isolated though powerful Republic, finally lead? And where shall the path upon which we have now entered finally lead?

Who will say that justice is not boldly subverted at the present time, when the burden of expense in maintaining the government, state, national and municipal, is cast upon one-half the property of the country, and the other half, that existing in the form of chatels and money, almost wholly escapes taxation?

Who will say that our government is sufficiently strong, when a difficulty between employers and employes in a single city can embarrass and nearly paralyze the commerce of the entire country?

Who can say that the well being of the people is sufficiently protected, when combinations of capital are able to increase or diminish the supply of food, and regulate the price of all the necessaries of life?

Who will not say that we have not already too much freedom, when the voice of the vagrant and the criminal counts for as much as the vote of the man who works and observes the holy requirements of law? And when the public funds are distributed by men who contribute nothing to the public funds, and who have no interest as householders or taxpayers in the maintenance of a safe, economical or just government?

The ship of state is not beyond the shoals. New questions and new dangers confront us daily. Is it any wonder that, foreseeing such a condition, the prophetic words of Alexander Hamilton were uttered? Taking up a book that lay on the table, he observed

'Ah this is the Constitution. Now mark my words. So long as we are a young and virtuous people this instrument will bind us together in mutual interests mutual welfare and mutual happiness but when we become old and corrupt, it will bind us no longer."

Lord Byron, meditating upon the ruins of ancient Rome, wrote thus

There lies the moral of all human tales
'Tis but the same rehearsal of the past
First freedom and then glory when that fails,
Wealth, vice corruption—barbarism at last
And history with all her volumes vast
Hath but one page and that is written here

There is but one safeguard against the disintegration of this noble Republic. Justice will be perpetuated and the Union maintained just so long as the majority of the people of this country are governed by motives, and their representatives and rulers are actuated by principles of truth, personal integrity and sterling honor.

It is the moral quality that made Washington a man of the people, and the moral quality alone in public affairs and private life can preserve the nation's existence.

A few months ago the Lord Chief Justice of England, Justice Coleridge, was a distinguished guest at Washington and New York. His first business was not the study of our wonderful material growth and progress, and his first pleasure was, not the sight of the granaries of the West, nor the grandeur of our eternal mountains. With reverent steps he turned his feet to Mount Vernon, where rest the remains of one whose fame is as well assured in foreign lands as in our own, and his visit to that sacred spot, the shrine of every true lover of liberty, was a pilgrimage creditable to him as an Englishman, and to every man in whose mind human character and personal worth are above every other possession

To night we are all pilgrims to the same sacred spot, and though we cannot participate in the principal exercises that are being conducted in memory of Washington, the soldier, Washington, the statesman, and Washington, the man and citizen, still, with the same elevated feeling of veneration for the most distinguished man of our land and time, we accord "honor, eternal honor, to his name"

DURANGO

Hall of Durango Lodge No 46, A F and A M,

Durango, Colo, December 15, 1899

Ed C Parmelee, Grand Secretary·

Dear Sir and Brother—I beg to submit the following report of the proceedings of this Lodge on the event of the Washington Memorial Exercises held on December 14, 1899

The Lodge met in Special Communication at its hall and was opened on the third degree, thence it proceeded under escort of the G A R Sedgwick Post No 12, of Durango, Colo, to the Presbyterian Church, where the enclosed programme was carried out, with the exception that Brother Burwell being absent, his part was omitted and the place supplied by the reading of a short account of Washington's life by Brother Chadsey. The Lodge then returned to the hall and closed in due form

Fraternally yours,

CLEMENT L. RUSSELL,

Secretary

PROGRAM

1799-1899

Durango Lodge No 46, A F and A M , Durango, Colorado

Music—(a) The Heavens Are Telling	Hesperian
(b) Our Washington	Chorus
Invocation	Rev L R Smith
Address—Washington and Masonry	Worshipful Master C A Pike
Annie Laurie (Dudley Buck)	Male Quartette
Letter from the Master of Alexandria Washington Lodge, Virginia	
	Past Grand Master J C Sanford
Selections from Washington's Farewell Address	Rev L R Smith
Soldiers' Chorus (Gounod)	Double Quartette
Washington's Last Illness, Written by His Private Secretary	Blair Burwell
Old Kentucky Home	Ladies' Quartette
Washington as a Citizen	N C Miller
America	Audience

ADDRESS BY BROTHER N C MILLER

Worshipful Master, Wardens and Brethren

It is fitting that an Order, enriched with so bright a jewel in its diadem, as the illustrious Washington, should assemble in public Communication throughout the nation on this centennial of his death, to do reverence to his memory

The old Greeks and Romans were accustomed to deify their dead heroes, and to assign them to constellations in the heavens Nor does this peculiarity wholly disappear as people become more civilized As years recede, only the stronger lines of the heroes' character stand out to view, and the rate at which they grow in our estimation affords some measure of their greatness It is a pleasant attribute of our nature to forget human shortcomings The effect is like that of leaving behind us the distant mountain, only the magnificent outlines appear on the horizon So when we view our hero of the past we see only the grand outlines of his character, and the manliness of his deeds, and in our love for a beautiful ideal, we fill in the minor parts with creations of a prejudiced fancy The tendency of posterity to magnify the character of illustrious statesmen who are dead, carries with it invaluable blessings It creates ideals which elevate citizenship inspire leaders and produce in the young the most lofty conceptions of patriotism A great nation must have its heroes of the past, their memories keep alive our pride and affection for our country

The simplicity, honesty and high purpose of our nation's heroes are its greatest treasures Washington, Hamilton, Jefferson, Franklin, Madison, Monroe, Jackson, Lincoln, Grant and General Sherman are some of the ideals of our people, and so long as we revere their memories and adhere to their teachings as the purest source of political wisdom, we are not apt to be driven into false doctrines during tempestuous political storms The fault is that the worst and best vie with each other in the attempt to trace their theories of government to the same illustrious source A great people create high ideals We do not look for great patriots in China In their flourishing period Carthage, Greece and Rome each had their generals and statesmen, whose appearance thrilled the people, and whose return from war was celebrated with pomp and splendor Those were the days when honesty, simplicity and patriotism were the boasted virtues of the people The same starry-decked heavens keep vigil watch over their homes now as then; air no less salubrious and bracing courses over their classic hills and valleys, their shores are washed by waves no less indulgent, and the same warm and benignant sun sheds its rays upon the land—but the greatness of the people is gone, and no longer do a liberty-loving people look to them for fresh inspiration

It is a happy country that can create a military hero without fear of militarism or revolution How many of the countries of the world could welcome home a Dewey, and invite the people to unrestrained expressions of joy and admiration without some fear of social disturbance? Surely England, possibly Germany, are there more? France stationed 8,000 soldiers near by, to insure peace on the announcement of the Dreyfus verdict The heroes of our country have been cradled, educated and matured in a land where the people are sovereign, and to whom never occurs the faintest notion of relinquishment, to any hero The land of the free and the home of the brave is more than a capricious sentiment It is the strongest national sentiment of our people, and the national air expressive of it, thrills the soul and awakens within us the strongest ties of country The sturdy spirit of our forefathers, who were seeking individual liberty as a reaction from the intolerable interference of the State in church and secular affairs, has established too firmly to be shaken, the confidence of the people in their independence

The progressive course of the world has always supplied the right man at the critical moment The insatiable ambition of Napoleon met the cool, calculating and unflinching Wellington It was part of the order of progress that Napoleon should be confronted by such a man at Waterloo The undulating wave of progress was then rising, free institutions were taking a strong hold on civilization, and the crest of the wave had not yet risen full high No man could overcome its force It matters not what errors Napoleon might have avoided, under ordinary calculations they were not errors The eternal forces of justice which always finally triumph, planted Wellington at Mont St Jean, an impassable barrier to unworthy ambition   The evolution of our national affairs required a Lincoln and a Grant, while the critical reconstruction period demanded the firmness of the latter

When we look at the narrow fringe of settlements whose people resisted with dauntless courage the attempt of George III to crowd upon the colonies his notions of the crown's prerogatives, we are filled with inexpressible admiration for the men and women of the Revolution   No task seemed too great, no trial too severe, unpaid, half clad, and starved, year in and year out, the descendants of Royalists in the South and Puritans in the North, fought, that the colonies might enjoy a free government   It is a false notion to picture to ourselves a serene and united spirit among the colonists   At times the greatest discord prevailed, threatening the very existence of the army, and the success of its cause   Men like Robert Morris, who expended their fortunes, and labored to arm, feed and pay the soldiers, are seldom counted among our great benefactors   Those were days when great men lived in America   If human perfection consists in each individual making the most out of his endowments, whether large or small, then, indeed, the men who were associated with Washington rose high in the scale of greatness   But when you consider men like Washington and Lincoln from the cradle to the grave, they appear enormities   Nature overleaps her accustomed yield when she produces them   They are part of the great plan of nature   Their brain, temperament and character were made to give a favorable turn to a great crisis   We admire them, we cannot understand them   Can you compare them to such men as Alexander or Cæsar, or any of the great heroes of the world who sought to quench their thirst for glory in conquest?   These were actuated by selfish motives, and the governments they instituted were almost as fleeting as their lives   Even the crusades, which have been called holy wars, were of a questionable spirit, for beneath the sentimental ambition of rescuing the tomb of Christ from the hand of Moslem, there lurked the barbarous pride of arms that characterized the fantastic chivalry of the Middle Ages   National aggrandizement, greed of territory, hope of plunder, the hollow glory of conquest, the insanity of revenge, these motives and such as these, have marshaled and sent forward the armies of invasion that have vexed the world and crowned the warriors with greatness   Nor can we picture as the idol of these patriots a general who was planning an empire for himself   The people of America were thirsting for civil and religious liberty, and a lesser man than Washington could not have fulfilled the destiny of this new civilization

If I were to talk to you of a typical American I would not choose as my ideal Washington   The traits of American character now familiar to us all, were not then blended in any one great man   Our people had not yet formed sentiments or habits free and distinct from the mother country   The gentleman of the age was in some sense an English gentleman. His ideas of living were cast in an English mould. His theories of government were colored by ideals borrowed from history, and America had no history. The principle of universal suffrage had not yet taken hold of the Colonial statesman, while the debates in the Constitutional Convention displayed honest distrust of the people as the safest foundation of free government. Washington's training, thought and action had not taught him to lean with unfaltering trust on the people.

Lord Brougham said he was the greatest man of his own or any age. The most wonderful thing about Washington was his majestic and beautiful character, which towered matchless and unsullied in its serenity and strength above all his countrymen, a man of faultless judgment, endowed with a high sense of justice, actuated by a spirit too broad and generous to descend into factional quarrels, living and doing so as to impress the people that his sole ambition was to make America free and great, he was the one man on whom all factions would unite and harmonize. Soothing the factious spirit of discord, ever manifesting amidst the gloom or glory of war a profound reverence for the laws of peace, with the magical charm of his placid but firm character, moulding the pioneers of America into a brave and loyal army, now worrying the enemy with his strategical marches, now harassing them by his bold sallies, fitted to meet every emergency, unnerved by no discouragement, General Washington, at the surrender of Yorktown, was the idol of the army and the oracle of the people. At the zenith of his military glory and power, with a patriotism unexampled, he returned to Congress his sword, in an address full of wisdom and patriotism, and with the respect and love of all, he sought the quietude of his Mount Vernon home, and the familiar scenes of his boyhood. Where in all history has another general written letters to the people in such a spirit of paternal care and solicitude, and the people received them with such filial respect? When his soldiers, tempted into sedition by disappointment and want of appreciation on the part of their country, which was then too poor to fittingly honor them, offered to make him king in the West he spurned the offer in an address ringing with patriotism and devotion to his country, and laden with tender affection for the soldiers, half clad and starved, who had clung to him with unfaltering courage and loyalty, amid the cold and hunger of the winter about Valley Forge. No wonder we cling to his memory to-day, with a fond admiration which sees no peer among the patriots of his day. His character and deeds are the glory of our free institutions, he is the bright star in that firmament of patriots who founded a new government on new principles, which are still maturing and growing and carrying the people forward to new conceptions of national greatness. Undoubtedly, there have been brave, wise and good men before Washington, but I do not know of another instance in history, where the hero of his people won so completely their affections and confidence, and at the very height of his glory and prestige surrendered every vestige of power and became their wisest and safest counselor. No sectional hatred, no dogma, no bias, no rivalry, no jealousy changed his purpose; he loved America and his countrymen, and they lavished upon him the most precious honors. Without a dissenting vote, he was made chairman of the convention that framed our Constitution at a time when the jealousy between the rival States made the delegations suspicious of the fairness of any other man, and after its adoption he was twice unanimously chosen President, and with a keen foresight for the future safety of the new nation, he established a precedent which even the hero of Appomattox could not transcend.

His was a turbulent time. It was an epic period in our country's history; the great nations of the earth were tossing on the raging billows of the political sea, and out of the chaos came forth the only enduring Republic the sun ever shone on. The wonder is that a single nation ever was evolved out of the turmoil. When the storms of passion raged fiercest, and the blasts of calumny sounded loudest, with wise discretion and dignity unbroken, he nursed and fostered with paternal care the new experiment in government, and with his wise counsel and courageous demeanor overcame much of the jealousy between the States. With his matchless letters of wisdom, he blazed the pathway for future years, and on his deathbed, calm and hopeful, in anxious and grateful remembrance of his country, he died, the bright consummate flower of our early patriots. We revere his memory to-day for the rich treasures of wisdom left us; for the sublime example of the pure and unselfish motives actuating him in public and private life; for the grandeur and honesty of his character, which rallied all parties about him, and carried the country through the vexatious and perilous period of infancy; and planted it firmly and permanently on the solid foundation of the Constitution. Such a man belongs to no one people or section; his teachings are a legacy to the world; his fame is imperishable, and will go down the ages of eternity challenging admiration and growing in brilliancy as the love of liberty and respect for the equal rights of man sink deeper in the human soul. "His resting place will be the world."

EATON.

Eaton, Colo., December 23, 1899.

Ed. C. Parmelee, Grand Secretary:

Dear Sir and Right Worshipful Brother—Acknowledging receipt of Dispensation, and acting upon the suggestions therein contained, Abdallah

Lodge, U D , made an effort to comply to the best of its ability   The secretary was ordered to procure a life size picture of General Washington,
and have it placed in the place of meeting, properly draped with crape and
the American colors, which was done

A programme was arranged and various members of the Lodge were
assigned the respective parts   The public was invited to attend, through
a notice published one week previous   The members of the Lodge met at
Brother Steel's store, and marched in a body to the Congregational Church,
where the exercises were held   The procession was led by the Tiler, followed by the brethren wearing their aprons   The Lodge occupied the platform   The following programme was then rendered:

Invocation	Rev Carson
"My Country 'Tis of Thee"	The entire congregation
Solo	Miss Smith
Reading—"The Last Illness of Washington"	Brother W L Petrikin
Reading of a letter from the Master of Alexandria-Washington Lodge,	
of which Washington was the First Master	Brother G W Atkinson
Reading of a Letter Dictated by Brother Adna A Treat, possibly the	
oldest Mason in the United States	Brother G W Atkinson
Violin Solo	Miss Dulbridge
Select Reading—The Character of Washington	Rev Carson
Address—"Masonry"	Brother J M Price
Benediction	Rev Carson

Attest: G W Atkinson,
                                                                Secretary

GEORGETOWN

Georgetown, Colo , December 24

Ed. C Parmelee, Esq , Right Worshipful Grand Secretary.

Conforming to the order of the Most Worshipful Grand Master, I
herewith return details of our Washington Memorial Exercises, held December 14, 1899.

We were unable to present an address on the "Idea of the Equality of Men," etc, but in all other respects the Grand Lodge committee's recommendations were carried out to the letter

The exercises were conducted jointly by Nos 12 and 48, the latter being then in annual session, No 12 met with them, the officers being equally divided between Nos 12 and 48—Brother D R Hatch, Master of No 12, acting as Worshipful Master. About forty brethren, being clothed and bearing the Great Lights, formed in procession and marched to the Presbyterian Church After concluding the exercises, the Lodge re-formed and marched to their hall, where the Lodge was duly closed on the third degree A large number of citizens filled the church and manifested much interest in the exercises

We desire to especially invite attention to the very able address of Worshipful Master Dorus R Hatch on ' The Services and Character of Washington," and trust it may be found worthy of distinction.

Fraternally submitted,

HENRY H NASH,
Secretary

GEORGETOWN CENTENNIAL

Of the Death of

GEORGE WASHINGTON,

Thursday, December 14, 1899

Ancient Free and Accepted Masons

Washington Lodge No 12   Georgetown Lodge No 48

PROGRAM

Opening Prayer   Rev George Darley
Letter from the Master of Alexandria Washington Lodge
.   Read by W M Fletcher

Quartette—'Sleep, Peacefully Sleep"
Letter from Brother Treat   Read by H H Nash
Lear's Account of Washington's Death   Read by Mary I Fletcher
Solo—"The Grave of Washington"
The Farewell Address   Read by Fred Dewey
Services and Character of Washington   Address by D R Hatch
"America"   Congregation

Benediction

ADDRESS BY D R HATCH

We boast of what America has done of important inventions and great dis-
coveries of ingenious appliances to save time and labor, to increase wealth and
comfort We call them the crowning efforts of man's progress in his struggle with
the powers of nature These are noble achievements but they are not the greatest
glory of our nation Nor are material things, however ingenious and wonderful,
wealth, however vast, or knowledge, however profound, the chief possession of a
people Let a nation boast of the men it has produced for unless successive generations are of a noble breed, unless they are of a better quality of mind unless
they are of a finer moral fiber, all progress in wealth and knowledge is in vain
The chief glory of these United States is the men they have produced

From 1607 to 1763 from the settlement of Jamestown to the close of the Old
French War, America was known to the world only as a howling wilderness, inhabited by fierce beasts and fiercer men In all that time no poet no philosopher, no
warrior no statesman had arisen But that century and a half did not elapse in
vain Its generations were not unfruitful There was breeding a race of men, the
like of which the world has never known a race of warriors patriots and constructive statesmen, whose writings surpass the masterpieces of antiquity, whose nation
building was fraught with greater moment to the world than that of Alexander or
of Cæsar Of all the men who ever lived on earth fit to perform that ancient and
heroic work the founding of a State they were the fittest, and among them Washington was first

> What constitutes a State?
> Not high-raised battlements or labored mound
> Thick wall or moated gate
> Not cities proud with spires and turrets crowned
> Not starred and spangled courts
> Where low-browed business wafts perfume to pride
> No Men—high-minded men—
> Men who their duties know
> But know their right and knowing dare maintain

The world has need of such as these, and God had prepared the crisis, the hour, and the men

Athens of old boasted that her citizens sprang from the soil, were sons of Mother Earth So are all men Nature, in her outer aspect, marked the man The soil, climate, the mountains, the sea, the forest, these determine the occupations and mould the mind of man Our forefathers were set where Nature taught her grandest lessons Before them rolled the limitless expanse of ocean, behind them the endless forests covered the innumerable hills which measured the distance to the mountains and beyond—men yet scarce knew what, but vast, illimitable, and in it the possibility of future empire All this they saw with broadened minds Nature also taught them the homelier virtues She taught them simplicity from their necessities, she taught them self-reliance from the dangers of the wilderness, she taught them industry to wring bread from a reluctant soil, and best of all, she taught them independence, the love of liberty was in the air they breathed Years of Washington's young life were spent in close and solitary companionship with nature—by day the immeasurable and stately forest, the eternal hills, the majestic river, by night, the stars and all the hushed teachings of a midnight stillness in the forest From these he drew his thoughts, and reasoned back from creation to Creator

The age demanded a form of government free from the caprice of princes, free from caste and class, free from the servility and superstition of the past The colonies had worked a century and a half on this problem The instinct of self government they had as an Anglo-Saxon inheritance They had resisted the aggressions of kings, they had enacted and altered constitutions, they had made their own laws Virginia had defied the Crown, she had thrust a worthless royal governor out, she had rebelled against another The Colonists had stood upon their rights as Englishmen and men, all the while working unconsciously toward that nice grant of, and delicate balancing of, governmental powers, whereby a multitude can rule itself To all this experience Washington was heir He had occupied public positions, he had sat among the burgesses, he had represented them in two Continental Congresses Such a preparation was to be had nowhere else on earth Thus nature and experience had educated the Colonists to become the builders of a nation They rendered a service, not only to their country, but to us their posterity, and to the world, whose effect shall reach to the end of time

The part of that service performed by Washington is matter of common knowledge to the American people Streets and towns, cities and counties colleges, societies and men by thousands, bear his name throughout our land His statue adorns our parks and halls His picture hangs on every wall His deeds are part and parcel of the folklore upon which our children feed at mother s knee

In recounting the deeds of men we are accustomed to tell of disadvantages and hardships We say in spite of lowly birth, of poverty, of grinding toil, they rose to greatness Surely nothing could be more in error We should say by the aid of lowly birth, blessed by poverty, and educated by grinding toil, they rose to greatness For surely there is no hindrance like a long line of pride-stuffed ancestors, there is no sedative like wealth, and there is no stimulus like poverty, no education like that of grinding toil, no courage like that of difficulties overcome For the leader of a great democratic people, no man was ever born to greater disadvantages than Washington He was handicapped by birth, by wealth, by religion, and by the social institutions of his State What need had he of honor and social position? A long line of worthy ancestors, honest and honorable every one, had bequeathed him that What need had he of wealth? The finest plantations of Virginia were his by inheritance What need had he for effort, for the education of grinding toil? A hundred slaves were born to do his bidding He was born to a family of cavaliers, whose guiding principle was loyalty to the house of Stuart His great grandfather had fled from England to escape the wrath of a so-called commonwealth, because he loved monarchy and revered his monarch Washington was born to a State church, whose head was the King of England, whose chiefest tenet was passive obedience to the powers ordained of heaven He was born to a society of castes and classes, founded on slavery reaping where it had not sown, and eating where it had not toiled To all these malignant influences was he born

But he was not born to these alone, thank God There were those mighty powers at work which set at naught the monarchizing trend of church, and state, and aristocracy Those powers which made the Colonies the breeding ground of patriots and statesmen, Virginia, the mother of Presidents, and Washington, the father of a free people

There were three periods of his public life, there were three inestimable services performed As general he led the army to success and gained our priceless heritage of freedom, as a private citizen he persuaded his distracted countrymen to union, as President he based our government on such principles and organized its powers in such form as to secure our lasting happiness

We see Washington in war moulding an army out of diverse and unruly soldiers We see him holding that army together against almost insuperable difficulties We see him fighting always on his own terms, continually surprising the enemy, never taken unawares himself We see him directing every wise and brilliant movement of an eight years' war We see him opposing, checking, harassing, defeating, and finally capturing armies superior to his own in equipment, discipline and numbers Such deeds are done only by a military genius of the highest order

Frederick the Great of Prussia, himself a consummate master of the military art, pronounced them the most brilliant and daring of the century

Where shall we look in that long war, full of heroism and pathos, for the picture that shall show us Washington at his best and greatest—that shall show in him at once the genius of the general and the moral grandeur of the man? Many could be painted which would show his bravery, his genius, his wisdom, his generosity, his tenderness, his faith But there is none to equal in sublimity that Christmas night upon the Delaware There was no shadow of doubt, no moment of hesitation The fit of fate was on him In his breast the hope that gave earnest of to-morrow's victory, in his breast that courage that deserved success and won it, in his soul, I doubt it not, a serene and abiding faith in Providence There was a God in Israel Justice would prevail It is the sublimest picture in all history

The war ended, peace was declared, but there was no peace Independence had been conquered, but not tranquility and union Impoverished by war, with property destroyed, credit undermined, and occupations gone, the Colonists found that they had changed a stable, steady going government for a condition not far from anarchy The Congress was a shadow, without money, without credit, without authority—its requisitions refused, its decisions disregarded, unable to keep the peace at home, without respect abroad—the Confederation was a rope of sand The crisis fast approached Were they to be one nation, respectable and prosperous, or thirteen nations, contemptible and miserable? Was independence won so brilliantly, and at such a cost, to be thrown away? No, not so, while Washington, who won that independence, lived Argument, entreaty, warning, influence, radiated throughout the land from Mount Vernon as a center

Yorktown closed the first period of his life, so the Constitutional Convention closed the second He came at the head of the Virginia delegation The Convention met in the old State House in Philadelphia, in the room where the Declaration of Independence had been adopted Here again the wisdom of the people was assembled to give forth another immortal document Above in the belfry was the old bell, which bore upon its lip the legend, "Proclaim liberty throughout the land unto all the inhabitants thereof" Again it was to peal its proclamation, then of liberty, now of union

In his administration as President, Washington was confronted with a problem such as no man ever faced before The Constitution was made, but not the government The document was to be interpreted In this interpretation Washington was perforce a pioneer He believed that the arm of the national government should be long and strong It was not yet decided whether we were a nation, one and inseparable, or a mere confederation Nor was the question settled, except by the Civil War Washington set the precedent when he, by overwhelming force, crushed rebellion in Western Pennsylvania While he was President, there was no question but what we were a nation, and when the test of civil war came, the chief executive was another such as he Lincoln, putting forth the mighty power of an expanded nation to crush rebellion but followed on the lines laid down by Washington

Thus it was his wish that this nation should become strong and great It was to become strong and great that it might lift its head among the powers of earth and show forth a model of free government But it was to become strong and great by inward expansion, not by conquest Let other nations seize here and seize there, let them scramble for the possession of weaker people He would have none of it This policy he followed when he made the treaty with England Half the people would ally with England and fight France, half would ally with France and fight England He decreed a strict neutrality, and the wisdom of his decision abides Thus the two principles, that of strong central government, and that of strict neutrality, from which has flowed our welfare as a nation, originated with Washington

To lead an army to success, to form a nation, to establish its government on just and lasting principles, these things may have been done before, but never in the face of such tremendous difficulties, never with such pure and lofty motives, never with such glorious results And for these deeds history will forever ring with the love and fame of Washington

No long analysis of character is needed It is blazoned in his works What he was, he did, and what he did, he was Genius alone could perform his feats of war Intensity, persistence and great force alone could persuade a people to unite Great wisdom, indomitable will, and moral heroism, alone could have established an untried form of government Only honor, generosity, and goodness could have enshrined him in the affections of a whole people Only lofty aims and great endeavors, moral purity and constant self sacrifice could have enkindled that reverence akin to worship, with which we still regard him

Great passion slumbered in his breast and anon flamed forth in terrible invective, but only when some base cowardice or mighty injustice had been done Did not the Master curse the Pharisees? The supreme lesson of his life is self control, and that is the lesson that he sends adown the years to you and me, it is the only safeguard of a self governed people His character is massive in its strength We see him as a tower in the storm The key to it was duty, clearly he saw what he ought to do, and did it well, more than that, can no man do Such self control and devotion to duty can spring only from an abiding faith in God Such faith he had, and because he had faith in God, he had faith in men He lived a pure and blameless life, vice touched him not, he occupied high place and power, yet ambition did not disturb his slumbers, and all the ends he aimed at were his country's, his God's and truth's

A hundred years ago to-day, "soothed and sustained by an unfaltering trust," he passed away as "one who wraps the drapery of his couch about him and lies down to pleasant dreams "

Now stand with me upon the stately porch of the mansion at Mount Vernon The grassy slope drops gracefully away, its surface shaded here and there by trees   At its foot the placid Potomac rolls its placid waters in peaceful silence to the sea, beyond and far away and blue the hills of Maryland   The scene is that of beauty, the air is that of peace   God's benediction rests upon the spot, and here in shaded nook, in ivy-covered tomb, the great heart sleeps   The rulers of the nation, the mighty of the land, were there to day, with uncovered heads and bowed they stood   The spirit of the Master was upon them, and they took away, as I trust we shall take away, aspirations for a nobler life

GLENWOOD SPRINGS

CENTENNIAL MEMORIAL

OF

WASHINGTON'S DEATH

(Portrait of Washington)

Held at the

DURAND OPERA HOUSE,

Glenwood Springs, Colorado,

by

Glenwood Lodge No 65, A F and A M ,

Thursday evening, December 14, 1899

PROGRAMME

Prayer—Brother, the Rev Hiram Bullis, Pastor of the Episcopal Church of
    Glenwood Springs
Music—"'Solemn Strikes the Funeral Chime "
Exhortation—Right Worshipful Brother, David W Rees, Master of Glen-
    wood Lodge No 65, A F and A M

Music—"Thou Art Gone to the Grave "
Prayer—Grand Master's ceremony
Music—"O Lord, Our Fathers Oft Have Told "
Address—Right Worshipful Brother Marshall H Dean, Grand Junior
    Warden
Music—"My Country, 'Tis of Thee "
Benediction

ADDRESS BY MARSHALL H DEAN

Worshipful Master, Wardens, Brethren and Friends

We have met here this evening to pay our respects to the memory of our Worshipful Brother George Washington, whose death occurred at Mount Vernon, Virginia, at twenty minutes past ten o'clock, P M , December 14, 1799, in his sixty-eighth year

The Masonic fraternity of the United States have assembled at Mount Vernon on this day, represented by the Grand Masters of the several jurisdictions of this country, and have re-enacted the solemn ceremonies that took place there one hundred years ago

Having been designated by my Lodge to prepare an address for this evening, I have compiled a few facts relative to George Washington's Masonic life, which I hope may prove of interest to our audience, and especially to the brethren of the Craft here assembled to do honor to the memory of our departed Brother

One hundred and forty-seven years ago George Washington was initiated into the sublime mysteries of the Masonic institution, the scenes enacted on that day in a small and obscure Lodge of the Old Dominion, were then, while the dark veil of the futurity was still undrawn, supposed to be of an ordinary character

The minute book of the Lodge at Fredericksburg, Virginia, presents no more than the usual record, that on the fourth day of November, 1752, George Washington was initiated as an entered apprentice Mason

The youth, who, though even then, had been honored by a distinguished appointment in the military service of his native State, had not yet developed the germ of his future greatness, passed undoubtedly through the solemn ceremonies of initiation into our mystic rights, without any suspicion on the part of those who assisted in bestowing on him the light of Masonry, that the transaction then occurring was to become an era in the annals of our institution, but time, whose lessons are always progressive, are often unexpected, has since taught us that the event of that evening was among the most important in the history of American Masonry It has furnished a topic of angry discussion to the enemies, and of grateful exulta-

tion to the friends, of our institution It has given an abiding testimony to the
virtuous principles of that society among whose disciples "The Patriot, the Hero
and the Sage" did not disdain to be numbered And while time shall last and
Masonry shall endure that old but distinctly legible page in the record book of
Fredericksburg Lodge No 4 of Virginia, will be pointed to with proud satisfaction by
every Mason as indisputable evidence that the wisest of statesmen, the purest of
patriots, the most virtuous of men, was indeed his brother, and bound with him in
one common but mystic tie of fraternity and love

In the ancient book of Fredericksburg Lodge No 4, at Fredericksburg, Virginia, will be found the following entries

"November 4, 1752 This evening Mr George Washington was initiated as an
entered apprentice and the receipt of the entrance fee, amounting to two pounds three
shillings is acknowledged "

'On the 3rd day of March, 1753, Mr George Washington is recorded as having
passed a fellowcraft

On the 4th of the succeeding August 1753 the transactions of the evening are
that Mr George Washington and others whose names are mentioned are stated to have
been raised to the sublime degree of Master Mason "

The records of the early Masonic career of Washington are inestimable to the
Mason as memorial of the first connection of the Father of his Country with our
institution

But if the history of that connection had there ceased, if admitted to our
Temple he had but glanced with cold and indifferent eye upon its mysteries, and
if then unaffected by their beauty, untouched by their sublimity, and unawakened
by their truth, he had departed from our portals, the pride with which we hail him
as a Brother would have been a vain presumption, and this tribute to his memory a
senseless mockery But the seeds of Masonry which were sown on the evening of
that November fell not on barren soil It grew with his growth, and strengthened
with his strength, and bloomed and ripened into an abiding love and glowing zeal
for our Order, nor ever withered or decayed amid all the trials and struggles, the
perils and excitements of a long life spent, first in battling to gain the liberties of
his country, and then in counseling to preserve them The evidence of all this is
on record, and the genuineness of the record cannot be disputed

Whatever the enemies of Masonry may say to the contrary, however they
may have attempted in the virulence of their persecution to insinuate that his connection with our Order was but accidental and temporary, first formed in the
thoughtlessness of youth, and then at once and forever dissolved, there is abundant
testimony to show that he never for a moment disowned allegiance to the Mystic
Art, and never omitted on every appropriate occasion by active participation in our
rites, to vindicate the purity of the institution, and to demonstrate in the most
public manner his respect for its principles

Years after his initiation, when he held the exalted rank of leader of our
armies in those perilous days, which have been so well defined as "The times that
tried men's souls," notwithstanding his responsible duties, his arduous labors, his
mental disquietudes, he would often lay aside the ensigns of his supreme authority
and forgetting for a time "the pomp and circumstances of glorious war," would
enter the secluded tent and mingle on a level with his brave companions in the
solemn devotion and mystic rights of some military lodge, where, under the sacred
influence of Masonry, the God of carnage found no libations poured upon his altar,
but where the heartfelt prayer for the prevalence of harmony and brotherly love
was offered to the Grand Architect of the Universe

We have the authority of a distinguished Mason of Virginia, who has elab-
orately investigated the Masonic life of Washington, for saying that "frequently,
when surrounded by a brilliant staff he would depart from the gay assemblage and
seek the instruction of the Lodge," and on one of these occasions Captain Hugh
Maloy was initiated in the Marquee of Washington, the Commander-in-Chief himself presiding at the ceremony

In scenes like these the great Napoleon has been known to appear, and the
Lodges of Paris have more than once beheld the ruler of the Empire mingling in
their labors, a willing witness of the great doctrine of Masonic equality, but in the
founder of a new dynasty such condescension might, and possibly with some truth,
be attributed to the policy of winning public applause In our true-hearted, single-
minded Washington, no such subserviency to man worship could be suspected, his
only motives were deep love for the institution and profound admiration for its
principles

In the Forty-sixth regiment of the British army there was a traveling Lodge,
holding its warrant of constitution under the jurisdiction of the Grand Lodge of
Ireland, and after an engagement between the American and British forces, in
which the latter were defeated, the private chest of the Lodge, containing its
jewels, furniture and implements, fell into the hands of the Americans The cap-
tors reported the circumstance to General Washington, who at once ordered the
chest to be returned to the Lodge and regiment under a guard of honor

The surprise says the historian of the event (himself an Englishman and Mason) the feelings of both officers and men may be imagined when they perceived the
flag of truce that announced this elegant compliment from their noble opponent, but
still more noble brother The guard of honor with their music playing a sacred march
the chest containing the Constitution and implements of the Craft borne aloft like another ark of the covenant equally by Englishmen and Americans who lately engaged
in the strife of war, now marched through the enfiladed ranks of the gallant regiment,
that with presented arms and colors hailed the glorious act by cheers which the sentiment rendered sacred as the hallelujahs of an angel's song

When the contest which secured the independence and freedom for his country was terminated, Washington, covered with the admiration and gratitude of his fellow citizens, retired like another Cincinnatus to the shades of private life, but he did not abandon then his interest in the institution of which he was an honored member In 1788 he united with others in presenting a petition for the formation of a new Lodge at Alexandria, Virginia, and the warrant of constitution, as the instrument authorizing the organization is technically called, is still in existence, preserved in the archives of that Lodge That warrant commences with these words

"I Edmond Randolph Governor of the State, and Grand Master of the Grand Lodge of Virginia do hereby constitute and appoint our illustrious and well beloved Brother George Washington, Esq late General and Commander-in-Chief of the forces of the United States of America and our worthy brethren Robert McCrea William Hunter, Jr and Joseph Allison, Esq together with all such other brethren as may be admitted to associate with them to be a just true and regular Lodge of Freemasons, by the name and title and designation of Alexandria Lodge No 22

The Lodge is still in existence, and in active operation, but in 1805 its name was changed in honor of its first Master, to that of Alexandria-Washington Lodge

The Honorable Timothy Bigelow, in an eulogy delivered before the Grand Lodge of Massachusetts, two months after Washington's death, when there were still living witnesses, supplies us with further evidence of his Masonic character He says

The information received from our brethren who had the happiness to be members of the Lodge over which Washington presided for many years and of which he died the Master, furnished abundant proof of his persevering zeal for the prosperity of the institution   Constant and punctual in his attendance, scrupulous in his observance of the regulations of the Lodge, and solicitous at all times to communicate light and instruction, he discharged the duties of the chair with uncommon dignity and intelligence in all the mysteries of our art.

Incidents like these, interesting as they may be, are not all that is left to us to exhibit the attachment of Washington to Masonry On repeated occasions he has announced in his letters and addresses to various Masonic bodies his profound esteem for the character and his just appreciation of the principles of that institution into which at so early an age he had been admitted   And during his long and laborious life no opportunity was presented of which he did not gladly avail himself to evince that he was a Mason in heart as well as in name   Thus in the year 1797, in reply to an affectionate address from the Grand Lodge of Massachusetts, he says

My attachment to the society of which we are members will dispose me always to contribute my best endeavors to promote the honors and prosperity of the Craft

Five years before this letter was written, he had, in a communication to the same body, expressed his opinion of the Masonic institution as one whose liberal principles are founded on the immutable laws of truth and justice, and whose grand object is to promote the happiness of the human race

In answer to an address from the Grand Lodge of South Carolina in 1791, he says

I recognize with pleasure my relation to the brethren of your society, and I shall be happy on every occasion to evince my regard for the Fraternity

In writing to the officers of St David's Lodge at Newport Rhode Island, in the same year, he uses this language

Being persuaded that a just application of the principles on which the Masonic fraternity is founded must be promotive of private virtue and public prosperity I shall always be happy to advance the interests of the society and to be considered by them as a deserving brother

And in a letter addressed in November, 1798, only thirteen months before his death, to the Grand Lodge of Maryland, he makes this explicit declaration of his opinion of the institution

So far as I am acquainted with the doctrines and principles of Freemasonry I conceive them to be founded in benevolence and to be exercised only for the good of mankind I cannot therefore upon this ground withdraw my approbation from it

If I have paused thus long upon these memorials of the past, and if I have borrowed thus largely from these evidences of Washington's opinions, it is that so far this audience at least may know of his sincere attachment to our Order, and that Washington was in very truth a Mason in heart, in affection and in allegiance, not merely in name and in outward bearing, but one who wrought with us in our hours of labor, and whose visits to our temple were prompted by no idle curiosity, but by warm devotion to the interests of the Craft, and a philosophical admiration of our mystic system And is it not a noble eulogy of our institution that it should have numbered among its faithful disciples one so stainless in morals, so devout in religion, a patriot so pure, a statesman so virtuous that his life was the admiration of the world, his death the desolation of his country?

There is, indeed, in the whole pervading spirit of Freemasonry, something of that beauty of holiness which must have been congenial to the character of such a man as he His heart was irresistibly drawn to it by the purity of its principles and the sublime beneficence of its design He could not but love it because it was holy, and he could not but admire it because it was intellectual Unfaltering trust in God, an humble dependence on the wisdom and power of the Supreme Controller of the Universe, is the first as well as the most indispensable moral qualification of every candidate for our mystic rites, and this virtue the foundation and suggestion of every other, was a distinguishing feature in the religious constitution of Washington

In all his private and public letters, in his official correspondence with the government and in his orders to the army, this firm reliance, this trustful dependence on Divine Providence, is prominently and frequently referred to as though it were a topic on which he could not too often dilate

Of charity, which has been aptly called the capstone of the Masonic edifice, and which, like the virtue already spoken of is taught in the most important ceremony of initiation, Washington was an illustrious example   He uniformly acted whenever the poor and deserving were presented to his notice   Under the influence of that great doctrine of our Order, which teaches us "To sooth the unhappy, to sympathize with their misfortunes, to compassionate their miseries, and to restore peace to their troubled minds," brotherly love, that sublime principle of philanthropy by which, as it is defined in our ritual, "We are taught to regard the whole human species as one family, the high and low, the rich and poor, who as created by one Almighty Parent are to aid, support and protect each other," was admirably exemplified in his humanity to the prisoner   His was indeed the character to win kindness from an enemy or to secure fidelity in a friend

But why extend this catalogue, or why protract this eulogium of him whom now to praise were indeed ' to paint the lily or to gild fine gold?"   May we not, in viewing this goodly audience and this large assemblage of the members of a mystic fraternity offering up the holocaust of their whole heart s veneration, and that, too, not here alone, but in all the widely separated segments of this vast empire, in the North, in the South, in the East and in the West, be all animated by one common feeling of joyous exaltation, and that the most loved and honored of our mighty dead was with us and of us, bound willingly and cheerfully himself in our bond of fraternity?   Looking thus at all that is around us in this public display, and all that is in us and about us in the sentiment of honest pride, that as Masons warms and animates us, may we not point to this day and to these services as a monument to the memory of our own, our venerated brother?

The fact that Washington was an active and devoted member of our fraternity is in itself a source of congratulation   But while we thus peculiarly honor the greatest man of his age, and assert that in uniting with us he vindicated by his own virtue the purities of his principles, we may be permitted to indulge in the consoling consciousness that such a vindication was not altogether wanting, but that both before and since the connection of Washington with the Craft Free-masonry has presented a catalogue of glorious names inscribed upon its proud escutcheon   It is indeed with truth that the ritual of our order declares to each

Initiate that ' the greatest and best of men in all ages have been encouragers and promoters of the art, and have never deemed it derogatory to their dignity to level themselves with the fraternity, to extend their privileges, and to patronize their assemblies "

General Washington never forgot Masonry when a soldier He encouraged and visited camp Lodges, and participated in their labors, frequently officiating as Master

It was at the old Freeman's Tavern on the green of Morristown, New Jersey, in 1777, that Washington himself made General Lafayette a Freemason Washington became a Royal Arch Mason in the year 1755, in a military Lodge connected with a British regiment in the command of the ill fated General Braddock So deeply, so fully was he impressed with the solemnities of the degree, that the Bible on which he sealed his obedience to the Order was henceforth to him not only the venerated word of God, but the sublime witness of his Royal Brotherhood This volume, which witnessed the exaltation of the august companion, is now in the possession of a Lodge in Manchester, England, where in the years 1834 and 1852 it was exhibited in solemn procession which moved three times around the Temple, and accompanied by a guard of soldiers

On the roll of workmen who have labored in the erection of our mystic Temple there are found many eminent and honored names, names that have been conspicuous in the history of our race, and which are often repeated when the great achievements of the past are recounted The records of Masonry are adorned with such on almost every page, we need not go back to remote antiquity to search for distinguished craftsmen among its traditionary legends, though such are not wanting even there

Frederick the Great of Prussia, George the IV of England, with all his uncles and brothers, Oscar of Sweden, Christian of Denmark and Ernest of Hanover may be named among the kings and princes who have not only been the patrons but the disciples of our art Napoleon, with every marshall and general of his camp; Nelson, Wellington, Collingswood and Napier, and every distinguished leader of England's army and navy have worn the Masonic badge and learned the Mason's sign In our own country the role of distinguished Masons is not less honorable to the fraternity In the Revolutionary War all the generals of the American army, and those noble and kindred spirits who came from France, Germany and Poland to assist us, were bound together, not only by the glorious bonds of the common struggle, but by the additional cords of Masonic fraternity And when, in after days, Lafayette, that patriot of the two hemispheres, had returned to the home from which for our cause he had so long been in exile, he could find no better token of his grateful recollection to convey to Washington, his venerated father in arms, than a Mason's scarf and a Mason's apron, and which, wrought by Madam Lafayette, a Mason s wife, were long treasured and worn by him to whom they were presented, and are now preserved as sacred relics by Alexandria-Washington Lodge No 22

In civil life we claim an equally noble catalogue More than fifty of the signers of the Declaration of Independence, several of our Presidents, including President William McKinley, also many of our judges and distinguished statesmen, have been initiated into the rites of Masonry Henry Clay is recorded in our annals as a Mason of unfaltering devotion, who years ago sacrificed the aspirations of ambition to his love of the Craft and refused the nomination for the Presidency by what was then supposed to be a powerful party, when the price of his support was to be a renunciation of Freemasonry

The records of the Craft are full, not only of noble names, but of the noble deeds of those who have shared in our labors and participated in our mystic rites, such names as Joseph Warren, Thomas Smith Webb, Sir Christopher Wren, James Anderson, Joseph Brandt, the Duke of Sussex, DeWitt Clinton, Benjamin Franklin, Marquis Lafayette, Israel Putnam, Paul Revere, David Wooster, Albert Pike, Dr Oliver, Robert Morris, Dr Mackey and a host of others too numerous to recite in this brief address, men whose hearts have swelled with pure emotions, whose strong arms and great souls have been the bulwarks of their country's rights and freedom, and whose living thoughts on science, philosophy and ethics have flashed like sunbeams on the intellect of the world, men who have adorned all professions that are honorable, and won distinction in every field of legitimate employment Among all these we find those who were proud to be numbered among the royal Craft, and hailed by them as Free and Accepted Masons

But why prolong this glorious theme to men, to minds, to hearts like these coming up in their devotions to our altars from all times and from all countries? Masonry may proudly point, as Cornelia did of old to her children, and say, indeed, with truth, "These, these are my jewels"

A century has passed since George Washington's immortal spirit passed beyond How many old empires have passed away, and how many new ones have been ushered into existence' How many dynasties of kings and kaisers have been blotted from the herald book of history, and how many others have been inscribed upon its pages of mundane glory' How many of the wise and good, the noble and the great, have drifted in the shattered bark of life to the shores where all is dumb' How many hearts that then beat with all the hopes of youth, or with all the ambition of age have ceased to pulsate, and all their throbs of joy and love, or hate and grief, been stilled in the silence of the tomb'

What millions of that busy throng who then peopled the earth s surface have buried a l their struggles and found a certain rest for all their varied labors in the grave? What revolutions have there not been in nations, what changes in arts and science, how many old theories have been proved to be fallacious, how many new ones invested with truth since that memorable day when George Washington our brother was laid to rest and he too with all his energy and endurance, with all his wisdom and purity, with all his power and popularity even he has passed away has gone from us forever leaving his glory and virtues as a legacy to his country

But time which has thus drawn into the vortex of its mighty gulf the perishable fabrics of man's device and buried in one common wreck the inventors and their inventions the players and the stage on which they strutted their brief hour has beaten in vain with all its billows against the impregnable rock of Masonry

Though other things have passed away that still remains now as it ever has been indissoluble immutable no land marks subverted no fragments dissevered from its perfect mass its columns still standing in strong support its lights still blazing with their sacred fires its truth still pure as in the days of its birthhood and when the cycle of another century shall have revolved and you and I and all that are elsewhere meeting on this Ceremonial Day shall have gone down to the dust from whence we sprung another generation will be here again to meet upon a second ceremony of the two hundredth anniversary of the day when the brotherhood lost the noblest of her sons

Deep and solid he laid the foundations of this mighty nation His was "square work" even when tested by the severest rules of art. He proved himself a Master Workman wherever and whenever he applied his strength and skill. and at near the age which Providence usually allots to man at peace with the world in the bosom of his family in a green and honored old age, he laid him down and died in full hope of a glorious immortality and was buried on his own ground on the shores of the noble stream so dear to his heart

> Disturb not his slumbers let Washington sleep
> Neath the boughs of the willows that over him weep
> His arm is unnerved but his deeds remain bright
> As the stars in the dark vaulted heaven at night.
>
> O wake not the hero his battles are o'er
> Let him rest, calmly rest on his own native shore
> While the stars and the stripes of our country shall wave
> O'er the land that can boast of a Washington s grave.

GOLDEN

GOLDEN, COLO , December 23, 1899.

Right Worshipful Brother Grand Secretary

I regret to say that this Lodge held no observance of the one hundredth anniversary of the death of Brother George Washington on December 14, 1899, as suggested by our Most Worshipful Grand Master, and, therefore, I have no report of proceedings to make

Fraternally yours,

GEORGE K KIMBALL,

Secretary

GRAND JUNCTION

(Picture of Washington)

MEMORIAL EXERCISES

Mesa Lodge No 55 A F and A M,

Grand Junction, Colorado,

December 14, A D 1899

PROGRAM

Music

Prayer	Rev O E Ostenson
The Washington Memorial Exercises	Horace T De Long

The Influence of Masonry on the Development of the American Idea
of the Equality of Men   Rev R Sanderson

Music

A Letter to the Lodges of Colorado from the Worshipful Master of
Alexandria Lodge, of which Lodge Washington Was the First
Master Under Its Virginia Charter   Oscar D Stewart

An Account of Washington's Last Illness, from the Diary of His Secretary   Lovias F Ingersoll

My Recollections of Grand Marquis de Lafayette, the Warm Personal
   Friend of George Washington, by Adna Adams Treat of Denver,
   now in the 103rd Year of His Age   William I Hammond
                        Music
Washington s Farewell Address   Heman R Bull
The Personal Character and Public Services of Washington.
                                          Prof W H Miller

                        Music
Benediction   Rev John M P Martin
America—"My Country, 'Tis of Thee," etc

GREELEY.

A special communication of Occidental Lodge No 20, A F. and
A M , was held in Masonic Hall, December 14, 1899, at 8 30 p m , A L
5899, for the purpose of holding Memorial Exercises upon the centennial
of the death of Brother George Washington   The Lodge opened in due
form on the third degree, and was then called from labor to refreshment,
and the public invited to the Lodge room, where the following programme
was rendered

Opening Prayer   By Brother Joseph Moore
Response   By M E Church Choir
Reading Personal Letter to the Lodges of Colorado from the Worship-
   ful Master of Alexandria Lodge, of which Lodge Washington Was
   the First Worshipful Master Under Its Virginia Charter
                                          By Brother H T West
Music—Banjo selection   Brother A W James
Reading—Personal Character and Public Services of Washington
                                          Brother Frank Maddon
Solo—Mount Vernon Bells   Miss M Nora Boylan
Reading—Personal Letter from Adna Adams Treat of Denver
                                          Brother S Atkinson
Reading—An Account of Washington's Last Illness, from Diary of His
   Secretary   J M B Peterkin

Memorial Hymn   M E Church Choir
Reading—Washington's Farewell Address   Brother Z X Snyder
Song—"America"   By the audience

The public having retired, the Lodge was then called from refreshment to labor, and closed on the third degree in due and ancient form

SHARON ATKINSON,

Secretary

ADDRESS BY BROTHER FRANK MADDON

The private character of George Washington was to a great degree molded by his surroundings, and the influences with which he was environed   Left fatherless at the age of ten years, he fell under the influences of his brother Lawrence, his senior by some fourteen years, a man who had received a finished education in Europe, and who, because of his abilities and acquirements, held a commission in the British army   It is no wonder, then, that the young ambition of George should be stimulated to admiration by the well bred, graceful, easy and polished manners of his tall and distinguished-looking brother   To his associations with his brother Lawrence, his biographer states, is due, in a great measure, his inclinations toward a military life

With visions of ultimate fame on the field of battle young Washington, no doubt, at this early day, looked forward with no little anxiety for opportunities where he might distinguish himself in the profession of arms, and much of the methodical manner with which he conducted his own private affairs is due to the discipline to which he devoted so much time and attention, both in early and after life, while in command of his troops in the several campaigns in which he was engaged

To him the past is not an oblivion   The silence of the tomb echoes the acclamations of his countrymen, as, in that distant day, he was just such a personage as would excite the admiration of both citizen and soldier alike   A man of magnificent presence, wanting in what, at the present day might be termed a university training, yet because of his natural gifts and rare qualities of mind he successfully met and gained the esteem of the most distinguished diplomats of the Old World   In his intercourse with men as a private citizen, he impressed all with respect and admiration, not only because of his excellent qualities, but on account of his unerring judgment, strong appreciation and consideration of the rights of others, and withal a delicacy so admirable as to call forth favorable criticism from all those with whom he conducted business. A man not gifted with eloquence, yet because of his honesty of purpose, both of heart and mind, he inspired his hearers with that confidence that carries with it conviction.

Thomas Jefferson tells us that "His stature was exactly what one would wish, his deportment easy, erect and noble, the best horseman of his age, and the most graceful figure that could be seen on horseback." Washington was essentially a man of affairs. His life was a busy one. Idleness was not one of his faults, if, indeed, he was possessed of any erroneous characteristics, his business affairs were always attended to with scrupulous exactness.

The tongue of scandal never whispered to the foul breezes anything derogatory to his private or domestic life. He stood before his fellow countrymen and the world a man of integrity, admirable in his rare gifts as a citizen of the new Republic, a model, so to speak, on which future generations might predicate a perfect type of American manhood and citizenship.

In speaking of the private character of General Washington, it is in a measure difficult to imagine him other than the hero who fought the battles of the nation, notwithstanding he was afterwards such a distinguished figure in her public affairs, and, we might add, the most illustrious personage that occupies a place in the history of modern times.

As to his public services, they have been so great and so varied, and at the same time so well known, that it seems almost useless to rehearse them to an audience composed of American citizens. All are more or less familiar with the history of the Revolution, where Washington's greatest talents were first called into requisition to their fullest extent, and the history of which never could be written were we to eliminate the name of George Washington, the central figure, round which cluster all those events which have made the sum total of the history of the birth of the American Republic. His personality, strange as it may seem, is mirrored on every department of this nation from the Atlantic on the east to the Pacific on the west, from the perpetual snows of the north to the sunny land of Beulah on the south. All bespeak the characteristics so indelibly stamped on his nation, and to the existence of which he contributed so much and so unselfishly.

Draper tells us that struggle as we may to change the inevitable trend of human progress, the time comes when such conditions are no longer possible as had heretofore existed, and the history of the world, for that reason, is the more rapidly made, and we may fairly assume that at this critical time the struggle heretofore waged by the mother country against the independence of the colonies, was by Washington, the instrument in the hands of Providence, brought forth in greater perfection than it might have been had the change taken place at an earlier day

Notwithstanding his limited acquirements he was so gifted by nature as a soldier that he met every emergency and turned them to his own advantage, as often did Napoleon the Great Again Jefferson tells us that he was rather slow to reach a conclusion, but when he had once fixed on his course of action, no man's judgment was more sound It was conceded by those who knew him as a soldier that he was wholly devoid of fear on the field of battle However, he never acted without due and mature deliberation, and once having seen his way clear no power could turn him from his purpose, whatever that might be The confidence and esteem in which he was held by his countrymen is evidenced by the positions of trust and responsibility to which he was so frequently called, and while serving his country, both as a soldier and legislator, his counsel was so often sought and held in such high esteem No scandal growing out of any of his public acts, as is too often in our day made manifest, has been left to posterity, or to his fellow countrymen as an inheritance, and when he finally retired to his home on the banks of the Potomac it was with a full sense of having done his whole duty, and with the grateful commendation of his felow citizens for work well and faithfully executed

The farewell address, to which we will listen, is characteristic of the man, wise, temperate and considerate of the destinies of the new-born nation In the language of another "In the production of Washington, it does really appear as if Nature was endeavoring to improve upon herself, and that all the virtues of the ancient world were but so many studies preparatory to the patriot of the new Individual instances, no doubt there were, splendid exemplifications of some single qualification Cæsar was merciful, Scipio was continent, Hannibal was patient, but it was reserved for Washington to blend them all in one, and like the chef d œuvre of the Grecian artist, to exhibit in one glow of associated beauty the pride of every model and the perfection of every master As a general he martialed the peasant into a veteran, and supplied by discipline the absence of experience, as a statesman he enlarged the policy of the cabinet into the most comprehensive system of general advantage, and such was the wisdom of his views and the philosophy of his counsels that to the soldier and statesman he added the character of the sage' A conqueror, he was untainted with the crime of blood, a revolutionist, he was free from any stain of treason, for aggression commenced the contest, and his country called him to the command Liberty unsheathed his sword, necessity stained it, victory returned it If he paused here history might have doubted what station to assign him—whether at the head of her citizens or her soldiers, her heroes or her patriots But the last glorious act crowned his career and banishes

all hesitation Who, like Washington, after having emancipated a hemisphere, resigned its crown and preferred the retirement of domestic life to the adoration of
a land he might be almost said to have created?"

In conclusion let me say, that while constitutional liberty lasts he shall remain the most illustrious figure of his own or any other time, "the soldier hero
who redeemed the nation and cut man's chains assunder with his sword" From
the tumult and strife of revolution, from the broken power of the nations of the old
world, who with mailed hand had for centuries held undisputed their depend-
encies, sprang the great Republic of Republics, a nation founded on a constitution,
the beacon light of a new civilization, at the head of which stands our illustrious
fellow craftsman—George Washington

IDAHO SPRINGS.

Idaho Springs, Colo , December 16, 1899

E C. Parmelee, Grand Secretary :

Right Worshipful Sir and Dear Brother—Acting under the general
Dispensation issued by the Grand Master, Idaho Springs Lodge No 26,
A F and A M , met at their hall at 7 30 o'clock p m , December 14, 1899,
with thirty members present, including officers and visitors   The Lodge
was opened on the third degree, a procession was then formed and proceeded
to the Presbyterian Church, where the following programme was rendered :

Invocation	Rev Willman
Song	Choir
Address—The Early Influence of Masonry on the Development of the Equality of Man, as Expressed in the Declaration of Independence, and Its Culmination in the Independence of the American Colonies	William L Bush
Song	Choir
Reading of a Personal Letter to the Lodges of Colorado from the Worshipful Master of Alexandria Washington Lodge, of which Washington Was the First Master Under Its Virginia Charter	
	E M Moscript
Solo—"Star Spangled Banner"	Miss Baker

Reading—An Account of Washington's Last Illness, Taken from the
 Diary of His Secretary   F A Moss
Address—The Personal Character and the Public Services of Wash-
 ington   Rev John L Boyd
Reading—Washington's Farewell Address Geo T Waltman of the G A R
Song—"America"   By the audience
Benediction   Rev Willman

In view of the patriotic character of the exercises, the members of the G A R were invited to attend in a body, which they did to the number of twenty   In addition to the members of the Lodge and the G A R, there were about one hundred and fifty others present   The exercises passed off pleasantly and were a credit to the Fraternity

Fraternally yours,

WILLIAM L BUSH,
Acting Secretary

ADDRESS BY BROTHER W L BUSH

Before taking up the subject assigned to me, it might be well to state how the idea originated in the Masonic Fraternity of holding a Memorial Service on the centennial of the death of Worshipful Brother George Washington   At the session of the Grand Lodge of Colorado, held in September, 1893, Grand Master W D Wright, on the suggestion of Brother R W Woodbury, Chairman of the Committee on Jurisprudence, recommended that proper memorial exercises be held at Mount Vernon on this date   At that time a committee of three was appointed to place the subject before the other Grand Lodges of the United States   A sufficient number of Grand Lodges having signified to co-operate to make the exercises a success, the arrangement of the details was placed in the hands of the Grand Lodge of Virginia   And to-day, not only at Mount Vernon, but in hundreds of cities and towns throughout the United States the Fraternity of Free and Accepted Masons have met and done honor to the memory of him who was "first in war, first in peace and first in the hearts of his countrymen "

It seems fitting and proper that this suggestion should come from Colorado, on account of having been admitted to statehood in 1876, one hundred years after the signing of the Declaration of Independence

In order to show what influence, if any, Masonry had upon the development of the American idea of the equality of men, and in the independence of the American colonies, it will be necessary to give in a general way some of the principal doctrines and teachings of the organization, and what is required of its votaries The influence of an institution reveals itself most clearly in the lives of men who have honored its principles and cherished its observances This is the final test of all institutions in the eyes of the world Masonry's influence has always been a silent one Its work is like the works of nature silent but irresistible We can, therefore only judge of its influence on the history of this nation in its formative period by the men who were connected with the Fraternity and a comparison of its principles with those of the Declaration of Independence and the Constitution

First of all Masonry requires a belief in God Not in the narrow sense of any particular creed or dogma, but in that broad and liberal sense that permits the Christian Jew, Mohammedan and heathen to worship at its altar We are taught to implore His aid in all our laudable undertakings and to esteem Him as the chief good The right to worship God according to the dictates of the individual conscience has always been and always will be the indisputable right of every Mason

One of the cardinal principles of Masonry is equality Not by lowering but by elevating to a common platform where all meet upon the level with equal rights and equal duties Masonry regards no man for his worldly wealth or honors believing that it is the internal and not the external qualifications which should recommend a man to favor Around the Masonic altar all meet upon the level All, let their rank in life be what it may when in the Lodge room are brothers The official jewel of the Senior Warden in every Lodge is a familiar emblem of this equality and no Lodge is ever closed without hearing that principle reiterated from the lips of that officer

One of the qualifications essential in one who seeks admission to the Fraternity is that the breath of liberty must have nourished and inspired him from the hour of his birth To bondsmen and slaves Masonic light has ever been denied To be made a Mason a man must be free born and in every manner qualified for a career of usefulness This is the doctrine of liberty taught to all Masons Liberty that is not license for Masonry teaches men to govern themselves The institution has ever stood with the doctrine of liberty equality and toleration emblazoned on its banners to wage war against feudal institutions and the despotism of churches over individual conscience

These are some of the cardinal principles of Masonry as taught in her Lodge rooms from the very inception of the organization Long before the discovery of the New World these principles have been taught to those who knelt at the altar and took the Masonic vows But under the form of government in monarchial countries the very conditions of society the methods of earthly monarchs jealous of power, the growth of the organization was necessarily slow. There, conditions did not tend to the full and complete application of these teachings. Even under these adverse conditions ideas were sown, the development of which meant much to future generations

With the settlement of the New World came Masonry. The first Lodge was chartered in Boston in 1733, by the Grand Lodge of England. From there it gradually spread throughout the colonies. At the time of the declaration of war there were Grand Lodges in Massachusetts, New York, Pennsylvania, North and South Carolina and Virginia, with subordinate Lodges in nearly all the other colonies. Masonry found in this new field a congenial home. When the time came for the colonies to cast off the power of the mother country and declare their independence it is found that the names of nearly all those who took an active part in making the history of the country at that time, were enrolled as members of the Masonic Lodges

The unjust taxation and oppression of the British Empire had aroused a feeling of resentment and resistance in the Colonies. One of the first steps toward shaking off the chains of that oppression was the throwing overboard of the tea in Boston harbor. Masonic records of Colonial times go to show that this was done by Freemasons disguised as Indians. They further show that they went from a meeting of St Andrews Lodge for that purpose. Among those who were in attendance at that meeting were General Benjamin Lincoln, Robert Treat Paine, Peter Faneuil, Dr Josiah Bartlett, Paul Revere, Dr Joseph Warren, all names that have an honored place in the history of our country

Paul Revere, who was made famous by the midnight ride to apprise the citizens of Concord and Lexington of the intended expedition of the British, had received Masonic light, and was at one time Grand Master of Massachusetts

Peyton Randolph, President of the first Continental Congress, and John Hancock, president of the Second Congress, were both Masons

Thomas Jefferson, who was Chairman of the Committee to draft the Declaration of Independence, and who formulated that immortal document, was a Mason, as were also fifty-two of the fifty-five signers of it

All but one of the Generals of the Continental army had worn the lambskin as the badge of a Mason, and gauged their lives by the sublime principles of the Order

Benjamin Franklin, that sage and patriot, who was one of the committee to draft the Constitution of the United States, was Master of a Lodge in Philadelphia

The first President of the United States he whose memory we meet to-day to honor, the immortal Washington, said of the institution, in which he was proud to claim membership "The grand object of Masonry is to promote the happiness

of the human race " When inaugurated as first President, he took the oath of
office with his hand resting upon a Bible taken from a Masonic Lodge room This
Bible is still in the possession of St John s Lodge No 1 of New York City The
oath of office was administered by Robert R Livingstone, then Grand Master of
New York As Grand Master of Masons Washington laid the corner-stone of the
Capitol building in the city that bears his name, September 18th, 1793

Lafayette, who did so much in aid of the cause of liberty, and a close personal
friend of Washington, had taken the obligations of the Fraternity Acting as
Grand Master, he laid the corner stone of Bunker Hill monument, with the ceremonies of the Craft, on June 17th, 1825 Of the institution he said, "that in the
United States it affords an important pillar of support and union to its free institutions and happy form of government."

Thus it can be seen that those who were leaders in the great work of launch
ing a new nation, a great Republic, the only real Republic that has ever existed,
were also the foremost men in the Masonic Fraternity Wherever great public
questions have agitated the minds of men, and influences have been arrayed upon
different sides, Freemasons have been found as advocates of liberty and enlighten-
ment They have ever been defenders of public education and the freedom of conscience

There can be traced also a similarity in the form of the government of the
United States and that of the Masonic organization A fundamental principle of
both is that "All governments derive their just powers from the consent of the
governed " As another has expressed it, "Both are governed by a written constitution, both acknowledge the controlling voice of the majority, both admit no official superiors but such as themselves have chosen, both limit the terms of office by
the previously determined will of the electors A general and local government
are common to both The stranger from every clime may be naturalized and fra-
ternized in both "

From whence then came the ideas the development of which resulted in the
Declaration of Independence, the Constitution of the United States and our form
of government, if not from the principles and teachings of Masonry ? No other
country or people had attempted to form such a declaration of the rights of man
or established such a government It was not believed at that time that the people
were capable of governing themselves The doctrine of divine right of kings was
acknowledged by the world It was not believed that the government established
by the colonies would live It did live however, in spite of predictions to the contrary, and we stand to-day as the greatest nation of God-fearing, progressive and
happy people in the world of nations

Masonry had for many years prior to this time been teaching at her altar the same doctrines of the rights of man as are given in our national Constitution Liberty, both civil and religious, brotherly love, relief, truth, temperance, fortitude, prudence, justice and charity, in its broadest sense had ever been its cardinal principles What more reasonable to suppose than that the men who had been taught these principles at the Masonic altar should make them the political creed of the nation? Unconsciously, perhaps, was this done, but the greater credit to their Masonic virtue, if so Without scheme or plan, without aggressiveness or organized influence, by its own internal constitution and by its action on its own members, Masonry has always exerted an influence which places it at the head of the conservative and progressive forces of civilization We, who are members of and love the institution, firmly believe that its influence had much to do with the establishment of this government We believe that the same influence is being exerted to-day for the betterment of mankind Were it not for the principles that lie at the root of Masonry, the Republic would never have been born, or, when born, could not have existed and could not have grown to its present immense proportions

Brethren and friends, the past is secure, the story is crystallized in shining deed, in glorious achievement, in enduring history So mote it be

LAFAYETTE.

WASHINGTON MEMORIAL EXERCISES

(Picture of Washington)

Lafayette Lodge No 91, A F and A M

December 11, 1899

Yourself and ladies are cordially invited

to be present at the

Washington Memorial Exercises

to be held in Bauer's Opera House at

8 p m , December 14, 1899

W H Bittner,   A H Zook,
John Carruthers, James P. Miller,
H R Burns,   Committee

LA JUNTA

HALL OF EUCLID LODGE NO 64, A F AND A M

La Junta, Colo, December 14, 1899

AMERICA,

My country, 'tis of thee, etc,

PROGRAMME

America   By the audience
Prayer   Rev W H Haupt
Introductory Remarks   J C Talliaferro, Worshipful Master
Music   Selected
Reading—Account of Washingtons Last Illness   C A Beerbohm
Reading of Letter from Alexandria Lodge, Washington's Lodge
                                               M Z Farwell
Music—Solo   H E Clucas
Address—Early Influence of Masonry   Rev Robert Coltman
Washington's Farewell Address   G H Winchell
Address—Personal Character and Public Services of Washington
                                               F A Sabin
Music   By the Audience

HYMN
Sung at the Tomb of Washington

Dear shade of our brother descend from above,
And list to our song of affection and love,
For deep in our hearts doth thy mem'ry abide,
Thy virtue and goodness our footsteps shall guide

When the star of thy country was pale in the heaven,
When stout hearts were quailing, and weak ones were riven,
Thou trusted in God, and His arm was thy stay,
Till burst out of darkness the sunlight of day

And now—to that Father Almighty—that friend—
Let praise and thanksgiving, and glory ascend,
That He Washington gave us and formed him to be
The savior, the founder, the strength of the free

Let the union he founded forever remain,
Strike powerless that arm which would sever its chain,
In goodness, in greatness, oh, let it extend,
Till earth becomes chaos and time has no end

LEADVILLE

(Portrait of Washington on representation lambskin apron.)

MEMORIAL SERVICES

Commemorating the One Hundredth Anniversary

of the death of

BROTHER GEORGE WASHINGTON,

Under the Auspices of the Masonic Fraternity

of Leadville, Colorado,

Weston Opera House, December 14,

A L 5899.

Eight o'clock P M

War March of the Priests (Mendelssohn)	Orchestra
Introductory Remarks	Brother J L Wright
America	Sung by the Audience
Invocation	Brother J H Henley
The Holy City (Adams)	Robert Slack
Reading of a Letter from the Master of Alexandria Washington Lodge	
	Brother H W Woodward
Vocal Solo (Mascagni)	Miss Anne Jane Hendrie
Address—Influence of Freemasonry on the Early History of Our Country	
	Brother John M Maxwell

Selection   Orchestra
Piano Solo (a) Second Valse (Godard), (b) March from Tannhauser
                                                  Karl E Tunberg
Address—Personal Character and Public Services of George Wash
    ington   Brother L M Goddard
Dark Is the Hour (from Ermine)   Robert Slack
Extracts from Washington's Farewell Address   Brother R D McLeod
Vocal Solo—Pierrot (Hutchinson)   Miss Anne Jane Hendrie
Reading—An Account of Washington's Last Illness   Brother John A Ewing
Finale   Orchestra

COMMITTEES

Ionic Lodge No 35	Leadville Lodge No 51
R A Cruikshank, W M	J L Wright, W M
I Q Hobbs	F C Webber
R D McLeod	A R Milks
Dan Morrison	F W Hurd

America— My country, 'tis of thee," etc

ADDRESS BY BROTHER J M MAXWELL

It is not my purpose to enter upon a metaphysical discussion of the subject which has been assigned to me, although a determination of the effect or influence of any and all institutions must largely partake of the speculative and uncertain

To determine, however, even speculatively, the influence of an institution upon any given period of the world's history an intimate knowledge of that institution, of its principles, its teachings and its tenets is necessary

The time allotted to me will not suffice to place before you all of the principles, teachings and tenets of the institution of Freemasonry, and I shall confine myself to a presentation of only such matters as are germain to the subject and which must, from the very nature of the human heart and intellect, have greatly influenced the members of the Order in the early days of our nation's history

Again, the influence of any institution, whatever its principles may be, largely depends upon its membership, whether large or small, devoted or indifferent, influential or otherwise

Suffice it to say on this latter point that during the last half of the last century the membership of the Masonic Fraternity in this country was in proportion to the population That it was devoted and earnest is evidenced by the large number of military Lodges in existence, in addition to the regularly constituted Lodges in the larger towns and cities, and the representative and influential character of its membership is shown by the fact that Washington and many of his generals and other officers, a large number of the signers of the Declaration of Independence, and many members of the conventions which formed the Articles of Federation and the Constitution of the United States, were devoted and consistent members of the Craft

What then are the fundamental, underlying and all-pervading principles, tenets and teachings of Freemasonry as they have existed from time immemorial, were during the early history of our nation, are now, and ever will be?

When the "Free and Accepted Masons" emerged from "Ancient Craft" Masonry, they had nothing to conceal except a few archaic ceremonial forms, their signs and tokens of recognition and fellowship, their universal language, and they, therefore, cheerfully and without reserve openly declared and published their objects, aims and ends, and spread all their charges, constitutions and laws before the world, so that they might be read and known of all men They adopted as their watchword and emblazoned on their banner ' The Fatherhood of God and the Brotherhood of Man " The world stood amazed Tyrants alone feared and trembled, as they had long kept the masses of their fellow men in the darkness and servility of ignorance Screening in sinister secrecy their false assumption of authority, they had lorded it over man and his divine heritage

The neophyte in our order, of his own free will and accord, having assumed an obligation in no wise conflicting with his duties to his God, his country, his neighbor or himself, receives instruction in the three great tenets of a Mason's profession

Brotherly love for the whole human family created by one Almighty parent, uniting men of all countries, sects and opinions upon the level of equality

Relief to the unhappy, the unfortunate and the troubled is a duty particularly incumbent upon Masons, linked together as they are by the mystic ties of brotherhood

Truth, a divine attribute, the foundation of every virtue, is one of the first lessons and is made the corner-stone of Masonic life and conduct

By a beautiful system of morality, veiled in allegory and illustrated by symbols peculiar to itself, Masonry instils and enforces the sacred duties of temperance, fortitude, prudence and justice, of patriotism, loyalty, peaceableness and forbearance, to seek peace and to assuage the rigors of conflict

It inculcates all the mutual duties and obligations of man to man in all the relations of life, of the ruler and the ruled, of the high and the lowly, the rich and the poor

Freemasonry is a system of willing obedience and rightful rule Order is the first law It is a system of jurisprudence more noble and ennobling than that of Roman law and Grecian ethics, in that it is based upon the essential and inherent rights of all men, without qualification or condition, save that he who best works and best obeys becomes thereby best fitted to rule and govern his fellowmen It is a comprehensive system of government founded upon the equal rights of man, and exercised and enjoyed in the perfection of loyalty, patriotism and humanity Its mission is peace, progress and prosperity to all mankind in equal proportions, dependent alone upon the worth and deserts of the recipient

Not claiming total exemption from the errors and frailties of all things human, or the entire absence of unfilial members, Iscariot betrayers, self-seeking pretenders or emissaries seeking to destroy, and without pretensions to unattainable perfection, it ever and earnestly strives, by increasing the power of education, by steadfastly maintaining the doctrine of equality of man, by teaching loyalty and patriotism, to accomplish the great and all-pervading object of its existence

Based, as it is, upon immutable truth and right, it knows not the changes and shifts of expediency and opportunities, but remains unmoved as the rock upon which the tempest-tossed waves of ocean beat in vain It has survived, and will survive the commotions, downfalls and disappearances of kings, princes, principalities and empires, the same yesterday, to day and forever, as it is founded upon that eternal truth, the "Equality of Man"

It may be objected that these are but the idle boasting of a partisan, the unsupported statements and claims of one carried away by his zeal for an institution of which he is a member Let him who doubts the statements or calls in question their verity read and study at his leisure the published constitutions, charges, morals and dogma of the Order

Again, it may be said, that preaching is one thing, practice another and by this test the institution is ready and willing to be judged It has been written "By their fruits ye shall know them" Witness the long list of men, distinguished in every walk of life, who have been devoted and consistent members of the Order Witness the history of Great Britain, with its world encircling empire, from the advent therein of the ancient Craft, with the freedom and laws of their guild, from the days of Magna Charta, and from the establishment of the Grand Lodges of England, Scotland and Ireland Witness the history of the founding of this great Republic prior to and from the Declaration of Independence to the present time Witness also, like causation, correspondence and outcome, the result in every land

wherein Freemasonry has had, and has a welcome home, a cherished abiding place
Witness, too, the thick darkness pervading all lands wherein Freemasonry does
not exist, wherein its light does not shine, wherein the moral, social and religious
equality of man is not recognized   And it follows, as does the night the day, and
the least observant may know, that the history and future promise of the free and
enlightened nations of the earth, and the history, progress and beneficent work of
Freemasonry therein are one and inseparable

Briefly outlined, such was the institution of Freemasonry and such its teachings, as it existed and flourished in this country in the last century   That was a
momentous age, not only on this hemisphere, but throughout the world   It was an
age restless as the sea, wave after wave of change, or desire of change, passing
over it, under the imperious command of some great tidal force   There were vast
movements in society, in morals and in thought   There were the first sounds of the
conflict between ancient dynasties and the larger, freer principles that lift humanity upward in the scale of life in the individual and in the race   Men groping
in the darkness and almost despair, impelled by an unknown and unrecognized
force, toward the goal of freedom and equality   It was an age gifted in statesmanship and brilliant in political science   There were intellectual and moral giants
in those days, heroes in thought as in war, ready to do and to dare all for what
their conscience told them was right, the silent hosts that go forth to open the way
for a better civilization, for national progress for the elevation of the human race

Time will not permit me to enumerate the names of those leaders among men
in the halls of legislation and the councils of war and upon the battlefield which
were found upon the rolls of the Craft in this country, but, suffice it to say, that
from the first name signed to the Declaration of Independence, John Hancock, to
that of the Father of his Country, many, very many of the heroes, statesmen and
patriots of that period of our Nation's history met within the tiled recesses of the
Lodge, knelt around a common altar, learned the lessons, imbibed the principles
and practiced the virtues of an Order whose watchword was "The Fatherhood of
God and the Brotherhood of Man," the corner stone of whose foundation was the
"Equality of Man"

As Masons, they knew no sect, no creed, no politics, no South, no North, no
East, no West   By its obligations they were enjoined to love their whole country,
to conserve its peace and unity, to magnify the worth of brotherly love, relief,
truth, justice, patriotism and fortitude, to resist the aggression of the oppressor to
incite the people to noble, generous and self denying deeds, to wage war only as a
last resort, and for the maintenance and preservation of the equality of man

The immortal Declaration of Independence bears eloquent and potent witness
to the fact that Freemasonry had a controlling influence upon this period of our

nation's history. Its declaration that all men are created equal; that they are endowed with certain inalienable rights, among which are life, liberty and the pursuit of happiness; that governments are instituted to preserve those rights, and that governments derive their just powers from the consent of the governed, was the simple enunciation and declaration of those Masonic principles, which were the chief foundation stones of the Constitution.

We do not pretend to claim that these immortal truths were the exclusive property of Freemasonry. We do not assert that Masons alone prepared and signed the Declaration of Independence, but we do assert and claim, without fear of successful contradiction, that every religious institution of that age, that every sect, creed and denomination, with a few exceptions, subscribed to and taught the doctrine of divine right of kings and the subservience of man to the constituted authorities, and that Freemasonry alone, as an institution, taught the "Equality of Man."

Furthermore, the lives of these men, their acts of self-denial, their heroic valor during the seven desperate years of struggle for independence, testify most eloquently to the influence of the teachings of Freemasonry. Fortitude, that great attribute of the Order, was displayed beyond measure by that noble band of patriots; that fortitude which is the courage which dares, and the steadfastness which follows every object to the end; that fortitude which has always been an underlying motive in personal and public greatness.

The splendid strength of national character, the supreme grandeur of national virtue, have grown out of and have been developed by, the lives and deeds of those who have pursued truth with this fortitude and made it the shining goal before them.

Justice, one of the brightest jewels of Freemasonry, that power which embraces all the forces of right, morality and truth, and sets forth the dignity of order and the supremacy of law, was always a controlling influence with these men.

The patience, that holds its steadfast watch in perplexity, the tireless courage that overcomes difficulties, the zeal and love that conquer and win to higher uses, the fidelity to principle, that assures moral victories, the faith in God that falters not amid confusions which baffle the human understanding, were practiced and displayed in an eminent degree by all those who bore a part in the magnificent struggle for independence, and who guided the young Ship of State through the troublous sea of the early formative period of its voyage.

Such being the principles, teachings and tenets of Freemasonry, such being its membership, such the devotion and acts of heroism of its members, can we not with consistency and force claim that the institution had a far-reaching, potent and incalculable influence upon the early history of our nation?

But Freemasonry is not given to boasting, nor is it necessary for it to claim that to which it is entitled. We cannot impart to you the absolute knowledge we have of the influence of Freemasonry upon its members. Such knowledge is reserved for those only who have penetrated its mysteries. We know that it constitutes a great brotherhood of men of many tongues and races, cherishing for each other a warm affection, cultivating the sympathies which make the hearts of thousands beat in unison. We know that it is the advocate and defender, all the world over, of free government and liberty of conscience. We know that it stands for the equality of man, love of God, country and humanity, and loyalty to government. We know that, with a steadfast purpose, it has pursued these objects from time immemorial. Knowing these things, we assert that the influence of Freemasonry, during the early period of our history as a nation, was for those sublime principles set forth in our Declaration of Independence.

And to-day and for the future, with the influence of over a million American Freemasons, the American people, the brave and just people who made the immortal declaration and who maintained with life and fortune their sacred honor, who established our wonderful Constitution, have not changed and will not change their character or their principles in the twinkling of an eye under the temptation of any base motive of personal advantage or under the excitement of war. They are subject, doubtless, as all masses of men are subject, however intelligent or however upright, to great waves of emotion, but their sober second thought is to be trusted. Their deliberate action will be wise and just, and the islands of the sea, which have been cast upon us by the fate of war, will yet rejoice in the blessings of liberty under the stars and stripes, and the great Republic will remain a Republic still.

ADDRESS BY BROTHER L. M. GODDARD

I esteem it an honor, as it certainly is a most pleasurable privilege, to take part with you upon this occasion in honoring the memory of George Washington. It is peculiarly fitting that the centennial of his death should be commemorated as it is to-night throughout the length and breadth of this country, under the auspices of an Order of which he was an illustrious member, and the beauty of whose tenets and teachings he exemplified in his public career and private life, for no man ever displayed the virtue of self-control to such a degree, under trying circumstances, as Washington, or excelled him in the observance of all the other virtues that Masonry seeks to inculcate and enforce.

However much his numerous biographers may differ as to his merits as a general or a statesman, they all concur in according to him the virtues of temperance, morality, benevolence and incorruptible patriotism, and represent him as one whose judgment ever sits enthroned above his impulses

There was no savor of chivalry about Washington's leading his tattered and half-starved army on those campaigns made memorable by indescribable hardships, and leaving the bloody trail of patriot soldiers' unshod feet, there was no appeal to fancy in the sufferings of the drenched soldiers crossing the icy waters of the Delaware, but far down among our heartstrings, the deeds of such soldiers and their dauntless leader clutch us with a hold strong as the passion of our souls or hero worship

He did not seem to know the sensation of fear   He exposed himself to danger and death whenever he deemed his presence necessary, with the same disregard of personal danger he manifested in his early campaigns, verifying in his life the truth of his favorite quotation from Addison   "'Tis not in mortal to command success"   He despised cowardice in others, and always spoke of it with contempt, even in an enemy   When the two New England regiments ran away from a small party of the British at Kipp's Bay he lost his self-control their "dastardly behavior," as he characterized it, and riding among them sought to stem the retreat, but finding this of no avail, he wheeled around in front of the enemy, and there, like Murat before the Russian battery, stood alone, with the bullets whistling around him, preferring death rather than life with disgrace   And at Monmouth, finding Lee retreating, and exasperated with his treachery, General Scott says that "he swore like an angel from Heaven"

He was slow to anger, but when the flood burst its bound it was something terrible   Headley says

If his impetuosity was great and his passions strong his self control was still stronger   Violent passions and ardent feelings are seldom found united with complete self-command, but when they are they form the strongest possible character, for there is all the power of clear thought and cool judgment impelled by the resistless energy of feeling   This combination Washington possessed for in his impetuosity there was no foolish rashness and in his passion no injustice

Also speaking of his ability as a military commander, he says

Washington's military genius is sometimes called in question and although he is allowed a high rank he is not placed among the first military leaders of his age But he who investigates his career carefully will come to a different conclusion Indeed anyone can tell where the truth lies by attempting to put his finger on the man whom he thinks could have carried the country through the Revolutionary struggle as quickly, safely and successfully as he did

By his successful maneuvers he gained the admiration of the British themselves, who characterized him as the "American Fabius"   And Frederick the

Great of Prussia, in presenting him with his picture, wrote underneath the words "From the oldest General in Europe to the greatest General on earth."

It has become too much the fashion of the age to tear down the old idols, and to show them forth as having feet of clay. Homer never existed, William Tell was a myth, there was no Shakespeare, the heroes of the Spanish-American war never performed those feats of valor that thrilled the world a few short months ago, their plumes are drooping and their glorious banners are trailing in the dust kicked up by the fickle masses. Yet the Iliad will be a great epic while scholars live and human nature endures. William Tell still walks in spirit among the sky piercing mountains of free Switzerland, Shakespeare is immortal as the English tongue, and the heroes of our army and navy, who made Santiago and Manila famous, will grow in stature "with the process of the suns."

Perhaps no man who has ranked among the world's heroes has suffered less from the iconoclasm of the age than George Washington, upon whom was pronounced the greatest and tersest eulogy ever spoken of any man. "First in war, first in peace, and first in the hearts of his countrymen." Carpers there are who exult because he sometimes tripped in his spelling, but sure it is he spelled the words "country," "freedom," "victory," in letters standard for all generations, all the way from Monmouth to Yorktown, and the British learned to spell them, as they ran.

Had he not been human, we had never so loved and revered him. The buzzards of this world are ever hovering in their gruesome flight, over the graves of the great and gifted, whose virtues will not let them rest, to see if perchance they may not blot out some word of honor from their epitaphs. No hero of any age or time has held his place on the pedestal where a grateful people have enshrined him, with the immovability that George Washington has done. The traitors, the miners and sappers who worked during the Revolution to undermine his influence, to traduce his character, have passed away with their machinations, leaving "not a wrack behind," and only small wits of our day essay to sharpen their puny weapons upon the little foibles of a great man who was only human by reason of them, while his real characteristics are invisible to them by reason of their own littleness.

Yet he is everywhere "our George Washington," a man set apart and only to be thought of in connection with that which is ennobling and inspiring. Strength and simplicity were his crowning characteristics, and "the elements so mixed in him that nature might stand up and say to all the world. This was a man." That nobility of structure which we call character was his pre eminently—an imperishable building, made of all that he was, and had grown to be in the years of his brave and manly being.

He was a gentleman by birth and breeding, he might violate a rule of grammar, but never the law of honor, he might shatter the third commandment, on provocation, but never the faith of a friend who trusted in him

The Father of his Country, like the "great commoner" of England, lacked the subtle, charming gift of humor   Though most genial and companionable, he was too serious to indulge in the fantastic flights and antics of humor   But his steadfast equability was better to be trusted, in life long companionship, than the mercurial temperament of one whose witty flights are often made at a friend's expense

The keynote of his character was straightforwardness   His statement, "I never say a thing of a man that I have the smallest scruple of saying to him," might well be engraved in enduring letters on some imperishable shaft where all "who run may read "

Jefferson's description of him is a pleasing one   "His person you know was fine, his stature exactly what one would wish, his deportment easy, erect and noble "   His height was one befitting to so commanding a man, being six feet three   The minute details of Washington's personal appearance vary as depicted by different people, both by pen and pencil, they all concur in giving him an air of real distinction, in which dignity, power, resolution, benignity and a manliness untainted by any affectation, shone forth pre eminently

His personal courage was great, and it seemed that a providential care guarded his life through the manifold perils to which he constantly exposed himself—a life on which it seemed his country's welfare and success depended more than upon all others   For Washington to have fallen might have changed the history of the Western Hemisphere

By perhaps a wise decree of fate, he left no children in whom he might live for generations yet to be, for thus he became more pre-eminently "the father of his country," the great ancestor of all free men who detest tyranny and abhor oppression   Well it was for America that she had at the head of the Revolutionary army, to combat that other George, on whose head the crown fitted so closely—a George on whose brow Nature had set her own seal of sovereignty, a man whom no treachery could dishearten, no adulation spoil, no sophistry blind to the true proportions of right and duty

His judgment was dispassionate, his moderation absolutely free from motives of fear or favor, of malice or revenge   He did his best for his country, as his conscience approved and his reason dictated, and never swerved from the path of impartial justice to favor a friend or punish an enemy

Jefferson's estimate of his character was an exalted one

His integrity was most pure his justice was the most inflexible I have even known, no motives of interest or of consanguinity, or friendship or hatred being able to bias his decision He was in every sense of the word a wise, a good and a great man "

Tilghman spoke of him as "The honestest man that I believe ever adorned nature "

A man less strongly moved by a reason and judgment susceptible to suggestions of selfishness or vanity, or mortification if being denounced and misrepresented, as he so often was, in the cabals and factional quarrels of the Continental Congress, in a human desire to justify himself, and to retaliate upon enemies for injuries often grievous to be borne—Washington, like the gentle Nazarene, "was moved by none of these things " He stood on loftier ground, and almost invariably conquered his enemies by the vastness of his magnanimity

He was the cynosure to whom all eyes turned for guidance and light, as mariners on unknown seas turn to their polar star His countrymen trusted him, no sufferings or privations discouraged him, no dangers daunted him, only cowardice and time-serving brought forth the fierce anger of his controlled and finely poised nature The aspersions of his enemies he brushed aside as unworthy of his notice in the stress of his great and arduous duties, as the lion of the jungle spurns the crawling reptiles that cross his path

He was a great general, wresting victory from conditions presaging only defeat, a wise President, "whose appointments were made with a view to destroy party, not create it," even sacrificing personal preference to the high requirements of an uncorrupt and incorruptible administration He was a citizen honored and honorable, lending the prestige of his great career to ennoble and enlarge the walks of private life, he was a fond and faithful husband to the wife to whom, on his departure, life meant only "waiting for the end " He was the exemplar of all ages, showing that a man may be great and yet good, that he may become famous without transcendant genius

Without any artificial or meretricious acts whereby to command the admiring gaze of the world, George Washington, of his own inherent greatness and upright ness, by his ability for all emergencies, his wisdom in direct straits, his incorruptibility in all the varied offices and situations to which he was called in life, stands to day an uncrowned king among the illustrious men who have glorified this world by their presence, and whose sublime shadows lengthen with the increasing suns

Let me conclude by quoting from that beautiful tribute paid him by the peer less Irish orator, Charles Phillips

A conqueror, he was untainted with the crime of blood, a revolutionist he was free from any stain of treason, for aggression commenced the contest, and his country called him to the command Liberty unsheathed his sword, necessity stained and victory returned it   If he had paused here, history might have doubted what station to assign him, whether at the head of her citizens or her soldiers, her heroes or patriots But the last glorious act crowned his career, and banishes all hesitation   Who like Washington, after having emancipated a hemisphere, resigned his crown and preferred the retirement of domestic life to the adoration of a land he might be almost said to have created?

> How might we rank thee upon Glory's page
> Thou more than soldier and just less than sage?
> All thou hast been reflects less fame on thee
> Far less than all thou hast forborne to be

PUEBLO

(Portrait of Washington)

IN MEMORIAM

WORSHIPFUL BROTHER GEORGE WASHINGTON

December the fourteenth,

Seventeen hundred ninety-nine

Eighteen hundred ninety-nine

Ancient Free and Accepted Masons.

Pueblo Lodge Number Seventeen

South Pueblo Lodge Number Thirty-one

Silver State Lodge Number Ninety-five

Pueblo, Colorado

PROGRAMME

Most Worshipful Brother George W Roe, Master of Ceremonies

Processional	Mrs Jeannie McGregor Rettberg
Prayer	Rev Brother Thomas Stephenson
Music—America	Choir and Audience

Reading a letter from Alexandria Washington Lodge of which Washington was the First Master under its Virginia Charter, which Includes an Account of Washington's Masonic Life
    Most Worshipful Brother Cornelius J Hart

Music—I Cannot Always Trace the Way (Dow)   Masonic Choir

Reading—Washington's Farewell Address   Brother John F Keating

Address—The Personal Character and Public Services of Washington   Brother Michael H Fitch

Reading—Account of Washington's Last Illness, from the Diary of His Secretary   Worshipful Brother James Rankin Strugnell

Reading a letter from Brother Adna A Treat, who is one hundred and three years of age, and one of the oldest Masons in the world   Worshipful Brother William W Cooper

Music—Doxology   Choir and Audience

Benediction   Rev Brother O P Wright

Recessional

THE MASONIC LODGES OF PUEBLO

Fraternally invite yourself and friends to attend

the services

Commemorative of the One Hundredth

Anniversary

of the death of

WORSHIPFUL BROTHER GEORGE WASHINGTON,

on Thursday evening, December the fourteenth,

Eighteen hundred ninety-nine,

at seven forty-five o'clock,

at the First Presbyterian Church

ADDRESS BY BROTHER M H FITCH

I   The trend of latter day biography is toward personality   The public want to know, in addition to a man's public services, what manner of human organism produces great results in this world   The interests of science and philosophy also demand that the personality of eminent men be given in their biographies, alongside of their services   Biology, especially that branch of it treating of genesis and heredity, together with its connected science, psychology, has been built up as an inductive science by bringing together as cause and effect organic peculiarities and resulting mentality   This connection in the written lives of great men makes possible such truthful generalizations as that "Great mothers have great sons," "Organisms inherit the fixed functional characteristics of their ancestry," and that "A man is the organic registration of the predominant traits in the lives of his ancestry, back to the beginning of life on the globe"   Great advance in anthropological science must be simultaneous with equally important advance in its copious source of inductive facts, the personality of contemporaneous biography

II   In the case of General Washington, all his biographers, from Weems, who was amongst the first, and whose school history was so universal in my boyhood days, down to the elaborate "Life" by Washington Irving, said very little of his personal appearance and individuality—in fact, nothing that would be of importance in formulating any scientific inferences   Weems' ruling idea seems to have been to make him a model saint for children to pattern after   He, therefore, gave prominence to such fictions as his fervent devotion to religious rites, and the tradition of the hatchet and cherry tree   Until within the last few years I think Washington was regarded more as an ideal than a real character   Even the numerous artists who painted his portraits, instead of presenting him in his natural hair and every day clothes and postures, represented him in powdered wig, laces and impossible positions   Stewart's bust portrait, from which nearly all the modern prints of him are copied, is undoubtedly largely fanciful, with a face more of an anthromorphic demi-god than a plain Virginia farmer   Too many writers and artists seem to think it necessary to clothe greatness in other garb than the homely contour and habiliments of every day manhood   Washington was a plain man, uneducated in books, but endowed with unusual practical common sense   In the days of our country's fathers the art of taking sun portraits had not been discovered   Daguerre had not invented his process called the daguerreotype, followed long after by the present invaluable methods of photography   The latter presents the human face and form as it is in nature, except the colorings   One good photograph of Washington, as he was in his every-day attire at Mt Vernon, or in his camp at Valley Forge, for the purpose of studying his person, would be worth more than all the portraits ever painted of him Fortunately, there was a life mask taken from his face I examined this mask, or a copy of it, in one of the Eastern ait galleries It was exceedingly interesting It showed a peculiar rigidity of his face, which was undoubtedly tho facial correlative of that quality which gave so much dignity to his presence The chin was prominent, the whole lower jaw large and finely molded, the characteristic of firmness and persistence His nose was slightly Roman, indicative of executive foice The eyes were very large and wide apart, showing breadth of mental vision, the cheek bones large and prominent, characteristics of physical endurance, the forehead prominent in the lower portion and sloping back, showing him more of a utilitarian than an intellectual idealist We are told that his hair was a deep brown, his complexion fair and colorless, his face marked by small pox His eyes were blue and rather dull He measured six feet three and one-half inches in height, but was large boned and exceedingly well muscled, carrying himself, especially on horseback, most gracefully His hands and feet were very large, but not out of proportion Lafayette wrote that he had seen him sitting at table two hours after dinner eating nuts These details are very instructive, because they plainly indicate to the student of ethnology the true character of the man They are infinitely more valuable than the idle repetitions of mere neighborhood traditions by purposeful biographers They indicate a powerful human, not saintly, organism, adapted to succeed in any active, manly undertaking They are the visible signs of strong human traits, such as successful warriors habitually display It is not the make-up of a scholar nor a poet, nor a dreamer, nor a philosopher, such as was Benjamin Franklin, nor of John Adams, who was a lawyer and orator, nor of Thomas Jefferson, the author of the Declaration of Independence and a learned socialist But it was the organism of a statesman and soldier, who in the troublous times of the Revolution was far superior to all of these contemporaries in the practical power to grasp and put in operation the statesmanship and militarism necessary to the successful separation of the colonies of the mother country He not only carried the Revolution to a successful issue, but was a master workman in setting up the political machinery, that has needed but little repair for more than a century

Washington has now been dead a hundred years As illustrative of the wonderful correlation of his physical and mental powers I give the following analogues For sixty-one years after his death the nation looked in vain for another built upon the same plan But the seeking was more or less a blind hunt, principally because the people had access in his biographies, not to his personal traits and physical and mental organization, but only to his public acts, and to much fiction about his supposed ethical and theological opinions But in 1860, in a haphazard way, they stumbled on to the same type of greatness, embodied in the same kind of organism, the same height, large boned, less graceful in body and social functions, but containing a higher order of pure intellect, one who carried the nation through a much larger revolution and more difficult war than the Revolution Not, it is true, like Washington as commander in chief in the field, but from his office in the Capital City of the country

The coincidence of the physical and mental traits of the two greatest men in our history shows that there is much more in personality than was dreamed of by biographers a hundred years ago I say that Lincoln had a higher order of mere intellect than Washington, but was perhaps not thereby a greater man in the common acceptation of the word, for intellect is only a part of mentality For instance, to show the difference between the two, it seems to be pretty certain that Washington was only nominally the author of his "Farewell Address." Ford, in his "True George Washington," says, "First Madison was asked to prepare a draft, and from this Washington drew up a paper which he submitted to Hamilton and Jay with the request that they put it in proper form" Hamilton made numerous changes and wrote in the language in which we now have it He made its tone less personal and gave it its style and expression But Lincoln needed no one to revise his Gettysburg address, his Cooper Institute speech, or his second Inaugural—papers that will stand beside the "Farewell Address" to the latest stroke of time Another instance I met in the War of the Rebellion a great and most successful General (I think him the greatest military genius of the Civil War) who reminded me of the personality of Washington as I had read of him He was perhaps as tall, heavier, and had face and hair very much the same color He was also a Virginian His manner was grave, his movements slow, but he was never unprepared and never taken by surprise He never lost a battle when he had personal control of the entire forces engaged His name was George H Thomas, but I have called him "the modern George Washington."

I love to study the personal peculiarities of true men If the theory of organic evolution is correct, then the true character is more or less disclosed in what may be called the general make up, that is, in scientific language, the morphology and physiology of the organism Not only does the shape of the head and the physiognomy determine the character, but the shape of the body, the hands, the feet, the mouth, ears, nose, as well as the walk, the voice, the texture of the hair, every motion of every part of the body, the handwriting, the manner of shaking hands, in fact, the aggregate, both structural and functional of the organism, makes up character and determines what each particular person must necessarily do under any given circumstance all through his life For instance, Benedict Arnold, who was an officer under Washington, was perhaps a more intellectual man than Washington, but not having Washington's general makeup in other respects could not have accomplished what Washington did On the other hand, it was impossible for Washington to become a traitor To use a slang phrase, which at the same time has a broad scientific basis, it was because he "was not built that way" So that a proper study of a man's physique and differentiation from his fellow man is necessary to a proper interpretation of the causes of his successes as well as his failures

III Perhaps the predominant trait in Washington was thoroughness He was honest through and through, and brought to the performance of every duty, small as well as great, a resolute purpose to do his "level best" His correspondence, which was very voluminous, and which only lately has been compiled and published, was of the most painstaking and laborious character He did not dictate to a stenographer, but painfully wrote out every word with his own fingers, and with expressions of the most elaborate politeness His surveys for Lord Fairfax, made when a very young man, were most faithfully done He avoided no exposure to the weather and made long journeys into the western wilds, far from the comforts of home and the allurements of society, while other more showy young men were dawdling away their precious days in the pleasures of society, but who are now forgotten His farming at Mt Vernon is noted at this day as being the best and most successful of his time He laboriously and most intelligently mastered every detail of it, making maps of his fields and watching with his own eyes the progress of all its operations He incurred his last sickness while riding in a storm to make his daily inspection Washington had that love of the soil, that rural predelection so characteristic of, and which has given the Anglo Saxon his superiority to other races in the practical affairs of life The independence from patronage and paternalism that accompanies the pursuit of agriculture was next to his physico-psychical organism, perhaps the most potent factor in forming his character John Adams in his speech in the Congress nominating him for Commander-in-Chief of the Colonial Armies, made a strong point of this sturdy independence in Washington No public honors could wean him from his love for the real source of his personal power and independence, the fair acres of Mt Vernon In the midst of his most arduous campaigns as a soldier, he never neglected his farm He received long reports from his superintendent, and wrote him at times as many as sixteen pages of minute instructions covering every detail of farming operations He was eager at the termination of the war to return to his favorite pursuit But mark the result of such sturdy independence The people, while filled with admiration for his military career, were also unconsciously drawn to him by this and other exhibitions of unselfishness in one who might have made himself a pensioner and a dependent on the public treasury

They therefore determined to keep him in their highest service Honors came unsought to him, who had the manhood to turn his back on them It was his manly reliance upon personal effort in the great struggle of life, that made others ready to struggle for him Every duty of his life was faithfully done and thus he prepared himself for the next Therefore, he was equal to every call as it came, however great What would have been laborious and difficult to ordinary men, who never did small things well, came easy to him This trait stood him better than college education, of which he had none While he did not spell well, and spoke no language but his own, yet Patrick Henry said of him in the Congress of 1774, that "in solid information and sound judgment Col Washington is unquestionably the greatest man on the floor" History recites his public life, but I like best to dwell upon his private character, because his splendid public career was made possibly only because of these admirable traits faithfully cultivated in the obscurer and earlier half of his career His home was at Mt Vernon for forty-six years—two thirds of his life—but he spent only half of these years in the beloved quiet of its exquisite surroundings, the other half being devoted to public service away from home The twenty-three domestic years were the happiest of his matured manhood The plain country mansion, still preserved by the munificence of the patriotic women of our country in its colonial architecture, as it was when Washington trod its floors, was baronial only in its hospitality Compared with the stately homes of old England, it is simplicity itself But what it lacks in magnificence or gilded splendor has been more than made up by the affections of the American people, which have settled upon it one perpetual sunshine

I turn with reluctance from so fascinating a private character, but something more is expected to be said of his public career Not only the history of his country, but the world's history treats copiously of that So seldom have the centuries produced a really great man, that Carlyle in his "Heroes and Hero Worship," refers to only three really great kings Napoleon I and Frederick the Great are two of these They were dwarfs, in physical stature, beside the stately Washington, and compared with what the latter has done for mankind, their achievements dwindle into insignificance Washington never fought a battle for conquest, yet he wrested a nascent imperial domain from the greatest power of the world, and handed it over to his fellow countrymen, for the benefit of themselves and their successors in common, in perpetuity, then, like another Cincinnatus, modestly retired to his farm, even refusing any compensation except his necessary expenses for such great services But what was worth more to him than gold, the affection of the common people of the whole world have enshrined his name for all time But Frederick and Napoleon bestowed the ill gotten territory and plunder of their conquests upon themselves and their families Napoleon I, who stands in history as a greater warrior, was conquered by the nation that Washington successfully resisted   He died a prisoner of that power, while Washington passed away in the peaceful and independent shades of his own home, in the midst of an independent people, made free by his own efforts, mourned and beloved by Christendom, including most of those against whom he had so lately fought   Every schoolboy knows the encyclopedic details of the public services of Washington, therefore, it would be mere platitude to recite them here, but I want to mention one significant fact, which shows what a dominating power he was in the events then passing   From that day in 1775, when under the tree that still stands in Cambridge, Massachusetts, he assumed command of the Colonial Army, by vote of Congress, till the declaration of peace in 1783, he was always in command and personally directed all the movements of the field   When battle reverses came, when his trusted officers deserted him, when Congress itself was in doubt whether a change of commanders might not be best, he did not lose heart but persevered to the end   He and Green and Knox were general officers who began at the beginning and fought without wavering to the close   Always at the front, amidst the uncertain fortunes of battle, when weaker officers lost their heads, Washington kept his eyes of faith, like those of the eagle's to the sun, upon the rising halo of triumph which he believed would ultimately fall like a benediction on the superhuman struggle that he and his ragged and foot sore yeomanry were then putting forth

His transcendant public services to his own country, looking back across the nineteenth century to the results, cannot be extolled too highly   But in what splendor of diction can one couch the indirect effects they have had upon the personal status of the masses throughout the world, in giving an impetus to the cause of Universal Freedom?   The French Revolution did not occur until six years after the achievement of the American Independence   The two came too close together not to have an inspirational connection   Little did Louis XVI imagine that his assistance given so opportunely to Washington in our struggle (not so much, however, to assist us as to punish George III) would so re act in so few years on his own person and throne in the way history records'   So, the influence of the public services we are now considering has permeated the atmosphere of every monarchy in the world for a century, making that atmosphere easier for the oppressed to breathe, and slowly corroding the chains that hold monarchial peoples in what was before a hopeless bondage

In this light, how can we measure the height and depth and breadth of the public services of Washington?   For it was he, next only to the all-pervading spirit of resistance in the small patriotic band of the people, that made our independence possible   Had he faltered, or had there been a defect in his organization, failure would have undoubtedly come instead of such glorious results   There would have een darkness instead of the dawn of Freedom There would have been sunset, nd not the rising light which will finally fill the whole world For this restless pirit of Freedom, really having its new birth on our shores, has already swept 1onarchy from this continent, and will, in time, do the same in the other When hat time comes, in the slow evolution of higher humanity, the paradox that nations f strong men as late as the dawn of the twentieth century, allowed themselves o be governed and oppressed by crowned tyrants, will be classed with witchcraft nd human slavery, as one of the delusions that have all through man's history at like "the old man of the sea" on the throne of human reason

In this sense, the public services of Washington take rank as almost a new orce in the evolution of human society Men of Eastern nations, having before hem the perpetual apparition of a great Republic, growing up beneath the setting un as the apotheosis of the immortal principles of the Declaration of Independ- nce, must, in time, conclude that all men should be thus conditioned That if here is any meaning in human existence, then every combination of men should e dominated by the will of its members only That no Divine command has ever een given to any man, or set of men, to govern and oppress the remainder That ll power, as fundamental law of society, must ultimately be derived from the onsent of those on whom the power so derived is to be exerted For—

> "Bequeathed from sire to son,
> Freedom s battle once begun
> Is never lost, but ever won"

WARD.

WARD, Colo , December 27, 1899

Ed C Parmelee, Esq , Grand Secretary, A F and A M :

Dear Brother—Mt Audubon Lodge No 107, at its regular communi- ation December 16, held Memorial Services in honor of Brother George Vashington Addresses were read and speeches made and the wishes of he Grand Lodge were carried out so far as it was within our power

Yours fraternally,

W. T McGinnis,

Secretary

WINDSOR

A special communication of Windsor Lodge No 69, A F and A. M, was held December 14, A D 1899, A L 5899 The Lodge opened on the third degree of Masonry with Brothers George H Frye, Worshipful Master, E U Minckwitz, Secretary, S L Getshell, Senior Warden, J H Springer, Junior Warden, T E. Bonifield, Treasurer, L Seaton, Senior Deacon, M W Kennedy, Junior Deacon, C S Toole, Tiler, and other brethren about the Lodge

After the Worshipful Master had announced what the call was made for, the Craft was ordered in funeral procession and marched to the I O O F Hall, where the following programme for the observance of Washington Centennial Memorial Day was rendered

Instrumental Music   Miss Ellie Rogers
Reading of an Account of Washington's Last Illness
       Brother F E Bonifield. Treasurer
Reading of a Personal Letter from the Worshipful Master of Washing-
     ton Alexandria Lodge, of which Washington Was the First Master
      Under its Virginia Charter   Brother S L Getshell, Senior Warden
Reading of a Letter from Brother Adna Adams Treat to the Most Wor-
     shipful Grand Lodge of Colorado
        Brother G H Frye, Worshipful Master
Song by Quartette
     Brothers A Hahn, T B Gormeley, W E Williams and F E Bonifield
Reading of a Sketch of the Personal Character and Public Services of
     Washington   G H Frye, Worshipful Master
Reading of a Portion of "Washington's Farewell Address"
        Brother L Seaton, Senior Deacon

Song by Quartette

After the exercises, the Craft marched back to the Masonic Hall, where the Lodge was regularly closed on the third degree of Masonry, peace and harmony prevailing

E. U. Minckwitz,
Secretary.

(Seal)

Approved December 19, 1899.

George H. Frye,
Worshipful Master

WRAY.

Hall of Wray Lodge No 71, A. F and A M

Wray, Colo, December 14, 1899

D C Parmelee, Grand Secretary, Denver, Colo.

Dear Sir and Brother—Memorial Services were observed by Wray Lodge to commemorate the one hundredth anniversary of the death of General George Washington The brethren assembled in the hall, and from here marched to the Methodist Episcopal Church, where an appropriate programme was carried out, after which the brethren returned to the Lodge, and closed in Ample Form

Fraternally yours,
J. N Counter,
Secretary.

Extracts from Proceedings
of Grand Lodges

Extracts from Proceedings of Grand Lodges.

Arizona's Review of Colorado.

The Committee on the Washington Centennial Memorial made their final report   This Committee was appointed seven years ago, when this project of having a Centennial Masonic celebration of the anniversary of the death of Worshipful Brother George Washington was first broached   The idea originated with this Grand Lodge, and it has all the reflected glory of such conception, and the Committee says   "The action of this Grand Lodge, in initiating this memorial, will long appear in its history as the most beautiful jewel that sparkles in its crown "

Canada.

In referring to the Washington Memorial Services at Mount Vernon the Grand Master says
To the Mason and courtly gentleman who was loved by all and whose memory we all revere, whose life was so pure that even with us of a different nationality his virtues and conduct are continually kept before us as worthy of emulation

Connecticut's Review of New Jersey

The Centennial Memorial of Brother George Washington marked an epoch in Masonic history   Its inception in the Centennial State—Colorado—and its culmination in the "Old Dominion" were creditable to both   Such tribute to the patriot and Brother is worthy of the Fraternity   From far and near were gathered representative brethren to do honor to the memory of the Father of this Country, men who had passed the meridian of life, veterans in the cause of Masonry, being in the majority

Georgia's Review of Vermont.

The Grand Master and Grand Lecturer O W Daley represented Vermont at the Washington Memorial Ceremonies A full and enthusiastic account is given, in which the opinion is expressed that "words would be insufficient to indicate the significance of this international testimony to the memory of the 'Father of his Country,' whose influence as a Mason is still extending, inspiring and uplifting the seekers for light"

Iowa's Review of Colorado.

The report of the Washington Centennial Memorial Committee is a noble document of genuine interest, and the historic value of the volume compiled by the Committee, containing the addresses at Mount Vernon, and those before Colorado Lodges, together with Memorial Circulars and photographs, is great, and will be increasingly so in after years The seven years of service by that committee were, in result, as that of Joseph in Egypt during a like number of years of plenty

Kansas' Review of Alabama.

The Grand Lodge was entertained by Brother W C Wheeler, Worshipful Master of Helion Lodge No 1, the oldest Lodge in that Grand Jurisdiction, by exhibiting a Masonic apron which was worn by Brother John W Thompson, late a member of Helion Lodge, at the time when the Marquis de Lafayette visited the Lodge and occupied the station of Senior Warden, Brother George Washington presiding as Worshipful Master This apron was tendered to the Grand Master for his use at the memorial ceremonies commemorating the one hundredth anniversary of the death of Worshipful Brother George Washington

Kansas' Review of New South Wales

Letters were produced from the Grand Lodges of Victoria, South Australia, Tasmania and New Zealand, relating to a representation at the Washington Centennial Ceremonies These Grand Lodges had been invited to unite with the Grand Lodge of New South Wales and send a personal representative to represent them on the occasion of the celebration of the one hundredth anniversary of the death of George Washington They decided to call upon their respective representatives in America to represent the Grand Lodge and present the necessary compliments on that occasion

Kentucky's Review of Virginia.

The Washington Centennial Commemoration has special mention, and large praise is given to the Grand Lodge of the District of Columbia for the part which it took in the ceremonies. A lambskin apron was deposited by Grand Master Small, of the Grand Lodge of the District of Columbia, upon the coffin of the illustrious dead, Brother George Washington, during the ceremonies of that interesting occasion, and subsequently removed from the coffin at the close of the ceremony. On account of the courtesy and kindness of the Grand Lodge of the District and its officers, it was suggested by the Grand Master that the apron be placed in the midst of an engrossed inscription, setting out the facts of the presentation, signed by himself and attested by the Grand Secretary, under seal of the Grand Lodge, and handsomely framed in massive oak, should be presented to the Grand Lodge of the District of Columbia at its next meeting.

Maine.

We feel that it was the most important event in which Masons, as such, have ever participated. So far as the outward world is concerned, the occasion gave a tremendous impulse to patriotism and veneration for the men who enrolled our country among the nations of the earth and laid the foundations for government by the people, and especially for him, who now, more than ever before, is hailed as the "Father of our Country."

Maine's Review of Colorado.

He (Burnand) gives a brief account of the Washington Centennial, speaking in very modest terms of the excellent address he delivered upon that occasion.

It will be remembered that the idea of commemorating this occasion was originated in the Grand Lodge of Colorado, and we believe by Past Grand Master Roger W. Woodbury, and the thanks of the Fraternity everywhere are due to Brother Woodbury and the Colorado brethren for the manner in which they aided in carrying out the plan originated by them.

The committee having charge of the matter made a report also, giving a very brief statement of what was done, and stating that the matter had been incorporated in a volume, made up, as we judge, like a scrap book. But we note that the matter of publishing the full Memorial was referred to a committee with power to have it published when a sufficient number of subscriptions should have been received. This is the first that we have noticed the matter, and we do not know whether the plan has been carried out.

Maine's Review of Iowa.

Referring to the Washington Centennial, he says that a concise history of the Masonic life and services of Washington was published in the library bulletin for November, 1899, and he issued an edict setting apart the 14th of December for Memorial Services, and while he himself went to Mount Vernon to attend there, a large number of Lodges observed the day. He says that "no occasion of Masonic import was ever so very generally observed by the Craft in that jurisdiction than was the Centennial Anniversary of the death of our beloved Brother George Washington." Of the centennial itself, he says. "Grand in its conception and successfully executed, the ceremonies at Mount Vernon on the 14th of December last stand without a parallel in the Masonic history of America, or in the world."

Maine's Review of Missouri

The Grand Master attended the Washington Memorial Services, and speaks of it in high terms, concluding as follows

"Concerning the appropriateness of such a service one hundred years after the death of Washington, there seemed to be only one opinion. Probably nothing in the history of our land has done more to place Freemasonry in its proper light before the American people as an institution which had so much to do with our beginning as a nation, and which is so closely interwoven with all that is best in American citizenship. The devotion of such a man as George Washington to Freemasonry for a period of seven and forty years is as good an answer as need be made to all cavilings that can be urged against our Order, and the Washington Memorial Service of last December, heralded so widely and reported so fully by the press, is worth vastly more to our Fraternity than all it cost in money, time and labor. Of the thousands of Masons who participated in those ceremonies there was not one whose devotions to the principles of our institutions was not quickened and whose spirit did not exult within him as he said, 'I, too, am a Freemason.'"

Maine's Review of Nebraska

He refers to the Washington Centennial Exercises, and does us the honor of giving, in his annual address, the greeting which we sent to the brethren of his jurisdiction. We think that almost everyone who was present was affected as he thus describes that he was

"As I stood that gray December day on that beautiful eminence which over-looks the broad Potomac and many historic spots hallowed with patriotic and fra-ternal blood, and listened to the last President of the United States, a Freemason, voice the affection and veneration of a mighty nation for the first President of the United States, also a Freemason, and one of the sublimest characters in all his tory, my bosom swelled with love and pride for ancient Craft Masonry, and I left the sacred place with a clearer and profounder conception than I ever had before of the power, grandeur, beauty and beneficence of our beloved institution "

Maine's Review of New Mexico

The Grand Master gives an extract from the report of his representative at the Washington Centennial, in which that Brother says "These memorial ser vices, in my opinion, were not only a grand demonstration to the world of the love and reverence of Masons generally for the name and memory of George Washing ton, but will result in great good for our Craft, as well as the world at large, in that many will be thereby inspired with better and higher ideals, and with greater respect and reverence for the institution of Freemasonry "

Maryland's Review of Virginia

According to the suggestions made a few years since by the Grand Lodge of Colorado, the Grand Lodge of Virginia invited the representatives of all the Grand Lodges in the world to assemble with it in the observance of the 100th anniversary of the death of our illustrious Brother George Washington Immediately after the opening of the Grand Lodge the distinguished representatives present were re-ceived and welcomed Nearly thirty-two pages of the proceedings are occupied by the speeches of welcome and the responses on the occasion

Montana's Review of Colorado

The Washington Memorial Observance, first suggested by Colorado, occupied much attention, and when Virginia asked further financial aid, a hundred Colorado Brethren subscribed $10 each The event has since transpired and we have read the addresses and transactions with much interest As Masons as well as citi-zens we cannot too often or too much recall the example and services of Washing ton Many of our Lodges held Memorial Services In spite of the fact that many of the fathers of our nation were members of the Fraternity our country witnessed later an anti Masonic crusade, such as the Pope with all his pretended authority has not been able to arouse in this era of light and more general intelligence Some of the difference is partly due to greater publicity of Masonic transactions and more still perhaps that its efforts are more directed to practical charity   "By their deeds ye shall know them "

Montana's Review of Utah.

The Grand Master and Grand Secretary attended Washington Memorial Services, and speak enthusiastically of the ceremonies and attentions received   Very generally in the Utah Lodges the occasion was observed at home in ample form

Nebraska's Review of Maryland

The Grand Master reported that he and his Grand Lodge took a prominent part and place in the Centennial at Mount Vernon, December 14th, 1899   It was an honor, he said, of which he gladly availed himself   The occasion was largely observed throughout Maryland by those who did not go to Mount Vernon

Nevada's Review of New Brunswick

It is well to contemplate what this Masonic demonstration teaches, that the virtues of the distinguished Mason are more permanent than political or military power

New Brunswick.

The one hundredth anniversary of the death of Worshipful Brother George Washington was a red-letter day in the Masonic calendar of our Brethren in the United States   In his native State, Virginia, the celebration assumed somewhat of a national character   Your Grand Master was most cordially invited to be present and take part, but was unable to accept, which he sincerely regrets   It is well to contemplate what this Masonic demonstration teaches, that the virtues of the distinguished Mason are more permanent than political or military power

South Carolina's Review of Pennsylvania

The Washington Centennial was unique in character, there has been, there will be no parallel case to fit it, it was a grand Masonic demonstration   It seems to us that on that one peculiar occasion the Pennsylvania traditions would have been "more honored in the breach than in the observance "

South Dakota

"The most notable event of the Masonic year has been the Washington Memorial Observance, a gathering of distinguished and other Freemasons to the number of thousands at Mount Vernon, in Virginia, the home of George Washington, the Father of his Country, and the Brother of Masons, to commemorate his virtues and his heroic life, and to testify in the strongest and most solemn manner possible to the great reverence and veneration we have for his memory Colorado first proposed this "Observance," to take place on the one hundredth anniversary of the death of our venerated Brother It was carried out by the Grand Lodge of Virginia The expense of the celebration was contributed to by nearly all American Grand Lodges, and representatives were commissioned to attend from many Grand Lodges from the world over, our Canadian and Australian brethren evincing the greatest interest in its successful execution Famous military bands discoursed touching and thrilling music, cannon boomed the solemn funeral salute, volleys were discharged by the Marine brigade, while ten thousand people thronged to aid the pageant Grand ceremonies by Grand Masters of Masons imparted dignity The beautiful funeral rites were repeated The President of the United States, Brother William McKinley, himself a Virginia made Mason, in simple, touching words, paid eloquent tribute to the memory of that grand soul, whose example shows that "to be truly great one must be truly good " Hearts swelled to suffocation, all eyes were filled with tears, and our Brethren turned homeward, richer and better and happier far because of that great experience "

South Dakota's Review of British Columbia.

The Grand Master and Deputy Grand Master attended Washington Memorial observance in a Washington Lodge, where the English and American flags were draped together This pleased them very much

South Dakota's Review of Colorado

Most Worshipful Brother Todd presented the lambskin apron, properly inscribed, that was worn by Grand Master Burnand at the Washington Centennial Memorial Exercises at Mount Vernon The Grand Lodge returned thanks It will be remembered that the Washington Centennial Memorial celebration had its origin in the Grand Lodge of Colorado It culminated in a great national event,

and our brethren in Colorado may well feel proud of it   The final report of the
Committee is interesting, and it is contemplated to incorporate all addresses, etc,
into a volume   Such an one will have great historic value   Resolutions of thanks
to the Committee were adopted by the Grand Lodge   The Chairman of the Committee then presented to the Grand Lodge a cane, inscribed as follows

ROGER WILLIAMS WOODBURY

Presented by the Ladies' Sewing Guild of Christ Church,

Alexandria, Va, December 14, '99

From the Wood of an Old Forest Tree, which Grew in the Yard of

WASHINGTON'S CHURCH

And asked that it be placed in the custody of the Grand Secretary and carefully
preserved, and that on the occasion of the Washington Memorial Services one hundred years hence it be carried by the then Grand Master of Colorado   The cane
was accepted by a unanimous vote, and the Grand Secretary directed to have a
plate attached, setting forth its presentation by Right Worshipful Brother Woodbury   The inscription is as follows   "Presented by R W Woodbury to the Grand
Lodge of Colorado, September, 1900, with request that it be carried by the Grand
Master at Washington Memorial Exercises in 1999   Accepted by the Grand Lodge
and the plate attached "

South Dakota's Review of New Hampshire

Although this Communication was held for the purpose of exemplifying the
work, the Grand Master gave a very interesting and entertaining account of his
visit to Virginia on the one hundredth anniversary of the death of Brother George
Washington   From it we learn that John Sullivan, first Governor of the State, and
first Grand Master of New Hampshire Masons, was the first to begin activity in the
Revolution by organizing a force and capturing Fort William and Mary, December
13, 1774   The same John Sullivan commanded the right wing at the battles of
Trenton and Brandywine, and also defeated the British at Germantown, a Masonic
ancestor of whom our Brother was justly proud

South Dakota's Review of Nova Scotia.

An interesting account of the Grand Master's visit to Washington to attend the Memorial Observance is given, in which he expresses much pleasure enjoyed from the hospitality of the Masons there He says "To me the scene and occasion of that moment were thrilling, surrounded, as I was, by all that was truly representative of our great Craft, and connected, as the event was, with the history of a nation "

Tennessee.

"My love for Masonry and patriotism for my country arose to the highest point To sum up the whole, it was inspiring from the beginning to the close of the grand ceremony "

Virginia's Review of Colorado.

In order to guarantee the appropriation of an extra thousand dollars asked for by our Centennial Committee, in view of the fact that the movement was, in its inception, Colorado's, and for fear the Grand Lodge would not vote the appropriation, one hundred Masons pledged $10 each The roll of honor appears on page 80, but the Grand Lodge met the issue, as Colorado might have been expected to do

Conclusion.

DENVER, July, 1903.

In closing this volume a few words seem necessary by reason of unforseen circumstances. The mind which conceived the idea of these exercises, and whose programme from inception to conclusion was practically carried out, not only in Colorado, but at Mount Vernon, was that of Roger Williams Woodbury, Past Grand Master of Colorado. Not only was it his mind to plan, but his hands to do, the consequent work. This Memorial Volume was entirely prepared by him, the copy all in the hands of the printer and a part of the proof read, when, without warning, "in the twinkling of an eye," he was taken to his long home July 11th, 1903.

The completion of the work consequently fell upon the remaining members of the committee, who finished the task as well as circumstances permitted, handicapped by their grief at the sudden taking away of their chairman, friend and brother. Much could be said of the character of Brother Woodbury, which, however, would not properly belong in this volume.

We take this opportunity of returning our thanks to Right Worshipful Brother Edgar A. Tennis, Grand Master F. & A. Masons in Pennsylvania, for his courteous and fraternal action in permitting us to use the Gilbert Stuart "Washington," which is the frontispiece of this volume, the steel plate being the property of the Grand Lodge of Pennsylvania, the portrait being considered one of the finest extant.

This volume is now submitted to the Masonic world in the belief that it has clearly told of the most interesting, impressive and important Masonic event of the last century.

WILLIAM D. TODD,
For the Committee.

Grand Secretary.

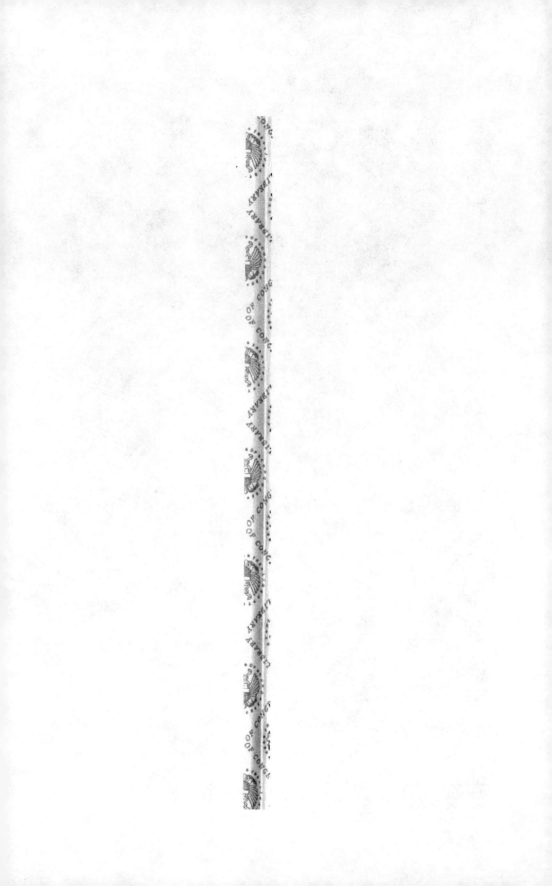

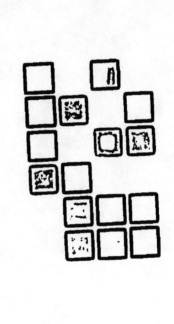

Printed in the USA
CPSIA information can be obtained
at www.ICGtesting.com
LVHW011931180823
755411LV00013B/531

9 781362 621744